"A definitive masterpiece describing the early travelling life of the world's greatest showman in magic. An explicit 'diary' of Harry Houdini during his first Maritime-Canadian tour, filled with details unlike any other historical documents previously published! Exciting and brilliantly written!"

—CORAL and PETER REVEEN, hypnotist, magician, performers, *The Man They Call Reveen*

"This is a book that will wow the magic world. Not only does it contain a wealth of never-before-published photos, but Bruce MacNab has drilled down into a relatively unknown period of Houdini's early life and uncovered facts, incidents, and artifacts that rewrite Houdini history. This is one of the most important books ever written about the great escape artist. It's also just a wonderfully told story. A standing ovation for *The Metamorphosis: The Apprenticeship of Harry Houdini*."

— JOHN COX, creator of *Wild About Harry* (www.wildabouthoudini.com)

"This is a terrific book. After reading *The Metamorphosis: The Apprenticeship of Harry Houdini*, I was left amazed by all the new details, photos, and juicy tidbits Bruce MacNab has uncovered. This book is well researched and a must-read for anyone interested in Houdini."

—DOROTHY DIETRICH, The First Lady of Magic, founder/director of The Houdini Museum, Scranton, PA

"No other performer captured the attention and entertained an audience during the vaudeville era as did Houdini. Bruce MacNab has done an amazing job in researching and sharing new information in his book *The Metamorphosis*. While Houdini toured with Marco the Magician for twelve weeks in 1896 throughout the Maritime provinces, he learned skills in the art of suspense and marketing that helped shape his career and made him the legend he is today. As the proud owner of one of Houdini's original Metamorphosis trunks, I am sure Houdini would agree that the book deserves a standing ovation."

— ROGER DREYER, CEO, Fantasma Magic and Houdini Museum, New York

THE METAMORPHOSIS

0324

THE APPRENTICESHIP OF
Harry Houdini

JUNE 1ST
1896

BRUCE
MacNAB
0324

GOOSE LANE

Cover and title page photograph: Harry Houdini (Harry Ransom Center, The University of Texas at Austin).
Edited by James Duplacey.
Cover and page design by Jaye Haworth.
Art direction by Julie Scriver.
Printed in Canada.
10 9 8 7 6 5 4 3 2 1

Library and Archives Canada Cataloguing in Publication

MacNab, Bruce, 1965-
The metamorphosis: the apprenticeship of Harry Houdini / Bruce MacNab.

Includes bibliographical references.
Issued also in electronic format.
ISBN 978-0-86492-677-7

1. Houdini, Harry, 1874-1926—Travel—Maritime Provinces.
2. Magicians—Travel—Maritime Provinces.
3. Magic shows—Maritime Provinces—History—19th century.
4. Maritime Provinces—Social life and customs—19th century.
I. Title.

GV1545.H8M35 2012   793.8092   C2012-902780-4

Goose Lane Editions acknowledges the generous support of the Canada Council for the Arts, the Government of Canada through the Canada Book Fund (CBF), and the Government of New Brunswick through the Department of Culture, Tourism, and Healthy Living.

Goose Lane Editions
500 Beaverbrook Court, Suite 330
Fredericton, New Brunswick
CANADA E3B 5X4
www.gooselane.com

*
   *   *
   *

For my parents, Ron and Mary,
who hiked the eight-hundred-kilometre
Camino de Santiago at the age of seventy.

May your walk together continue through eternity.

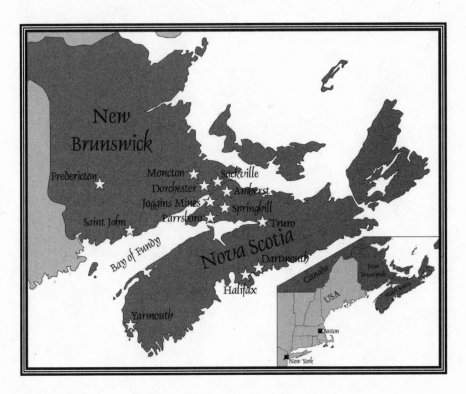

Map of northeastern North America. (Ron Macnab)

🖝 This series of photographs published in 1901 offer a rare glimpse of the Houdinis performing Metamorphosis. Note how Bessie exits the trunk wearing Harry's jacket. (Harvard Theatre Collection, Houghton Library, Harvard University)

CONTENTS

Houdini and Mrs. Houdini five years after their runaway marriage

$$* \atop {* \quad *} \atop *$$

FOREWORD

HARRY HOUDINI DIED IN 1926. By 1959 only three biographies detailing his life and legend had been published. Today, in 2012, there are literally hundreds of books about the great showman, and almost all of them share the same problem. They concentrate on the part of Houdini's life when he was a star, one of the most well-known personalities of his time, a time when he maintained an almost daily relationship with the press. He was one of the most photographed men of his time, but many of the best-known images were taken after he became famous.

The time in Houdini's life when he was finding his way as a performer, the years 1891-1899, generally receive minimal coverage, despite the fact that they are among the most interesting years of a most interesting life. One reason for this is that information about this period in Houdini's life and career has been very hard to find. Perhaps it was the challenge of tracking down the stories that no one else had been able to unearth that led Bruce MacNab to write this book.

Bruce was particularly interested in a tour of Nova Scotia undertaken by Houdini and his young wife in the second year of their marriage. All the information we had about that tour until now was some brief anecdotage from the

Harry and Bessie in 1899. Harry Houdini had trouble convincing others that Bessie was old enough to be his lawfully wedded wife. After they were married, they had difficulty renting an apartment because landlords believed Harry had robbed the cradle. (Library of Congress)

Houdinis themselves, so MacNab started there and has gone on to find more fascinating material about the early years of Houdini's career than anyone ever has.

Because Bruce feels that documentation is vital, not just for the biographer but for the reader as well, he has included documents he has found, and most of those have not been seen for over a hundred years. He has also made a great effort to illustrate with photos the people and events he is describing, and many of those photos have not been seen in a hundred years.

I personally believe that everybody who has ever read a book about Houdini —and enjoyed it—should buy this book. It is a great read, and it is filled with brand new revelations about a man a lot of people think they know about but who, in fact, remains largely mysterious. Bruce MacNab has very ably shed some light on the ever-mysterious Harry Houdini.

Patrick Culliton
May 14, 2012

*

*   *

*

PROLOGUE

HARRY HOUDINI'S FIFTY-TWO-YEAR LIFE straddled the nineteenth and twentieth centuries with perfect symmetry—twenty-six years in each. He lived the first half of his life with the horse and buggy and telegrams, the second half with automobiles, telephones, and the onset of radio. He lived twenty-six years mired in poverty and struggle, followed by twenty-six years of fame and riches.

Houdini left school in his early teens, but never stopped learning. He was the first man to fly a powered aircraft in Australia. He invented and patented a diving suit. He allied with police forces, teaching them the tricks of scammers. He dedicated himself to the war effort, training soldiers and selling bonds.

Houdini also started a motion picture company and starred in five movies. He tirelessly exposed the spiritualists who defrauded grieving widows. He was president of the Society of American Magicians for nine years and entertained presidents, kings, and children. He wrote ten books and published a magazine. He corresponded with Sir Arthur Conan Doyle and Alexander Graham Bell.

Houdini grew up speaking three languages and learned others on the fly, addressing foreign audiences in their native tongue. He practised physical fitness and athletic training half a century before the rest of the world understood the concepts. The original self-promoter, his methods are copied to this day by rock stars, mixed martial artists, and politicians.

And let's not forget, he was also an escape artist.

I first read about Houdini when I was a schoolboy in Dartmouth. Houdini's adventurous up-from-under story, even with its tragic end, was an epiphany for me. No, I didn't master locksmithing, handcuffs, or the straitjacket escape. Nor did I jump off bridges into icy rivers whilst chained to an iron ball. I owe a much more profound debt of gratitude to Houdini — he gave me the gift of reading and the need to discover.

For me, this is Houdini's greatest legacy.

His story has kick-started many young imaginations, inspiring them to read more and more books, unravelling the secrets of this world one page at a time.

Above all, he taught us how a mystery can be a far greater gift than an explanation. In his introduction to his book *Miracle Mongers and Their Methods*, Houdini stated, "Yet we are so created that without something to wonder at we should find life scarcely worth living." This is a powerful sentiment in an age where the Internet has all but replaced wonderment.

As a born-and-raised Nova Scotian, and proud Maritimer, I'm thrilled to know that Houdini walked our streets, boarded our steamships, and entertained our people long before the world knew his name. That's why I've enjoyed these many years unveiling the details of Houdini's visit to the Maritimes by combing through private collections, archives, museums, basements, attics, and libraries while tapping the knowledge and resources of folks from all walks of life, especially magicians, historians, and police officers.

And now, I am proud to share with you this story of Harry Houdini and his Maritime summer.

Let's ring up the curtain.

Images of Houdini from a youngster of three-and-a-half to an aspiring magician of 19. (Kevin Connolly Collection)

1877

3½ YEARS OF AGE

8 YEARS OF AGE

AGE 15

13 YEARS OF AGE

19 YEARS OF AGE

HARRY HOUDINI AT DIFFERENT AGES OF HIS CAREER

*
*   *
*

INTRODUCTION

WHEN HARRY HOUDINI LANDED IN NOVA SCOTIA on May 27, 1896, he couldn't possibly have foreseen the tumultuous summer that he would spend in the Maritimes.

Previous researchers and biographers have been largely indifferent to Houdini's pivotal 1896 Maritime tour, which had more than its share of embarrassing lowlights: shows were cancelled because of poor ticket sales, he performed for a handful of bored townsfolk in a wallpaper store, and was bumped from a church hall to make way for a pie-eating contest. Perhaps that is why one major biography, *Houdini: His Life and Art*, summarily dismissed Houdini's visit as "playing to sparse crowds in obscure places."

They should have looked closer—much closer.

It was in the Maritimes that Houdini met the very man who invented the handcuff escape act. On this tour, he encountered evidence of a real-life fortune teller and personally investigated a haunted house, an important development for a man who became famous for investigating supernatural claims. Yet, you can scour every Houdini book ever written and never learn of these remarkable incidents in the escape artist's life.

This rare photograph offers astonishing detail of Houdini's powerful hands and forearms. Remarkably, Houdini lived with a bullet lodged in his left hand after a shooting incident in 1897. (Harry Ransom Center, The University of Texas at Austin)

Most authors have agreed that Houdini discovered his famous straitjacket in New Brunswick, Canada. Inexplicably, others have tried to rewrite history. A 2010 television documentary claimed Houdini discovered the straitjacket in Massachusetts. The worst of the worst was a Houdini biographer named Ruth Brandon who wrote that Houdini made his career-changing discovery in St. John's, Nova Scotia!

In some ways, Harry Houdini himself is to blame. After all, he did have the tendency to meddle with the details of his own legend. For instance, Houdini always claimed his 1896 Canadian tour with the Marco Magic Company was doomed before it began. According to Houdini, a "bogus magician" named Markos had toured the region the previous year, spoiling the territory for Houdini and his similarly named boss, Marco. The truth? Markos was one of the most popular magicians who ever set foot in the Maritimes. The same, however, can't be said for Houdini's friend, the Nova Scotia-born Marco.

All legends aside, there is no denying that Houdini landed in Canada as a magician but left as an escape artist. It's also widely believed Houdini took his secrets to the grave.

Since that fateful summer back in 1896, he has certainly guarded his Maritime secrets well.

Until now.

PART ONE

SETTING THE STAGE

CHAPTER ONE

HOUDINI 101

New York, New York
1874-1896

"There is nothing mysterious about me or my work. I'm a New Yorker,
was born in Harlem, where I still live."
—Harry Houdini addressing Keith's Theatre, February 1906

HARRY HOUDINI HAD ALREADY LIVED an adventurous life by the time he
landed in Nova Scotia in 1896. Born Erik Weisz in Budapest, Hungary, the future
legend immigrated to America in 1878 at the age of four. Immigration officers
changed his name to Ehrich Weiss, but his family called him Ehrie. To his new
American friends, his nickname sounded an awful lot like Harry.

Growing up in Appleton, Wisconsin, he learned to speak English at school but
always spoke to his German-born mother, Cecilia Steiner, in her own language.
Ehrich also understood Hungarian and Yiddish, thanks to his father, Mayer Weiss,
a lawyer turned rabbi who served a small synagogue above a local harness shop.

At an early age, Ehrich was fascinated by circus entertainers. After watching a
small-time variety show that featured a tightrope walker called the Great Weitzman,
Ehrich strung a rope across his yard and tried the stunt himself. His first attempt

A twenty-something Harry Houdini posing with his magic props with a
Metamorphosis poster showcased on the wall behind him. A pair of Bean Giant handcuffs
can be seen on the table at left foreshadowing his future career as an escape artist. (Corbis)

at wire walking didn't end so well. "Down I went with a crash so I could barely get up again."[1] Ehrich learned an important lesson from his accident—sometimes what looks easy takes an enormous amount of knowledge supported by years of experience. But he was hardly discouraged. Showing astonishing determination for a child, he practised for hours by hanging upside down and picking up sewing needles off the floor with his eyelashes.

When a new Appleton synagogue opened in 1883, the congregation hired a more progressive-minded English-speaking rabbi. Mayer Weiss suddenly found himself unemployed with a wife and seven children to support.

Appleton offered few prospects so Rabbi Weiss moved his family to Milwaukee. The family fell into hard times and lived in at least five different rentals, constantly moving to keep ahead of bill collectors and unpaid landlords. For a short time, Rabbi Weiss worked on the killing floor of a slaughterhouse in order to put food on the table for his family. Later in his life, the memories of these rough years were still too painful for Ehrich to discuss. "Such hardships and hunger became our lot that the less said on the matter the better."[2]

Milwaukee was a favourite stop for the big-time circus tours. After attending one of the shows, Ehrich's neighbourhood friend Jack Hoefler was inspired to start his own circus and invited Ehrich to perform. Mrs. Weiss used her sewing skills to fashion a pair of tights by sewing red stockings to a pair of long johns. The short-lived Jack Hoefler's Five-Cent Circus offered Ehrich a chance to perform as an acrobat called Ehrich: Prince of the Air.

The circus was an inspiration for Ehrich, but it was another visiting show that really caught the boy's attention—a magician named Dr. Lynn. Awestruck after watching the British magician work his apparent miracles, Ehrich had found a new life's goal—to become a magician himself.

Young Ehrich was starting to demonstrate that he drew no line between obsession and commitment in his many pursuits. He played hooky from school and worked a number of jobs, including selling newspapers, shoe-shining, and delivering groceries. By the age of eleven, he had amassed a then-impressive savings of ten dollars.

In 1885 Ehrich's half-brother Herman died from tuberculosis in Brooklyn, New York. Ehrich dutifully stepped up and donated his savings to help bury his twenty-two-year-old sibling.

During his family's struggles in Milwaukee, Ehrich would sometimes run away from home. Aside from a desire to ease the financial pressures on his parents, he

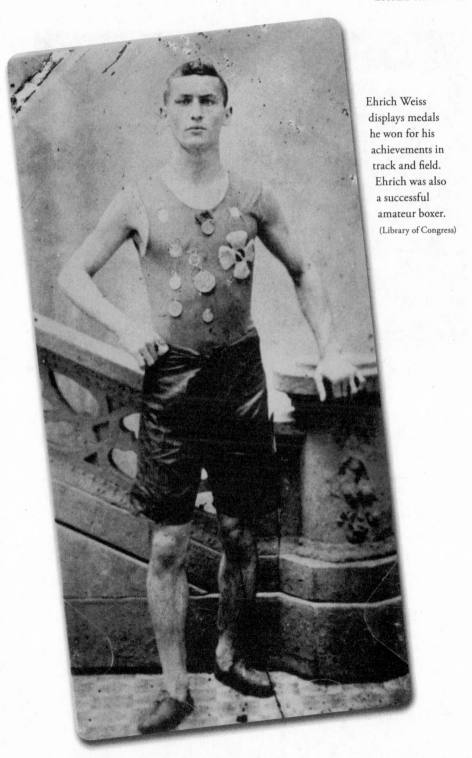

Ehrich Weiss
displays medals
he won for his
achievements in
track and field.
Ehrich was also
a successful
amateur boxer.
(Library of Congress)

Houdini demonstrates a "back palm" sleight-of-hand move to his brother Theo (Dash) while his brother Nat looks on. (Harry Ransom Center, The University of Texas at Austin)

later wrote, "I guess it was the wanderlust that made me leave home then."[3] At one point, he returned to Appleton where, at eleven years old, he briefly apprenticed with a gun dealer named John Hanauer, who also offered locksmith services. Many legends have sprung from Ehrich's time at Mr. Hanauer's shop; Houdini was happy to embellish, if not invent, many false lock-picking stories later in his career.

Ehrich also rode the rails for a time, following a cavalry regiment. His activities during these years remain largely a mystery. It's possible he hooked up with a circus or simply travelled and shined shoes. One clue to Ehrich's vagabond travels survives —a postcard mailed to his mother from Missouri in 1886, giving an update on the twelve-year-old's ambitious plans. "I am going to Galveston, Texas, and will be home in about a year. Your truant son Ehrich Weiss."

After years of frustration in Milwaukee, Rabbi Weiss moved to New York City. Eventually, the rest of the family joined him there. In his early teens, Ehrich joined New York's Pastime Athletic Club where he excelled as a member of the track team. A natural athlete, he won a prestigious road race but was disqualified on a technicality. The race result did not keep Ehrich's spirits down for long. Because by now, he was seriously pursuing another hobby aside from athletics — magic.

In 1888 fourteen-year-old Ehrich joined the working class in the garment district. He put in long shifts of manual labour at H. Richter's & Sons as an assistant lining cutter on the necktie line. There the young worker's interest in magic blossomed thanks to his workmate, Jacob Hyman, an amateur magician three years older than Ehrich.

In spite of his factory pay, the money Ehrich needed to develop a proper magic act was in short supply. For a while, even Rabbi Weiss had to work at the necktie factory to keep the Weiss household afloat. But poor family finances would not stop Ehrich. He simply learned to improvise.

Unlike the star magicians who used exotic birds in their stage shows, Ehrich could only afford an ordinary bantam chicken. The little chicken, named Banjoe by Ehrich's mother, became a beloved family pet and developed an unusual talent of his own. "When we would whistle it would come to us like a dog," Ehrich recalled years later in a letter to his brother Theodore.

After cobbling together enough gear to mount a show, Ehrich, with his sidekick Banjoe, gave his first magic performance at the Pastime Athletic Club on East 69th Street where he billed himself as Eric the Great. On that night, a small audience of male wrestlers and track athletes watched as Ehrich took his first turn at magic on any stage.

Then, around his sixteenth birthday, Ehrich discovered a book that would change his life's journey. But first, the journey had to end for Ehrich Weiss.

THE BIRTH OF HOUDINI

The *Memoirs of Robert-Houdin* is the autobiography of France's legendary magician, Jean Robert-Houdin (1805-1871). Before Robert-Houdin, magicians performed as clown-like wizards wearing comical robes. Robert-Houdin transformed the image of a magician from Merlin-inspired silliness to eloquent theatrical performers who dressed in formal evening dress. The impact of this single book on young Ehrich cannot be overstated. Years later, he wrote, "My interest in magic and conjuring and my enthusiasm for Robert-Houdin came into existence simultaneously. From the moment I began to study the art, he became my guide and hero. I accepted his writings as my textbook and my gospel."[4]

Even at work, Ehrich couldn't stop talking about Robert-Houdin. He later recalled, "By this time I had re-read his works until I could recite passage after passage from memory."[5] Finally, his work friend, Jacob Hyman, made a suggestion. According to Jacob's limited grasp of European languages, adding an "i" to a surname meant you were "like" that person. Ehrich needed no further convincing. "I asked nothing more out of life than to become in my profession 'like Robert-Houdin.'"[6]

Neither Ehrich Weiss nor Jacob Hyman realized that Houdin was properly pronounced as "who-dan." Instead the boys had been pronouncing the name as "who-deen." With the addition of Hyman's *i*, thus was born the name "Houdini," pronounced "who-dee-nee."

Ehrich's nickname, Ehrie, permanently became Harry. And in an instant, the world's most famous stage name came to life on a factory floor in New York's garment district. Harry Houdini was born!

With his new stage name, Harry joined forces with Jacob and developed a magic act called the Brothers Houdini. The "Brothers" had limited success but did manage to book the occasional show around New York City. By April 1891 seventeen-year-old Harry was confident that he could earn a living as a magician. He left the necktie factory on good terms and worked solo and as half of the Brothers Houdini.

In October 1892 Rabbi Weiss died following cancer surgery. By this time, the partnership between Harry and Jacob Hyman had fallen by the wayside. For a few shows, Jacob's brother Joe filled in for his older brother. Ultimately, blood was thicker than water and Harry recruited his real brother Theodore to join him as a full partner in the Brothers Houdini. By now, Theodore was known to his family and friends as Dash, a variation of his Hungarian name, Deshö.

Dash and Harry found plenty of small-time work for the Brothers Houdini, especially at Brooklyn's Coney Island. Their show took a huge leap forward when they acquired a mysterious trunk illusion that they named Metamorphosis.

In May 1893 the Brothers Houdini set their compass for Chicago where the enormous World's Columbian Exposition was celebrating Columbus's arrival in America. Along with countless other acts, the brothers set up shop at the fair's

🐚 Robert-Houdin (1805-1871) is considered the father of the modern art of conjuring. Born Jean Eugene Robert, he took his wife's name, Houdin, for business reasons. This photo is inscribed by Harry Houdini. (Harry Ransom Center, The University of Texas at Austin)

Simonetti

Robert Houdin

in 1861 when living in
retirement in Blois France.

I doubt if another photo like this is in
existence. I met Pierre Petit in Paris who
took the above Photo & he could not
find the old negatives. H. Houdini

Midway Plaisance, where jugglers, snake charmers, and dancers competed with magicians, musicians, and artists for nickels and dimes.

Within a week, the midway entertainers were threatening to strike over problems related to dirty washrooms and the lack of nighttime lighting. American girls were refusing to wear their "exotic" costumes and the streets of the midway were filthy from the droppings left by camels and other animals. Wisely, the Brothers Houdini did not stay long. The boys found a booking at a local dime museum in Chicago then spent the rest of the year playing third-rate theatres throughout the northern states.

By February 1894 the Brothers Houdini was near the top of the billing at the 9th and Arch Museum in Philadelphia. The act was featured along with Fitima, a female snake charmer, and a host of other acts both eccentric and common. Once called variety entertainment, the booking of so many diverse acts at one theatre at the same time was by now called "vaudeville."

By the time Harry celebrated his twentieth birthday, he had become quite comfortable in his role as "Professor" Harry Houdini. His commanding stage presence, coupled with his genuine likeability, was winning over the small audiences he was entertaining. This actually worked against the Brothers Houdini at Vacca's Theatre at Coney Island. The manager noticed his customers were so interested in Harry Houdini that they weren't buying enough beer during his act. The brothers were promptly fired, leaving theatre patrons a choice between acts called the Smilax Sisters and Ferry, the Frog Man.

In spite of the Brothers Houdini's success, everything changed in the spring of 1894. That's when twenty-year-old Harry met and married a Brooklyn singer named Wilhelmina Beatrice (Bessie) Rahner. Dash soon lost his job with the Brothers Houdini. There simply wasn't enough income from the act to support three members. In a matter of weeks, Dash found himself replaced in the act by his new sister-in-law while eighteen-year-old Bessie became the fifth performer to appear onstage as a Houdini. Afterwards, nineteen-year-old Theodore found himself performing solo at Farmer Dan's, one of the smallest theatres at Coney Island. To add insult to injury, he was billed below a dancing duck and a human-faced chicken.

With Bessie as his assistant, Harry's prospects took a giant leap forward. Although Theodore was a skilled magician and escape artist in his own right, he was much taller and bulkier than Harry. This made it difficult to pull off illusions where a magician had to be concealed. Bessie, at four feet nine inches, was an ideal

Wilhelmina Beatrice Rahner
(Library of Congress)

assistant. Not to forget, Bessie was an attractive young lady. Given a choice, any savvy theatre manager would prefer a lady on the bill over two men.

The young Mr. and Mrs. Houdini had taken their first steps together on an adventure that would take them to the top of the world. But it would be a long and difficult climb to get there.

>⟶•○•⟵<

The RAHNERS, Americas
Greatest Comedy Act.

[?] PICTURE 189[?]

WHEN HARRY MET BESSIE

The captivating Beatrice
(Bessie) Rahner *(above)*
and the dapper Harry Houdini
(facing page) (Library of Congress)

HARRY HOUDINI was lovestruck at his first sight of a petite brown-haired showgirl named Wilhelmina Beatrice (Bessie) Rahner. On that spring day at Coney Island, Houdini had one major problem—his new obsession already had a man. And Bessie's boyfriend was certainly no stranger to Houdini.

In a 1945 article in *Conjuror's Magazine*, Houdini's ex-partner in the Brothers Houdini, Joseph Hyman,

recalled the night Houdini first laid eyes on Bessie: "We were all at Coney Island together. There was Harry and his partner (my brother Jack); they were the original 'Bros. Houdini.' One day 'Dash' turned up with a new girlfriend to whom he proudly introduced us. Houdini took one look at [the] really handsome young miss! Dash was immediately minus his girlfriend and Harry had found a wife!" The bloke named Dash who lost his girlfriend to Harry was Houdini's younger brother, Theodore Weiss.

Within two weeks of their first meeting, Bessie and Harry eloped. The newlyweds told family and friends that their marriage ceremony was performed by a Coney Island official who had once done business with Bessie's late father. However, no marriage certificate has ever been found. And the supposed marriage official was actually doing time in Sing Sing prison on the wedding day, June 22, 1894. Bessie also claimed the couple was married two more times in an attempt to satisfy both families of the Jewish/Catholic couple.

Houdini indulged in his own share of misdirection with the details of his marriage. In a September 5, 1916, letter to his friend Quincy Kilby, he wrote, "Never made a mistake. Saw a young girl passing down the boardwalk. She never gave me a look. Three days after she was my wife." Bessie rarely spoke of the wedding; although, she once commented privately to Dorothy Young, one of Houdini's later assistants, "I sold my virginity to Houdini for an orange."[7]

Bessie was warmly welcomed to Houdini's family by her new mother-in-law, Cecilia Steiner Weiss. When Harry introduced his Brooklyn bride to his mother, he spoke in fluent German. Bessie, a daughter of German immigrants, had yet to reveal a secret to Houdini about her own linguistic ability. "He spoke in German, my own family tongue, though at the time he did not know that I could understand."[8]

Love easily overcame any religious differences between Harry and Bessie. But the same can't be said for the Rahners. Bessie's family wasn't exactly thrilled with her choice of husband. "In our austere German standards of respectability, public entertainers were beyond the pale—and I had married a showman. Besides,

though the matter had not been mentioned, I gathered from Ehrich's appearance that he was a Jew, and in our simple Catholic upbringing a Jew was a person of doubtful human attributes."[9]

From their first moments together at Coney Island, Bessie and Harry Houdini's romance would last thirty-three years. But Harry never apologized for stealing his brother's sweetheart. Instead, he always said, "That was the best turn Dash ever did for me."[10]

Harry and Bessie Houdini with Harry's mother Cecilia Steiner Weiss. Houdini saved all of his beloved mother's letters which were sewn into a pillow and placed under his head in his coffin.

(Harry Ransom Center, The University of Texas at Austin)

CHAPTER TWO

WORKING ON THE RAILROAD

Pennsylvania and Points North
October 1895 to May 1896

"We have starved and starred together."
—Letter (excerpt) from Harry Houdini to Bessie Houdini,
San Francisco, June 22, 1919

OVER THE NEXT YEAR, Harry and Bessie paid their dues as entertainers, performing together almost the entire time in sketchy, small-time venues. After playing at one sleazy dive, Houdini wrote, "We opened and when I found out what kind of a theatre it was, good night and good bye."[1] Another time, Bessie simply refused to go on stage with her husband at a classless New York City venue. Harry took her decision in stride and noted in his diary, "Bess refused to work...I put up stuff and worked alone."[2]

After a gruelling spell playing vaudeville theatres from New York to the Deep South, the young couple signed on for one of the toughest apprenticeships show business had to offer.

Bessie and Harry Houdini arrived at Lancaster, Pennsylvania, in late April 1895. In the darkness of a miserable rainy evening, the couple wandered through

The cast of the Welsh Brothers Show. Harry and Bessie are seated at right. Ringmaster Clinton Newton is seated second from left. (Library of Congress)

the unfamiliar town. Shivering and drenched to their skin, the Houdinis finally arrived at a railway siding in the industrial outskirts of town. The sight of a few colourfully painted train cars meant their rain-soaked ordeal was over. This was the winter quarters of the Welsh Brothers Circus.

Mr. Welsh, a giant of a man with a walrus moustache, greeted the young couple and invited them on board a rattletrap railcar that had seen much better days. After Bessie and Harry kicked the mud off their shoes, they were led down a dark narrow hallway as Mr. Welsh announced, "Here are the Houdinis!" Above the din of the rain pounding on the car's roof, the couple heard someone shout a greeting out of the shadows, "Welcome to our city!"

Bessie and Harry should have been well prepared for the cramped lifestyle the circus offered. After all, Harry grew up in a family with six brothers and a sister while Bessie had lived with eight sisters and one brother. But the moment Mr. Welsh showed the Houdinis their makeshift sleeping quarters, Bessie was overwhelmed with despair. Over thirty years later, she provided the following recollection:

> Our lodging was a mere cupboard partitioned off in the car, with a flimsy curtain for a door. Within was just a cot, no chair, table or bureau. In fact there was room only for a cot. A cardboard partition separated us from the next apartment, in which low voices rumbled. Still soaking wet, dismayed at the strange environment, the darkness, the cramped quarters, I fell on the cot sobbing. Houdini soothed me. He was already engaged in thinking out little rimes for my songs, and acted so thoroughly at home that I was shamed out of some of my terror.[3]

Harry and Bessie had joined the Welsh Brothers Circus in time for its fifth season—set to open May 1, 1895—signing on for the entire five-month season at a salary of twenty-five dollars a week. The Houdinis became part of a roster that featured an eclectic group of entertainers including clowns, freaks, a fire-eater, gun jugglers, a ventriloquist, contortionists, trapeze artists, and a marching band. Aside from a few trained dogs, some performing doves, and an educated donkey, the circus featured only human performers.

Nineteen-year-old Bessie Houdini soon overcame her first-night trauma with help from her circus co-stars. "The two other women with the show were very kind

John and Mike Welsh. "I still look back with pleasure upon that season's
work as being one in which we had an abundance of clothes to wear and
good food to eat, for the Welsh Brothers certainly fed their artists extra well."
— Harry Houdini reflecting on the 1895 Welsh Bros. season
(Harry Ransom Center, The University of Texas at Austin)

and did everything to make me feel at home. One of them fashioned a little dress
for me to wear in the concert, and they lent me other things."[4]

A wide range of Bessie and Harry's many talents was tapped to entertain in the
main tent, which could seat two thousand in collapsible bleachers. They performed
their trunk act, along with several comedy numbers and a mind-reading act. Bessie
took turns as a singing clown while Harry was pressed into service as "Projea, the
Wild Man of Mexico." Dressed in old burlap sacks with blue stripes painted on his
face, Houdini flailed about a cage pretending to eat scraps of food thrown between
the bars of his pen. Harry's career as the Wild Man came to a sudden halt after one
"feeding" by the ringmaster that left Harry with a serious injury. "Clint Newton
threw me some raw meat to eat, he hit me in the eye, and I would not look at him
for three weeks, as my eyes were closed. That caused me to become tame, and
someone else had to play wild man of Mexico."[5]

In his 1894 booklet *Mysterious Harry Houdini Tricks*, Houdini wrote: "Whenever you do any small coin trick if possible borrow the coin, and borrow as much coin as possible and try to forget to give it back."
(Harry Ransom Center, The University of Texas at Austin)

The Houdinis performed in towns from one night to one week throughout the circus route. In some Pennsylvania towns like Lancaster and York, the show exhausted its audience from the local neighbourhood. Undaunted, they simply pulled up their stakes and moved the operation across town to cash in on new customers.

Harry was allowed to make extra money by selling a weekly paper along with various soap products. Between acts, Bessie sold the circus songbooks by singing some of the more popular numbers found inside. Bessie's pay for shilling the songbooks was an extra two dollars per week. She was delighted with the extra cash. "My, but I was proud of that money! I felt that I earned it all myself."[6]

With their meals and accommodations provided, the young couple could save most of their pay. But almost half of the Houdinis' salary was sent home to Mrs. Weiss in New York City, who used the money to finance medical school training for Harry's youngest brother, Leopold.

Unlike most performers working the circuits, Houdini never drank alcohol. A few weeks before he died, Houdini told a Boston luncheon, "I have never touched nor tasted a drop of liquor in my life."[7] Although Houdini made countless preposterous claims in public, this one was never disputed by anyone who knew him or toured with him. But there was one incident where he accidentally became intoxicated and almost drowned while escaping from a container filled with beer.

BIG TOP TO BURLESQUE

Through the smouldering heat of a Pennsylvania summer, the Houdinis honoured their circus contract, but when the soaring temperature and the crude train lodgings became unacceptable to Bessie and the rest of the talent, the Welsh Brothers responded by scrambling to buy a proper sixty-foot sleeper car.

The Welsh Brothers finally closed their season in Lancaster on September 23 with two charity shows. By the end of the final night, Bessie and Harry had performed their act twice a day for 113 days in 65 different towns.

A stone's throw from the Welsh Brothers Circus tents, at Lancaster's Fulton Opera House, Harry Newman, Harry Houdini's cousin on his mother's side, was packing up after a performance by his fledgling burlesque company, the American Gaiety Girls.

In a risky business gamble, Harry and Bessie invested their hard-earned circus savings in the burlesque show and became part owners of the production. And without a moment's rest, with the circus summer behind them, the hard-working couple was back on the road for another new season.

When Bessie and Harry Houdini joined the American Gaiety Girls at the close of the Welsh Brothers season, they found themselves riding with a debt-ridden burlesque company struggling at the start of its second season. The actors had grown accustomed to booing and hissing during their performances, which one newspaper called, "not only monotonous, but simply disgusting."[8]

Early on, the Houdinis discovered that several members of the company were hopeless alcoholics. When two of the singers were too drunk to go on, Harry Houdini and his cousin, Harry Newman, filled their slot. In perhaps his first and last attempt at singing on stage, Harry Houdini was roundly booed by the audience for his less than tuneful effort.

On another evening, a child actor named Tiddlywinks was pressed into service to replace an inebriated player in an act that involved the kidnapping of Bessie Houdini. It wasn't until the kidnapping scene arrived that everybody, including Bessie, realized the boy was too small to abscond with his leading lady. To salvage the skit, Bessie picked up the boy and dashed offstage while the audience convulsed with laughter. For the rest of the tour, Bessie's impromptu gag remained in the sketch.

Within the space of two weeks, Houdini and Newman revamped the show. The drunken troublemakers were ousted and new talent was signed. Houdini later boasted, "I had the finest, cleanest and largest show of its kind on the road that season or any other season before my time."[9] Theatre reviewers of the day, however, critiqued

Houdini's show somewhat differently: "The Company was inferior in number, talent and beauty. The music was poor and the alleged wit loud and coarse. The house that greeted them was small but much better than the company deserved."[10]

The tour covered New York State and New England in a dizzying schedule of one- and two-night stands in mostly smaller communities. The tour continued to play the coast and central Massachusetts up until Christmas. After a short break to celebrate the New Year, the American Gaiety Girls resumed their tour in Pennsylvania.

The 1896 tour limped through the northeastern states without generating enough profit to properly feed the troupe. Bessie and the other burlesque girls were forced to accept charity from admiring but wishful-thinking men who paid to have sandwiches and drinks sent backstage.

On February 27, 1896, the American Gaiety Girls rolled into Hartford, Connecticut, but the Houdinis and the rest of the troupe went virtually unnoticed.

After the American Gaiety Girls pulled out of Hartford, the troupe welcomed May Morgan, a "handsome and shapely" female wrestler, to the show. With fifty dollars in prize money up for grabs, Miss Morgan accepted wrestling challenges from both women and men.

Sadly, wrestler May did little to bolster the show. In March, a newspaper review of the American Gaiety Girls claimed that, "An aged egg was one of the ecomiums [sic] from the crowd." An indignant Houdini kept the article for his press book but hand-noted, "a lie no eggs were thrown HH."[11]

By mid-April, the American Gaiety Girls were appearing in the largely French-Canadian populated city of Woonsocket, Rhode Island. The troupe's business manager, Fred Harvey, was charged with fraud related to some unpaid salaries. The arrest of Harvey cued the final curtain for the floundering company when a newspaper exposed the troupe's precarious finances. "The company came here in hock, owing $20 for railroad fares."[12] Houdini and Harry Newman cut their mounting losses and unceremoniously folded the American Gaiety Girls.

Dejected and broke, Harry and Bessie retreated to their flat in New York City.

By coincidence, they were looking for bookings just as a church organist named Edward James Dooley was on the hunt for talent for his touring magic show.

Dooley, who had formed an elaborate company called the Marco Magic Company, was preparing to go out on tour. With good luck firmly on his side, Dooley found an able assistant in Bessie and a gifted performer in Harry Houdini.

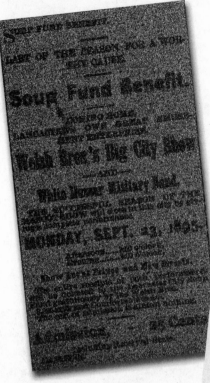

Both the American Gaiety Girls and the Welsh Bros. were performing in Lancaster, PA, on September 23, 1895.

(Public domain, images courtesy of State Library of Pennsylvania)

FULTON OPERA HOUSE.
Monday, September 23.
American Gaiety Girls,
INTRODUCING
THE BLOOMER CLUB.
Bright Specialties, Pretty Girls, concluding with the laughable burlesque,
Rob-Hip-Hur-Roy.
See the Trilby Dances, Grand Amazon March.
A show up to date.
PRICES.................15, 25, 35 and 50 Cents

Exactly how Houdini and Dooley connected is unclear. What is known is that Dooley was stocking his Marco roster around the same time Harry and Bessie Houdini performed four shows in his adopted hometown of Hartford with the American Gaiety Girls. When they finally did meet, Houdini was impressed with Dooley and his commitment to his Marco show and later recalled, "Marco was a gentleman if ever there was one. For years he had planned to have a show on the style of the one presented by Herrmann the Great, and had invested quite a sum of money to get together a truly honest and good show."[13]

Houdini and Edward James Dooley had something else in common besides magic—both were immigrants to America. Now Dooley was taking his newly staffed Marco Magic Company back to his home and native land.

And Harry Houdini was going to Canada.

>—⊶⊶—◦—⊷⊷—⊰

EDWARD JAMES DOOLEY liked burning the candle at both ends. Aside from his organist duties, the Nova Scotia-born musician was also a choirmaster, a lecturer, a theatre producer, and the leader of the orchestra at the Hartford Opera House. He was a founding member of Hartford's Catholic Club and an active member of the Elks Lodge. And he was a respected teacher who was known to his students and friends as Professor Dooley.

In his private life, the forty-two-year-old Dooley lived and breathed magic. While leading the Hartford Opera House orchestra, he watched from the pit as the greatest magicians of the day, Alexander Herrmann and Harry Kellar, worked their magic on the Hartford stage.

Professor Dooley, a confirmed bachelor, had practised magic for

A CANADIAN YANKEE

(*left*) In 1890, "E.J." Dooley briefly ran a store that specialized in keyboards and photographic supplies in Hartford, CT. (from microfilm: Connecticut State Library)

(*right*) Edward James Dooley had looked forward to forming his own touring company ever since leaving his hometown of Halifax, Nova Scotia, as a boy in 1870. (Harry Ransom Center, University of Texas at Austin)

many years, polishing his amateur act at the various men's clubs that proliferated in Hartford. Over time, he had developed an elaborate magic show and a stage persona: Marco, the Monarch of Mystery.

By 1895 Dooley was ready to take his magic show on the road and the Marco Magic Company was born. The professor planned on touring the Canadian provinces and set up a tour that would see him visit Nova Scotia and New Brunswick. Dooley started advance promotions for his tour that featured himself as Marco the Magician with a lady assistant called Miss Belmont, the Thought Reader. The dignified professor sent his colourful lithographs, featuring himself as a superhero clad in red tights, on to the eastern Canadian cities of Halifax, Saint John, and Yarmouth.

The 1895 tour never happened.

Professor Dooley claimed an illness forced him to cancel the tour. But there was another reason why the tour was a bad idea. The world-famous clairvoyant, Anna Eva Fay, was touring the same territory in 1895 and selling out theatres at every stop. Fay would be a tough act to follow for any magic company with similar

material, especially an amateur show fronted by a middle-aged organist. But Professor Dooley's magical stage dreams didn't die. He simply spent another year building his show and buying bigger and better illusions.

In February 1896 Dooley was again planning a summer tour of the Canadian Maritime provinces. As a trial run, he put together an ambitious variety show at the Foot Guard Armory in Hartford billed as "The Mammoth Minstrel Show." The production featured an orchestra, comedians, the Hartford banjo club, and several large choirs. And of course, it also featured plenty of magic acts, including Hartford's leading magician, Fred Jewett.

Dooley's grand show went off without a hitch and won kudos from the city's press corps. "There was certainly entertainment enough, with over eighty minstrel performers on the stage at one time, and a great deal of it was excellent judged by standards higher than those of an amateur."[14] Unfortunately, as the reviewer noted, "It was a good show, but not a very large house to see it."

Unfortunately for Professor Dooley, he would see plenty more small houses before his career was over.

THE HOUDINIS

No 1

No 2

No 3

PRESENT THEIR

MARVELLOUS MYSTERY

HARRY

BESSIE

No 4

No 5

No 6

METAMORPHOSIS

→ EXCHANGE MADE IN 3 SECONDS ←

The Greatest Novelty Mystery Act in the World!

All the Apparatus used in this Act is inspected by a Committee selected from the Audience.

Mons. Houdini's hands are fastened behind his back, is securely tied in a bag and the knots are sealed; then placed in a massive box which is locked and strapped, the box is then rolled into a small cabinet, and Mlle. Houdini draws the curtain and claps her hands three times, at the last clap of her hands the curtain is drawn open by Mons. Houdini and Mlle. Houdini has disappeared, and upon the box being opened She is found in his place in the bag, the seals unbroken and her hands tied in precisely the same manner as were Mons. Houdini's when first entering the bag.

Just think over this, the time consumed in making the change is THREE SECONDS,!

We challenge the World to produce an act done with greater Mystery Speed or Dexterity.

Respectfully yours THE HOUDINI'S.

CHAPTER THREE

NOVA SCOTIA BOUND!

Lewis Wharf, Boston Harbour
Tuesday, May 26, 1896

"The woman in the act was a little brown-haired bit of humanity,
and the man a handsome undersized youth, stockily built,
with deep set eyes and a wealth of black curly hair."
— *Pittsburgh Post* describing Harry and Bessie onstage

AS THEIR TRAIN ROLLED to a stop in Boston, the Houdinis were confident their days as theatrical bottom-feeders were finally over and hopeful about their upcoming season with the Marco Magic Company. Now they were key members of a major magic company going on their first tour outside the United States with a regular salary and without the worries and frustrations of running a bush league burlesque troupe.

Unlike last year's season with the Welsh Brothers, there would be no more sleeping in a tiny cubicle on board a stuffy and smelly train. And this summer tour would be much better than the vaudeville circuit. No more dirty halls or saloons filled with drunken losers looking for an eyeful of lovely little Bessie in her stage tights. No more tawdry showgirls, snake charmers, or hustlers. Professor Dooley was a bona fide college-educated man and a respected teacher. The long-time Catholic

One of the Houdinis' first posters for their Metamorphosis illusion. (Library of Congress)

45

church employee was nothing like the riff-raff taking up space in the lowly curio theatres and travelling sideshows.

It was a sensible decision for Professor Dooley to work the Canadian Maritime theatre circuit. He knew his hometown territory well and still had contacts in Canada. Besides, the theatre market in the northeastern states was highly competitive, especially in the major cities like Boston. There was little room for a new and unproven magic company no matter how promising it might appear.

Many of the vaudeville companies now playing in Boston toured relentlessly throughout North America. And plenty of them would swing through the Maritime provinces as well, offering the Houdinis and Dooley some formidable competition. Two large American productions had a head start on the Marco Magic Company and were already touring Nova Scotia and New Brunswick.

Rufus Somerby, a long-time show manager from Cambridge, Massachusetts, was once again covering his favourite territory in the Maritime provinces. This season, Somerby was presenting a brand new attraction called Professor Wormwood's Monkey Theatre. The American Gaiety Girls' former burlesque competitors, Rose Sydell's London Belles, had also begun their Maritime tour and were currently performing in Saint John, New Brunswick.

Back at the Lewis Wharf, the forty-two-year-old proprietor of the Marco Magic Company surveyed the scene with pride. Dooley was promoting a fantastic show that he claimed was "a hundred years ahead of the times." This was debatable. But he had certainly put together a show that was ahead of his finances. The show had exhausted Dooley's savings, forcing him to find a working partner named Jack McKierney to help bankroll the Marco Magic Company. Now with his finances in order, Dooley could focus on his actors and stagehands.

Through his connections at the Hartford Opera House, Dooley had assembled a young but experienced troupe to round out his roster.

CASTOFF AND CREW

Harry Houdini had two roles to fill. Aside from being Dooley's stage director, he would also appear onstage in two of the six acts.

Another promising young magician, seventeen-year-old Albert Kilby, would appear onstage in novelty acts with Dooley. The New Britain, Connecticut, boy, who normally worked in a box factory, went by the name Burton or Bert. Dooley chose an entirely new stage name for Kilby. Inspired by Kilby's uniform, a cadet coat that featured three rows of buttons, Dooley had christened the boyish performer, "Buttons."

Proper stage lighting and power were essential to the success of an elaborate presentation like the one Dooley had put together. Professor Dooley hired a Hartford electrician, Edward "Budd" Trout, to handle the electrical duties on this Maritime tour.

Dooley's stagehands each had duties aside from packing and unpacking gear and setting up the stage. J.M. Whitehead, who went by the nickname "the Irishman," acted as treasurer and kept accounts as well as occasionally collecting from the box office. George Turner was master of properties. A part-time Hartford magician, Stanley Orriss, was appointed manager of the entire company.

Another teenaged assistant, Chas Bryant, was already an experienced stagehand. For Dooley, Bryant would serve as a humble stage boy and business manager. His duties included collecting the company's take after the box office closed each evening. Dooley's entourage was rounded out by a capable thirty-three-year-old stagehand named John C. Kenney.

Harry and Bessie arrived at Boston's Lewis Wharf hauling their trunk packed with a collection of Harry's props and their wardrobe, which wasn't much. Harry travelled with two suits and a few white shirts. Bessie brought her stage tights and a homemade dress.

With Dooley's troupe assembled and his gear stored on board ship, it was finally time to sail. Plenty of vacationers waited in line with the Marco Magic Company to board the SS *Yarmouth*. Moments after boarding the steamship, Houdini started questioning his seaworthiness. His colour drained away and his rock-steady magician's hands began to shake. Sweat beads popped from his forehead and his normally dark complexion turned deathly pale and then darkened to a noticeable green.

Harry Houdini was seasick.

On this day, Houdini would have to endure at least fifteen hours on board the steamship as it crossed the Gulf of Maine before landing in Canada. The crossing could take up to seventeen hours, depending on the seas. At noon, the SS *Yarmouth* and the SS *Halifax* steamed out of Boston Harbour side by side. The Marco Magic Company was on its way to the southwestern Nova Scotia town of Yarmouth, while the other steamship was bound for Nova Scotia's capital city, Halifax.

Harry Houdini and the Marco Magic Company sailed from Boston to Nova Scotia aboard the SS *Yarmouth*. Here, the ship is rounding the Yarmouth Light at the entrance to Yarmouth Harbour. The steamship still carried masts and sails for emergencies and for saving fuel.
(Bruce MacNab Collection)

The two vessels increased their speed as they hit open waters. The *Halifax* was slightly ahead of the *Yarmouth* but the smaller boat was catching up quickly. Could the SS *Yarmouth* live up to its reputation as the fastest steamship plying the waters between the United States and Canada? A crowd rushed to the starboard rail just as the *Yarmouth* pulled alongside the *Halifax*.

The race was good fun; a correspondent from a Nova Scotia newspaper jotted down notes so he could write an account of it along with a description of the "cool breeze and charming weather."[1] Once the smaller of the two steamships, *Yarmouth*, had pulled ahead for good, the passengers looked up to the wheelhouse and applauded the *Yarmouth*'s captain.

Not everybody on board the SS *Yarmouth* was having a good time. As the steel-hulled steamer continued across the Gulf of Maine to Nova Scotia, Harry Houdini became violently ill. The magician alternated between lying on the deck and stumbling to the rail. Of the hundreds of passengers on board the large steamship, Harry was the first to lose his lunch. Years later, Professor Dooley had a bit of fun informing him, "You were the first to worship Neptune."[2]

Later that evening, under a clear sky lit by a full moon, the steamship sailed out of American territory and into international waters. It was the first time Houdini was outside his adopted country since his family immigrated to the United States from Hungary in 1878.

Now, eighteen years later, Harry Houdini was about to take his first steps in Canada.

>–⚬–<

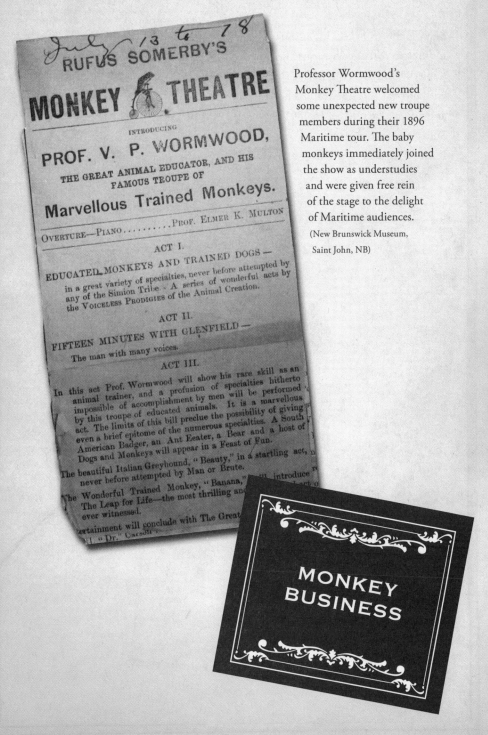

RUFUS SOMERBY'S

July 13 to 18

MONKEY THEATRE

INTRODUCING

PROF. V. P. WORMWOOD,

THE GREAT ANIMAL EDUCATOR, AND HIS
FAMOUS TROUPE OF

Marvellous Trained Monkeys.

OVERTURE—PIANO . . . . PROF. ELMER K. MULTON

ACT I.

EDUCATED MONKEYS AND TRAINED DOGS—

in a great variety of specialties, never before attempted by
any of the Simion Tribe. A series of wonderful acts by
the VOICELESS PRODIGIES of the Animal Creation.

ACT II.

FIFTEEN MINUTES WITH GLENFIELD—

The man with many voices.

ACT III.

In this act Prof. Wormwood will show his rare skill as an
animal trainer, and a profusion of specialties hitherto
impossible of accomplishment by men will be performed
by this troupe of educated animals. It is a marvellous
act. The limits of this bill preclue the possibility of giving
even a brief epitome of the numerous specialties. A South
American Badger, an Ant Eater, a Bear and a host of
Dogs and Monkeys will appear in a Feast of Fun.

The beautiful Italian Greyhound, "Beauty," in a startling act,
never before attempted by Man or Brute.

The Wonderful Trained Monkey, "Banana," . . . introduce
The Leap for Life—the most thrilling an . . .
ever witnessed.

ertainment will conclude with The Great
. . . "Dr." Carson . . .

Professor Wormwood's Monkey Theatre welcomed some unexpected new troupe members during their 1896 Maritime tour. The baby monkeys immediately joined the show as understudies and were given free rein of the stage to the delight of Maritime audiences. (New Brunswick Museum, Saint John, NB)

MONKEY BUSINESS

SINCE STARTING his career more than forty years earlier, Rufus Somerby had toured the Maritimes with offbeat acts like trained horses and a Japanese village. In 1891 Somerby's feature attraction was Prince Tinymite, a thirteen-year-old midget named Dudley Foster from Hampton, Nova Scotia, whom he exhibited with Miss Maude Muller, a woman who reportedly weighed 865 pounds.

Described as a dignified Quaker elder — complete with

PRINCE TINYMITE.

Prince Tinymite, born in Hampton, Nova Scotia, was Rufus Somerby's star attraction in 1891. (Stuart Fisher Collection)

Rufus Somerby signed his name as a professional manager in box office statements for over 40 years. (New Brunswick Museum, Saint John, NB)

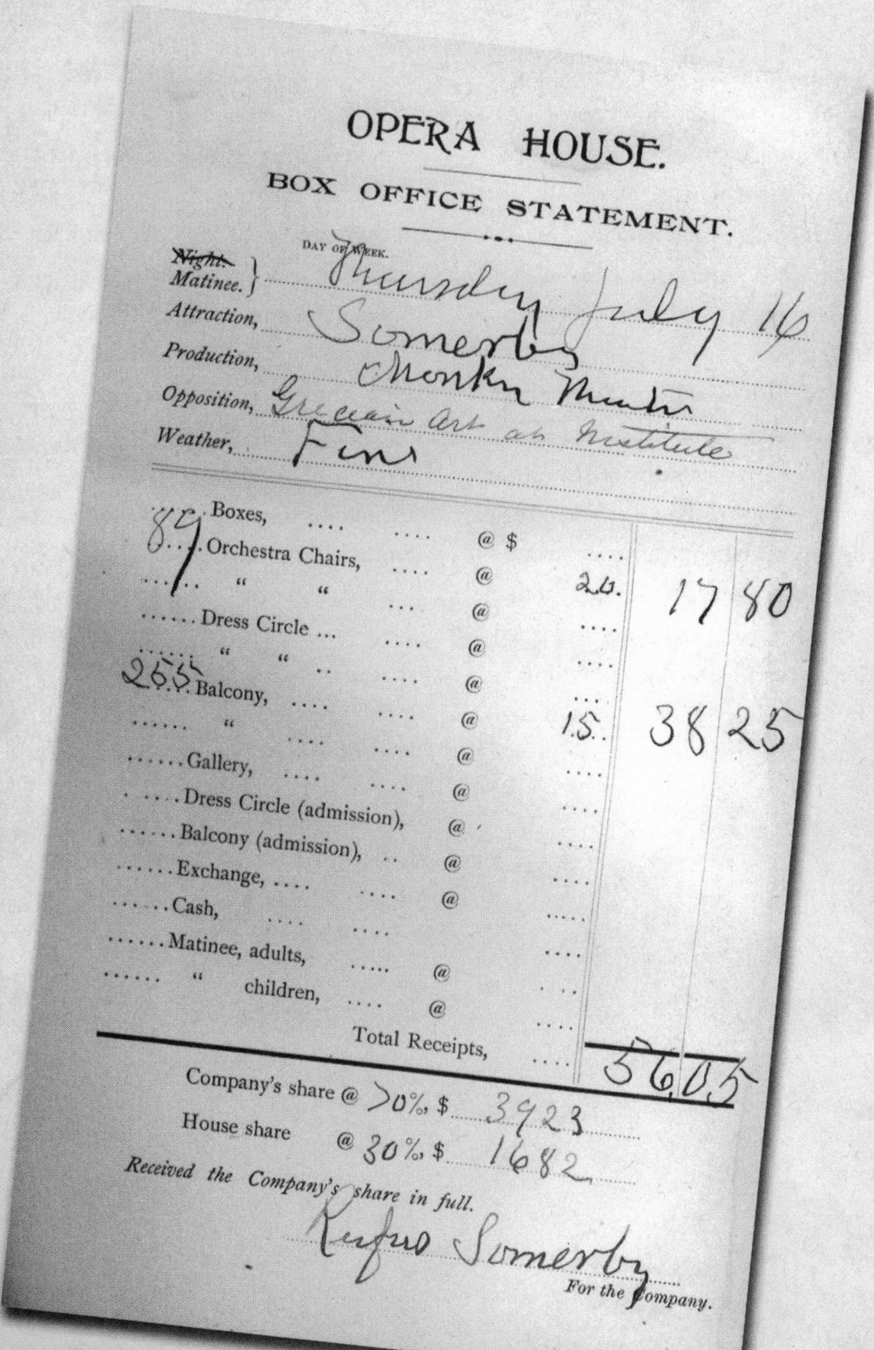

OPERA HOUSE.

BOX OFFICE STATEMENT.

Night.
Matinee. } *Thursday July 16*

Attraction, *Somerby*

Production, *Monkey Music*

Opposition, *Grecian Art at Institute*

Weather, *Fine*

85 Boxes,	....	@ $	....	
Orchestra Chairs,	....	@	20.	17 80
" "	....	@	....	
Dress Circle ...	....	@	....	
" "	....	@	....	
255 Balcony,	....	@	15.	38 25
Gallery,	....	@	....	
Dress Circle (admission),	....	@	....	
Balcony (admission),	....	@	....	
Exchange,	....	@	....	
Cash,	....	....	....	
Matinee, adults,	....	@	....	
" children,	....	@	....	
	Total Receipts,	....		56 05

Company's share @ 70% $ _3923_

House share @ 30% $ _1682_

Received the Company's share in full.

Rufus Somerby

For the Company.

a wide-brimmed felt hat and long white hair—sixty-three-year-old Rufus Somerby played the role of show manager flawlessly. A fashionable man who lived in Cambridge, Massachusetts, he favoured a Prince Albert coat with a white silk tie.

Professor Wormwood's Monkey Theatre was Somerby's new venture —and what a venture! No fewer than twenty-four monkeys, twenty dogs, a badger, and an anteater comprised the animal troupe. The talented monkeys were dressed in costumes and acted out scenes portraying everything from elegant violinists to doctors and nurses. In other acts, the monkeys boxed, rode bicycles, and danced. In one scene monkeys jumped in little wagons harnessed to dogs and raced across the stage.

Somerby opened his 1896 monkey theatre tour in Yarmouth, playing dozens of towns and cities throughout Nova Scotia, Cape Breton Island, New Brunswick, and Quebec. Somerby began every show with a religious-flavoured lecture about the intelligence and treatment of animals. Commenting on Somerby's lecture, a reporter in Woodstock, New Brunswick, wrote, "He hoped that every man after the show would go home and try to get a more comfortable place for his dog to sleep."[3]

PART TWO

YARMOUTH, NOVA SCOTIA

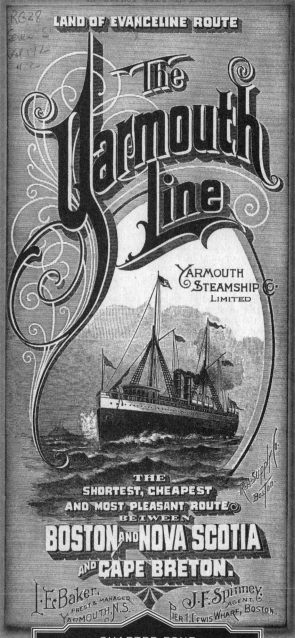

LAND OF EVANGELINE ROUTE

The Yarmouth Line

YARMOUTH
STEAMSHIP Co.
LIMITED

R.A.Supply Co.
Boston.

THE
SHORTEST, CHEAPEST
AND MOST PLEASANT ROUTE
BETWEEN
BOSTON AND NOVA SCOTIA
AND CAPE BRETON.

L.E.Baker,
PRES'T & MANAGER,
YARMOUTH, N.S.

J.F.Spinney,
AGENT,
PIER 1, LEWIS WHARF, BOSTON.

CHAPTER FOUR

HOUDINI LANDS IN CANADA

Yarmouth, Nova Scotia
Wednesday, May 27, 1896

"I win all the sea-sick medals on board of all ships."
—Harry Houdini writing to Quincy Kilby
from aboard the RMS *Imperator*, July 9, 1920

HARRY HOUDINI DIDN'T NOTICE that the rising sun was doing its best to burn off the morning fog in Yarmouth Harbour. The only thing the magician cared about was how swiftly the steamship's gangplank could be set down in Canada. Houdini's fellow passengers likely let the obviously suffering young man get to the front of the line.

His seasickness was so spectacular that Professor Dooley vividly recalled it six years later in a letter he sent to Houdini in reply to one from him. "Your reference to your seasickness reminded me of that famous journey to Yarmouth. If you suffered as much as you did then, you were certainly to be pitied."

Once the ramp was in place and the gate opened, Harry Houdini and the rest of the passengers quickly disembarked on what the Yarmouth locals called the Boston boat wharf. The waterfront was especially busy on this day. The air

There was steamship service between Yarmouth and New England from the mid-1800s until Nova Scotia's NDP government ceased subsidizing the ferry in 2009. (Nova Scotia Archives)

was thick with the smell of cod splayed out on flakes to dry for export. Thousands of barrels of mackerel were being loaded by Yarmouth stevedores onto special steamers bound for Boston. Nova Scotia's coast was swarming with unusually large schools of the oily fish. Under the watchful eye of Canadian officials on Dominion cruisers, more than forty boats from Gloucester, Massachusetts, were raking in huge catches alongside the local fishermen.

Water Street bustled as carts arrived to pick up luggage, and family members welcomed home their people who were returning to Yarmouth after working and visiting in the Boston States. The dock filled quickly with trunks and suitcases as stevedores unloaded the steamship's cargo. Hacks and cart owners did a brisk business transporting passengers and their luggage to the railroad station as well as delivering fares to Yarmouth's hotels.

Bessie and Harry Houdini had landed in a prosperous town of six thousand that proudly boasted the Maritimes' first street railway. Yarmouth was booming thanks to the fishery and a solid manufacturing industry that produced everything from clothespins to anchors. If Harry and Bessie needed a reminder that they were no longer in the United States they didn't have to look far. The Union Jack fluttered at the top of flagpoles above Canada's flag, the Red Ensign.

In terms of entertainment, Yarmouth benefited from being a point of entry from the United States via steamship. Theatrical troupes knew Yarmouth had plenty of workers with money to spend on entertainment. As a result, American show companies often opened or closed their tours of Eastern Canada with performances at the Yarmouth theatre. The theatre, located on the third floor of a building owned by the Boston Marine Insurance Company, was known as the Boston Marine Hall.

Once back on his native soil, Professor Dooley had plenty on his mind besides memories of his Nova Scotia youth. The trunks labelled "Marco Magic Company" along with piles of rigging had to be hauled up the steep slope of Jenkins Street to the theatre, located across from Brown's Hotel, on Main Street. But first, the entire Marco Magic Company had to be bonded to perform in Canada. Immediately upon arrival, all foreign performers had to register with government officials and

🐚 An assortment of press clippings from the Yarmouth portion
of the Marco tour as displayed in Houdini's 1890s press book.
(Sidney H. Radner Collection, History Museum at the Castle, Appleton, Wisconsin)

Marco

Nr
Joined at Boston
may 24th, 1896

Marco died in may
1908 august

Canada

The Daily Telegraph

ST. JOHN, N. B., JUNE 5, 1896.

THE DAILY TELEGRAPH is published at 22 and 25 Canterbury street, every morning (Sundays excepted), by THE TELEGRAPH PUBLISHING CO., of St. John.

He is a Wonder.

"Mysterious" Harry Houdini who is in connexion with the Marco Company gave a grand exhibition in Chief of Police Clarke's office, last evening, and it is needless to say kept his guests wondering as to how he did the different tricks.

Mr. Houdini claims that there is not a hand cuff in the city that he cannot get free from without breaking. At his exhibition last evening before the chief of police and a number of newspaper representatives and friends, Captain Jenkins of the south end division put a number of different kinds of hand-cuffs on Houdini's wrists, and after being a short time in a private room, he would appear before the audience with the cuffs unlocked and himself a free man.

The last test that Chief Clark made was with a pair of new appliances used for the purpose of keeping insane persons from doing injury to themselves. The appliance looked and is very difficult, but the young magician, after a few minutes' work, was clear of the different straps, etc.

A newspaper representative then picked out a playing card from a pack and after seeing the number of figures on the front of it, sent a note by one of the police officers over to Hotel Stanley asking Madamoiselle Marco what card was chosen. In a short time she sent back a correct answer.

Mr. Houdini is represented here by his manager, Mr. Bert Kilby, who intends making a tour of Europe this season, leaving America in August.

YARMOUTH TIMES

YARMOUTH, FRIDAY, MAY 29.

The original Marco magic and mystery company arrived from Boston Wednesday and after two nights in Boston Marine Hall, next Monday and Tuesday, will spend a week at St. John opera house and a week at the Halifax Academy of Music. Last evening, a TIMES representative was given an illustration of how easily a magician escapes from handcuffs. Houdini, a member of the company, has a collection of curious handcuffs and manacles, leg irons, etc. He could almost instantly—a matter of seconds—release himself from any of them when locked upon him, without any key, handing the irons over unlocked. Chief of Police Griffin and Policeman Palmer were called into a shop and in the presence of several gentlemen they handcuffed Houdini, with their own up-to-date handcuffs. The magician retired for a few seconds to the back shop and returned free, handing the open irons over to the officers.

THE DAILY SUN.

ST. JOHN, N. B., JUNE 5, 1896.

CAN OPEN ANY HANDCUFFS.

There was an interesting seance at the central police station last evening. Harry Houdini, one of the prominent members of Marco's company, which will open a week's engagement at the Opera house on Monday next, called on Chief Clark by appointment at 7.30 p. m., and gave a most wonderful exhibition of his skill as a handcuff worker. As the first test a pair of the latest style handcuffs were locked on Houdini's wrists; he then stepped into the chief's private office alone, the door was closed, and in just ten seconds by a stop watch he walked out with the hand-cuffs unlocked. Then the chief produced a pair of padded leather wristlets, which were put on Houdini and the strap carried tightly around his wrist and locked in the middle of his back, with a patent lock, the most recent Chicago invention. Houdini again retired and after a short absence reappeared, streaming with perspiration, but with lock unfastened and the entire outfit taken to pieces. The third and most severe test of all was made with the safety apparatus for securing persons violently insane or prisoners who need protection against themselves. Houdini's hands were each forced into a stout, hard leather glove, preventing any movement of the fingers; the hands were strapped together at the wrist and the belt passed around his waist and fastened behind. He was then placed in the Chief's private office and the door closed. Everybody believed it impossible for a human being to throw off the gloves, but Houdini did it in a very few minutes. It was, he said, the hardest test to which he had ever been subjected in his life. After this, by way of amusement, he executed a lot of wonderful tricks with a pack of cards. Officer Killen says that, if Houdini is ever placed in his charge he will not trust to handcuffs, but will stand over him with a shillalah.

The Gazette.

ST. JOHN, N. B., FRIDAY, JUNE 4, 1896.

The GAZETTE is published at 21 Canterbury street, every morning, Sundays excepted, John A. Bowes, Editor and Publisher.

Spirits in Chains.

A most novel seance was given in Chief of Police Clark's office at the police station last evening by Harry Houdini, pupil of the wonderful Marcos, who open at the Opera house on Monday.

The mysterious stranger showed himself very clever in palmistry and sleight of hand as well as at mind reading, conjunction with Mme Marco who remained at the Hotel Stanley, yet told selected card picked out at the police court.

Perhaps the most wonderful exhibition of the night was Houdini's handcuff trick. Several pairs of wrist cuffs including the wonderful maniac cuff and belt, which Chief Clarke is trying to persuade the city to adopt were tried on the young man, each in turn were as easy to open though they were never locked.

This can be said of all the cuffs with the exception of the promise cuff with

St. John Globe

ST. JOHN, N. B., JUNE 5, 1896.

CAN OPEN HANDCUFFS. — Harry Houdini, one of the wizards who is to appear at the Opera House with Marcos, gave a wonderful exhibition of his skill at

Yarmouth's Boston Marine Hall as it appeared in 1896 when
Houdini performed there. (Yarmouth County Museum and Archives)

pay duty. The customs laws were designed to prevent American theatre troupes from
overstaying their welcome. Ninety per cent of the duty charged on stage properties
was refundable, but only if entertainers stayed less than one month. Dooley was
already booked past the one-month mark in Canada, thereby guaranteeing he would
forfeit the duty paid on his excessive amount of equipment.

The customs officials also targeted theatrical bill paper such as posters,
programmes, broadsides, and tickets for pricey non-refundable duties. There was
no guarantee that Canadian officials would welcome every foreign entertainer with
a smile. Both Canada and the United States happily turned back performers that
seemed less than professional. They had very little tolerance for organ grinders and
gypsy musicians. Magicians could also be denied entry. The popular conjuror Zera
Semon had a close call when a Canadian official suspected he was attempting to
mount a lottery show, where theatre tickets were entered in a draw to win trinkets

or cash prizes. The smooth Semon managed to talk his way out of trouble and won entry to his favourite Maritime market—where he promptly mounted a lottery show.

Professor Dooley issued a statement to the Yarmouth press that stretched the truth. "Yarmouth is the only city in which Marco will appear between Boston and Saint John."[1] In reality, Dooley was already booked into at least three other Maritime cities. And furthermore, he was actively pursuing more local dates to fill in some gaps in his tour schedule.

Dooley and Houdini would learn that many great magicians had held the boards at the Yarmouth theatre. Recently, the Richmond, Virginia-based Zera Semon had performed in Yarmouth with his wife and son. One of the most famous mystery performers in the world had also appeared here at the Boston Marine Hall, when Anna Eva Fay included Yarmouth as a one-night stop at the end of her sold-out 1895 tour of the Maritimes.

Yarmouth had seen some duds, too. In December a Boston-based magician named Sie Hassen Ben-Ali landed with an elaborate stage show. The two Christmas Day shows were poorly attended and were forgettable thanks to several bungled illusions.

To convince citizens of Yarmouth that Marco was a first-class performer, Professor Dooley wrote a rambling press release and submitted the fanciful article to the *Yarmouth Light* newspaper editor.

There will be an entertainment of particular interest at the Boston Marine Hall Monday and Tuesday nights when the wonderful Marco will mystify with his performance of magic and illusions. This Marco, who is the original from Egyptian Hall, London, should not be confounded with any of the imitators who have been using his name. In speaking of Marco's performances the *Hartford Post* said, "Herrmann and Kellar are good magicians, but there are others as was proved at the opera house last evening when Marco made his first appearance in Hartford. Marco performs several of the most difficult feats of the old time wizards, just enough to show that he is as clever as any of them and then he proceeds to give a performance of novelties, all of them of surpassing mystery. It is in this particular of originality that Marco excels—his tricks and illusions aside from the time honored experiments, without which a magic show would not seem complete, are evidently inventions of his own and the ingenuity of their conception and the artistic way in which they are worked out contribute to the belief indicated in the opening sentence that Marco is the equal, if not the peer of the more famous exponents of the black art. In the sleight-of-hand first part, Marco absolutely defied the closest attention and the quickest eye and not the least entertaining feature of his work was the bright and witty remarks that accompanied every trick.

Along with the write-up, Professor Dooley ran large advertisements for the Monday and Tuesday night shows in three different Yarmouth newspapers. His front-page Marco advertisement in the *Yarmouth Light* boasted illusions with names like Voodoo Temple of Brahma, Cremation of Floribel, Mystery of L'Hasa, and the Birth of Flora. Dooley set his ticket prices ten cents higher than usual at twenty-five, thirty-five, and fifty cents.

Professor Dooley had most certainly planned for a considerable build-up to his company's first performances on this Maritime tour. The SS *Yarmouth* made two round trips between Boston and Yarmouth every week. Professor Dooley could have departed from Boston on Friday, landing his troupe in Yarmouth early Saturday morning. Instead, the Marco Magic Company now had five-and-a-half days to spend in Yarmouth before Monday's opening at the six-hundred-seat Marine Hall.

EDWARD JAMES DOOLEY spent much of his life doubling as a Catholic church choirmaster and organist. And Dooley had formal training to back up his twenty years of professional musicianship. In 1870, at the age of fifteen, he enrolled at the College of Montreal where he spent six years earning degrees in business, music, and the classics.

Dooley's first stop after graduation was Portland, Maine, where he was the organist for the Immaculate Conception Cathedral, but he was soon recruited away to a cathedral in Buffalo, New York. Dooley returned to the east coast, organizing the chancel choir and introducing the Gregorian chant at the Redemptionist Mission Church in Boston.

Dooley finally settled down in Hartford, Connecticut, as the organist for St. Patrick's Church. With only four weeks' rehearsal, the thirty-year-old debuted at a sold-out concert, performing an organ recital and then conducting a performance of the Stabat Mater featuring an eighty-member choir and an eighteen-piece orchestra. A review of Dooley's performance in the *Hartford Courant* heaped praise on the talented Nova Scotian: "Mr. Dooley's organ playing showed much facility and was received with evident pleasure though applause is not permitted in the church."

Professor Dooley's mechanical knowledge of organs was just as impressive as his musicianship. A bishop once entrusted him to choose an organ for a New York

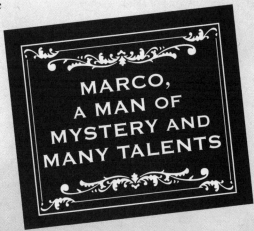

MARCO,
A MAN OF
MYSTERY AND
MANY TALENTS

Harry Houdini saved this early Marco letterhead in one
of his many scrapbooks. Houdini inscribed it "Prof. EJ Dooley
of Hartford, Conn." (Library of Congress)

State cathedral. Dooley responded by purchasing one of the finest organs ever built in the United States, a showpiece at the 1876 Centennial Exhibition in Philadelphia. And in 1890 Dooley opened his own Pearl Street store introducing Hartford to electric pianos and self-playing organs.

With his Marco Company, Dooley landed in Yarmouth just as the newly built Zion Church was planning a dedication celebration. The previous Saturday, the organ had been installed and tested in the five-hundred-seat church. They had spared no expense purchasing the custom-built two-thousand-dollar organ from Toronto. The instrument's enormous pipes were a wondrous sight to the townsfolk of Yarmouth. But, of course, the big organ pipes were more than familiar to Dooley.

Somehow Professor Dooley managed to steal the spotlight by organizing his own recital on

Saturday, May 30, 1896, a full week prior to the official dedication of the new church. The Zion United Baptist Church was packed with Yarmouth citizens of all religious stripes, anxious to hear the magnificent new organ for the first time. Professor Dooley was rewarded for his performance when a reporter from the *Yarmouth*

Light wrote, "Marco is also a fine organist and on Saturday afternoon he delighted quite an audience with his playing on the fine new organ in Zion Church."

Professor Dooley's life was indeed a paradox—an adored world-class musician who chased after fame and fortune as an amateur magician.

The Zion Church in Yarmouth where Professor Dooley performed an organ recital a week before the church's official consecration. The Parade Street church still stands in 2012.

(Yarmouth County Museum and Archives)

CHAPTER FIVE

HANDCUFF KING

Yarmouth, Nova Scotia
Thursday, May 28, 1896

"No one had ever trod the path of Escape until
I cut the pathway to fame, and may I add, Fortune."
—Harry Houdini writing to his friend Quincy Kilby, March 11, 1915

HARRY HOUDINI DIDN'T WASTE ANY TIME publicizing the Marco Magic Company. He spread the word that he would give a free handcuff escape demonstration in downtown Yarmouth on Thursday evening, the day after his arrival. Houdini set up at Scott's Bazaar, a general store that sold just about everything from wallpaper to sporting goods. More importantly for Houdini, the store at 379 Main Street was also selling the advance tickets for the Marco shows at the Boston Marine Hall.

Free shows like the one Houdini was planning for Yarmouth were an old stock-in-trade trick of promoters. Dime shows featured their finest attraction outside of the tent as bait to lure customers to pay admission to see the "wonders" inside. Likewise, every circus offered a free parade to generate excitement and flush out customers to visit the big top.

The image of Houdini posing in a formal tux while cuffed and shackled is as striking today as it was more than a century ago. (Library of Congress)

The handcuff act had been around for many years, and was still very much a fringe form of entertainment. Nobody had ever tried to build an entire career around escapes, but Houdini already had some success using his handcuff act to generate free publicity for the American Gaiety Girls.

Back in November, at the bustling Massachusetts fishing port of Gloucester, Houdini paid a lunchtime visit to the police station and easily escaped from the department's handcuffs. While the unusual stunt didn't exactly cause a sensation, it did get the Gaiety Girls a free paragraph in the November 21, 1895, edition of the *Daily Times* that complimented Houdini: "He is truly a marvel and his performance is most interesting."

Houdini's handcuff escape at the Gloucester police station made the leap from the amusement listings all the way to the news items, where it was printed alongside court reports and a story about a missing fisherman. Even though his handcuff handiwork was reported as "real" news, the Gloucester article still closed with a sentence guaranteed to make any promoter smile. "He will repeat the performance on the stage this evening." Pleased with his Gloucester success, Houdini visited the Springfield police station a week later and scored another write-up in the *Springfield Union*.

By the time Houdini signed on with the Marco Magic Company he had more than enough skill to escape from the regulation handcuffs used by most American police forces. And Houdini's correspondence with magic dealers of the day indicates he was still trying to improve his escape act in May 1896.

In the weeks before landing in Nova Scotia, Houdini had visited the navy yards in Brooklyn scavenging for more chains and shackles to use onstage. He already had several antique handcuffs and shackles that he couldn't open, so he sought the help of W.D. LeRoy, a Boston magic merchant. LeRoy asked Houdini to send him the irons and he would help devise a secret method to unlock them.

Mr. LeRoy, a magician who was no stranger to the Maritimes, wasn't pleased when he got word that Harry was bragging about how he escaped from some of his stage handcuffs. As a dealer in magic apparatus, LeRoy counted on his customers keeping his secrets. Just before Harry joined the Marco Company in Boston, he received a letter from LeRoy, sent on May 7, with a pointed reminder about the magician's code. "Don't tell anyone that you use keys or have any, let 'em guess."

On Thursday evening, Harry Houdini discovered he had some competition. A popular Scottish group had returned to Yarmouth and was presenting a concert

Harry Houdini gave his first-
ever international escape act
performance at Scott's Bazaar.
(Yarmouth County Museum
and Archives)

of Celtic music and readings in the town. Nevertheless, Harry managed to find an interested audience for his demonstration.

At Scott's Bazaar, Houdini easily escaped from his assortment of leg irons, handcuffs, and manacles. Among his curious collection was a prized pair of Lilly Irons, famous in America because they were used on the conspirators following the assassination of Abraham Lincoln. The Lilly Irons featured a straight iron bar between the wrists rather than a chain, making it impossible to reach one hand with the other. A Yarmouth reporter noted Houdini's prowess with the shackles. "He could almost instantly — a matter of seconds — release himself from any of them when locked upon him without any key."[1]

Although every escape ended with Houdini handing his unlocked restraints to the onlookers for examination, the spectators, including a reporter from the *Yarmouth Times*, were suspicious about a magician escaping from his own handcuffs. After all, they could likely be rigged to open by secret means without a key. The spectators were correct in their suspicions. A portrait photographer from Lynn, Massachusetts, appropriately named B.B. Keyes, had invented a pair of trick handcuffs that could be easily opened by any stage performer without a key.

Even Houdini was starting to have doubts about his own escape act. Less than a month earlier, Houdini had offered to sell his irons to Mr. LeRoy's magic shop because, as Bessie explained, audiences appeared indifferent to the escapes. "In fact all our acts went well with one exception. That was the handcuffs. Houdini was still unable to give the public a thrill with this pet trick of his own invention. Every week

Yarmouth policeman Harris "Had" Palmer was the first lawman outside of the United States to snap a pair of handcuffs on Harry Houdini. Harris lived in Dayton, and walked the two and a half miles to his job in Yarmouth.

(Yarmouth County Museum and Archives)

he seemed to be giving a more difficult and intricate performance with the irons. An audience of police chiefs would have been amazed at his skill and technique, but our small-town American spectators were utterly cold to it. The majority of them apparently assumed that Houdini was using prepared cuffs."[2]

So far on this evening in Yarmouth, it seemed as if Houdini's small-town Canadian spectators were also cold to the act. That suddenly changed when one of the onlookers decided to make life a little more difficult for Houdini. The shopper, who might have been an undercover member of the Marco Magic Company, had summoned policeman Harris "Had" Palmer and Chief of Police Michael Griffin to test Houdini's ability with a pair of real Yarmouth police handcuffs.

The crowd fidgeted as they watched the young magician's face carefully for any sign of nervousness now that he realized he was face to face with Yarmouth's finest. Houdini realized his audience was absolutely transfixed by the spectacle unfolding before them. This was exactly what Professor Dooley needed, genuine street-level publicity!

As policeman Palmer snapped the Yarmouth handcuffs on Houdini, the audience couldn't help but notice that the young showman's wrists, hands, and fingers were powerfully corded with muscles that could rival the working hands of Yarmouth's most venerable fishermen. When Palmer tightened the cuffs, the veins in Houdini's formidable forearms popped outward as if the cuffs were too tight and were blocking his circulation.

Houdini tugged hopelessly on the cuffs, then turned his back to the crowd. Chief Griffin and policeman Palmer smiled at each other as Houdini took a few tentative steps toward the back of the shop. Several of the spectators felt sorry for the dignified young showman. He had been very friendly and respectful to his small Yarmouth audience before the police got involved. It was a shame that he was going to be embarrassed by the real police handcuffs.

Within seconds, Houdini turned around and walked back toward the policemen and calmly handed the chief his unlocked cuffs. Chief Griffin looked at policeman Palmer in disbelief. The little crowd applauded and congratulated the young magician on his escape. Houdini couldn't hide his own smile now as he glanced at the troublemaking shopper's face. As planned, word of the mysterious Harry Houdini quickly spread throughout Yarmouth.

The *Yarmouth Times* published a small notice of Houdini's escape from the handcuffs. The eagle-eyed Houdini had another clipping for his collection. And this one was special; it was the very first of many, many international articles that would be written about the young showman in the future. Houdini pasted the short article in his press book and proudly wrote "Canada" above the story.

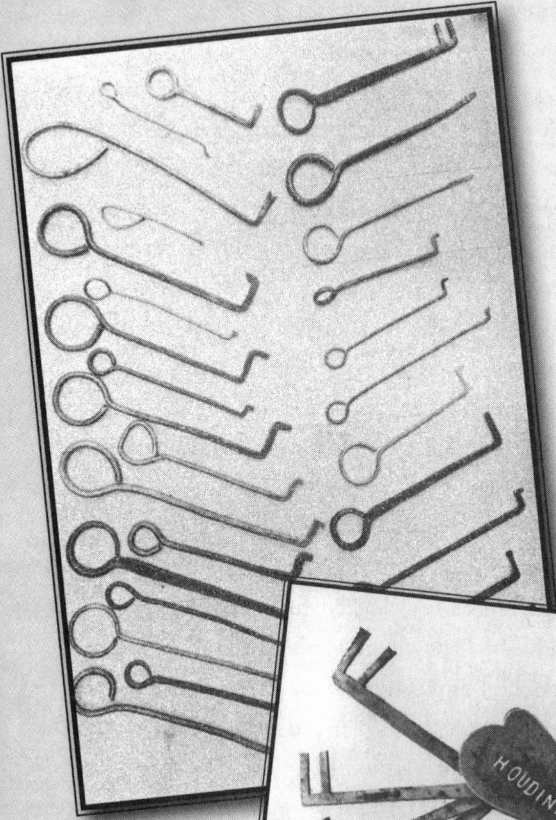

A selection of Houdini's
lock-pickers from his
book *Handcuff Secrets*.
(Public domain)

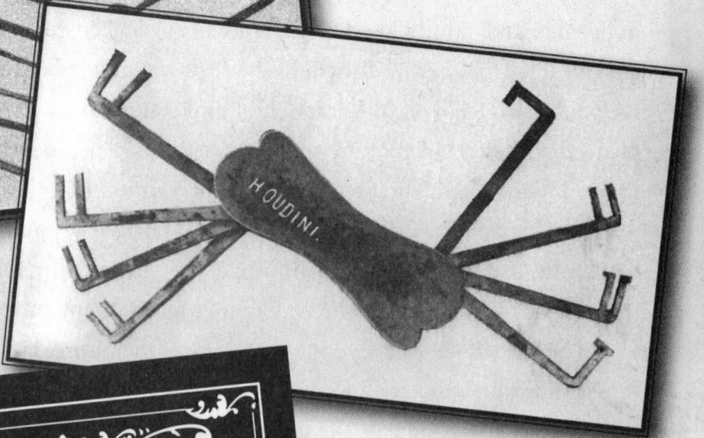

TRICKS
OF THE
TRADE

THROUGHOUT HIS CAREER, Harry Houdini compiled long lists of handcuff makes and models, with notes explaining how to open each and every one. Lock picks and hidden keys were fair game, but Houdini had other methods for opening handcuffs as well.

Early on, in an 1892 letter, Houdini's long-time confidant August Roterberg offered the young magician a tantalizing secret. "Do you know how to open the Tower Cuff without a key? If you don't know, I will write you how or at least the plan by which it is supposed to work." For a time, Houdini used a hidden lead plate sewn into his pants just above the knee. Once out of sight, he could strike certain makes of handcuffs on to the metal plate, quickly jarring them open.

Later on, after he had largely abandoned the handcuff act, Houdini told a Baltimore reporter he once concealed tiny pieces of rubber under his tongue or in between his fingers. While examining handcuffs prior to an escape challenge, he would secretly drop the rubber morsels into the mechanism, preventing them from completely locking. He also claimed that a small piece of bread would work in lieu of rubber.

Although he had a deep and thorough understanding of locks, Houdini's greatest strength as an escape artist was his showmanship. In his 1910 book, *Handcuff Secrets*, he warned budding new escape artists, "It is not the trick that is to be considered, but the style and manner in which it is presented."

Houdini in Chicago with his long time friend and lock advisor August Roterberg and Mr. Roterberg's wife.
(Library of Congress)

CHAPTER SIX

OPENING NIGHT

Boston Marine Hall, Yarmouth, Nova Scotia
Monday, June 1, 1896

"One of the cleverest acts ever seen…namely the Metamorphosis box mystery
as accomplished by the artists the Houdinis. A great many would no doubt
be led to the belief that they used supernatural power in conjunction with
their act. How two human beings can accomplish what they do in
3 seconds time is something mysterious."
— *Evening Sentinel*, Carlisle, Pennsylvania, August 3, 1895

BY MONDAY MORNING, the Marco Magic Company had spent five days preparing for the opening of their Canadian tour at the Boston Marine Hall. Houdini's handcuff act at Scott's Bazaar had won the company some much-needed press attention, and the third-floor theatre in the Boston Marine building was packed with patrons eagerly awaiting an "evening of wonder" provided by "The original, the only Marco, Man of Mystery."

Professor Dooley opened the performance at eight o'clock with some traditional sleight of hand with coins, silks, and cards. Dooley was an amateur magician, but thanks to years of experience as both a lecturer and musician, he was very much at home on the stage. In Yarmouth, a reporter noted Dooley connected with his

 Harry and Bessie pose with the Metamorphosis trunk. During the act, the trunk was placed within a curtained enclosure known as a "cabinet." (Patrick Culliton Collection)

audience from the start by performing some close-up magic. "He had the usual mechanical magic and sleight of hand tricks many of which he performed right down among the audience and all of which were cleverly done."[1]

After his sleight-of-hand routine, Dooley formally introduced Bessie and Harry Houdini to the Yarmouth audience. "As I am on my retirement tour it gives me great pleasure to introduce you to my successors, my daughter, Lady Marco, and her husband, the mysterious Harry Houdini!"[2]

The young couple was welcomed onstage with a warm round of applause. A murmur went through the crowd as some members of the audience recognized Houdini as the man who escaped from policeman Palmer's handcuffs.

The couple's stage presence was in itself a clever illusion. The dark-skinned Harry towered over Bessie by eight inches, creating the appearance of a much taller man despite his actual five-feet-and-five-inch height. Harry was often noted to be an undersized man but he was sturdily built and aside from being slightly bowlegged, he was a perfect specimen of male anatomy.

Bessie weighed just over ninety pounds and was still easily mistaken for a young girl. Tonight, she looked stunning in her homemade stage dress and tights. Her brown hair was parted down the centre and fell in natural curled ringlets on each side of her carefully made-up face. When she laughed, her smile revealed teeth that were gapped and slightly crooked.

THE MIRACULOUS METAMORPHOSIS

Standing in front of a curtained enclosure that measured six feet square, Houdini motioned to the wings and watched as two stagehands brought out a large steamer trunk. The steel-reinforced wooden box was unquestionably well-travelled; it had all the expected wear and tear marks on the protective wooden slats that criss-crossed its sides and tops. It stood thirty inches high and measured almost four feet in length. The box was just over two feet deep, allowing plenty of room for a magician to be locked inside.

While Bessie stood by, Harry introduced their Metamorphosis illusion, or as Houdini explained to his Yarmouth audience, "a quick change." While other performers would suggest the audience was about to witness spiritualistic forces at work, Houdini was unfailingly honest in his patter and announced that the Metamorphosis illusion was not achieved with the aid of supernatural power. This

Flyers like this, presenting "Mysterious Harry" and "La Petite Bessie" while promoting the Metamorphosis, were mailed to booking agents and theatre managers.

(Library of Congress)

opening confession was something Houdini started while with the Welsh Brothers Circus when he bluntly informed an audience in Carlisle, Pennsylvania, that the mysterious trunk act was "nothing but a trick."

Harry invited five members of the audience to come up on stage and form a committee to oversee the proceedings. Before performing the couple's signature act with Bessie, Houdini offered a demonstration as a prelude to the illusion. After asking the committee men to tie his hands behind his back, he entered the curtained enclosure. Within a minute he reappeared with his hands still tied behind his back but his coat missing.

Almost every member of the committee and the audience suspected Houdini had a trick coat in play. To vanquish that theory, Houdini asked a member of the committee to remove his coat and hang it in the curtained enclosure. Houdini re-entered the cabinet and appeared seconds later wearing the man's coat. When he turned around, the audience could clearly see his hands were still tied behind his back.

Now it was time for the main event.

Houdini instructed the committee to examine the Metamorphosis box, inside and out. Once the men reported the trunk was legitimate, Bessie handed them a large cloth sack to examine. After the men found the sack to be in good order, Houdini asked them to place it in the trunk. Next, Houdini stepped into the trunk

and asked the committee to pull the sack up and over his head. Bessie gave the men a few feet of quarter-inch sash cord and asked them to tie the bag securely at the top, above her husband's head. To ensure the cord would not be cut or untied, the committee was given some sealing wax to put on the knots.

Houdini crouched down in the trunk, allowing the men to close the lid. After locking all four of the trunk's built-in brass locks, the committee was coached to wrap rope around the trunk and make certain it would be impossible for Houdini to open it from inside.

The attentive Yarmouth audience watched as the committee placed the rope-trussed trunk inside the curtained enclosure and then stood off to the sides.

Bessie stepped into the curtain cabinet and spoke to the audience for the first time. "I now draw the curtain." Once the curtain was drawn, she clapped three times.

At the third clap, the curtain was flung open and Harry Houdini rushed out of the enclosure with his hands free and minus the committee man's coat. The stunned audience barely let out a collective gasp as their eyes tried to comprehend what they had just witnessed. How did the magician untie his hands, get out of the sealed sack, and exit the locked and rope-bound trunk?

And where was Lady Marco?

Professor Dooley's stagehands worked feverishly to unlock the trunk and fling open the lid. When the sack was revealed, Houdini asked the committee to examine the wax seal on the sack's cord for any evidence of tampering. After the rope was cut free, the sack was dropped and the audience gasped as one. There was Lady Marco! And she was wearing the same committee man's coat that the magician was wearing when he entered the trunk. When Bessie spun around, the audience gasped again. Her wrists were tied together.

After Bessie was freed from her bonds, she stood hand-in-hand with her husband at centre stage and took a slow and practiced bow as the audience continued applauding. More than a few audience members noticed sweat dripping off of Houdini's face and soaking into the stage floor.

The sweat was a testament to how hard Harry had struggled to free himself from the ropes while he was curled up in the trunk. Challenging rope work was something he had expected to face in Yarmouth, a fishing town populated with knot-savvy fishermen. As with the other towns where the Houdinis performed

A large poster used to promote Metamorphosis. (Library of Congress)

Metamorphosis, the audience now had a topic for endless discussion and theorizing about how the trunk act was accomplished. In the coming days, Yarmouth citizens would suggest explanations involving trap doors, mirrors, and body doubles. Others would honestly believe that the Houdinis had assistance from the spirits or had the supernatural ability to dematerialize and pass through solid materials.

The Marine Hall audience had witnessed one of the greatest acts in the history of magic. The very same Metamorphosis illusion would be performed by the Houdinis throughout their entire career. Back in Yarmouth, Professor Dooley had the unenviable task of following the Houdinis' brilliant act. Dooley returned to the stage and performed the Mystery of L'Hassa with Bessie. This was a mystifying levitation otherwise known as the Queen of the Air. The illusion was a difficult one to pull off successfully. The mechanical contraptions had to be worked perfectly and silently to fool an audience and, on opening night, the levitation went off without a hitch.

The Yarmouth audience applauded and cheered the entertainment until eleven o'clock, a half-hour beyond the promised show length. The theatre patrons buzzed with excitement as they spilled out of the building and chatted under the street lights on the corner of Main and Cliff. It was a memorable night in the history of the Boston Marine Hall, which stood until 1982 when it was demolished to make room for a YMCA.

The next day, Harry and Bessie's trunk trick was the talk of Yarmouth, guaranteeing another good house for a second show on Tuesday night. The *Yarmouth Times* provided a great clipping for Houdini's press book. The short review of the Marco show made a point of mentioning, "The metamorphosis or Egyptian trunk mystery by Mr. Houdini and Mdlle [*sic*] Marco is alone worth the price of admission. It is certainly a marvelously quick change."

With the tour off to an inspiring start in Yarmouth, the Marco Magic Company set sail for one of North America's oldest cities, Saint John, New Brunswick. The steamship *Alpha* made the short run between Yarmouth and Saint John twice a week, leaving at three o'clock in the afternoon. Houdini would have an opportunity to test his sea legs against the highest tides in the world in the Bay of Fundy.

Houdini would make extraordinary discoveries in Saint John—including one that would eventually ensure his place in history.

➤⊷⊹⊷⊙⊷⊶⊷⊰

PART THREE

NEW BRUNSWICK

Our Chireen Features from the MIDWAY.

THE WALTER L. MAIN

GRANDEST AND BEST SHOWS ON EARTH

3 RING CIRCUS. PARIS HIPPODROME, WILD WEST AND WILD EAST.

"Up she goes."

"Down she goes."

CHAPTER SEVEN
FOOTLIGHTS
AND FOG BANKS

Saint John, New Brunswick
Wednesday, June 3, 1896

"Why, Houdini would murder his grandmother for publicity."
—Overheard by Harry Houdini and noted in his diary, May 13, 1924

RIGHT OFF THE BOAT IN SAINT JOHN, New Brunswick, Harry Houdini and Professor Dooley realized they would be up against some stiff competition during their week-long stand at the Saint John Opera House.

Charles Bernard, the press agent for the Walter L. Main Circus, had visited the city just four days earlier with his own railcar and a crew of eighteen men, including a lithographer. Bernard and his poster brigade, armed with glue buckets and mops, had covered almost every billboard and dead wall in Saint John with circus advertisements.

The colourful posters featured plenty of wild images like Wallace the Wonder, a horse-riding lion, and the Mighty Bovalapus, otherwise billed as "the ocean's awfulest treasure." Now, every man, woman, and child in the city knew the big-time

> "A circus would not be complete without a menagerie, and no one knew this better than Colonel Main when he spent about a million dollars depleting the jungles and forests of five continents for beasts rare and ferocious, strange and beautiful, to people his vast menagerie" — *Saint John Globe*, June 11, 1896
>
> (Harry Ransom Center, The University of Texas at Austin)

railroad circus was coming to town on Friday, June 12—bad news for Dooley who was booked to hold the boards at the Opera House from June 8 to 13.

In the hustle and bustle of the city, the Marco Magic Company, with its arsenal of trunks and props, was spotted by a newspaperman who mentioned the company's arrival in the *Saint John Globe*. "The six advance stage carpenters arrived in the city today and with them was [*sic*] tons of apparatus and riggings that are used in the different illusions."

After their gear was dropped off at the theatre on Union Street, Professor Dooley and his company checked into the Hotel Dufferin on Charlotte Street. The brick hotel was located across the street from a beautiful public park, King's Square, which was designed with diagonal pathways and triangle-shaped gardens to mimic a Union Jack. As a bonus, the Hotel Dufferin was only two blocks from the Opera House, a short walk from the opposite side of the park.

TAKING STOCK IN SAINT JOHN

Saint John had four daily newspapers and Dooley planned to advertise in all of them. He had to promote six evening shows along with matinees on Wednesday and Saturday. As was the custom, with paid advertisements came additional publicity through short articles that promoted the performances. Dooley had an article ready to go for the next day's *Daily Gazette* under the headline "The Wonderful Marco."

> The announcement of the appearance of the original Marco, who will be seen for the first time in this city Monday evening next at the Opera House, has created considerable interest among theatregoers. Marco, who has been copied more than any other magician for a decade, will introduce some of the most marvelous illusions that have ever been presented. In Europe and America these illusions have been marveled at and have puzzled the most knowing minds. The public has but little idea of the immense amount of apparatus that is required for a performance of this kind so prodigious as Marco. This has been sent here ahead, tons of rigging and mechanisms, which are being placed by Marco's advance brigade of stage carpenters. Monday night Marco will introduce, for the first time on any stage, a new illusion, that he has been working to perfect for the last three years, and it is

The Marco Magic Company stayed at the Hotel Dufferin.
Like every well-fitted hotel of the era, the lobby of the Dufferin
was equipped with spittoons. (Heritage Resources Saint John)

promised to be a revelation in magic. In addition to the illusions he
will entertain with half an hour of "sleight of hand," a performance
in which he is said to be without a peer. Mlle. Marco will also do
some very wonderful things in mental occultism telling some startling
things while in a state of hypnotic influence. The sale of seats will
begin at the box office tomorrow morning.

Harry Houdini and Professor Dooley were only the latest in a long list of magicians
to visit Saint John. The city had hosted plenty of conjurors since one of Houdini's
lifelong idols, Signor Blitz, had visited the city in 1840. In more recent years,
Zera Semon, Anna Eva Fay, and Balabrega had mystified audiences in Saint John.

Houdini's Boston magic supplier, W. D. LeRoy, had also performed here five years earlier at the Parlor Musee, a grand exhibition staged by Rufus Somerby. LeRoy, a former violin teacher, won rave reviews from the Saint John press and citizenry for his flawless close-up magic that featured something new for a magician, as reported in the August 17, 1891, *Evening Gazette*: "Mr. LeRoy does his stage performance with his sleeves up."

Aside from promotional work, Professor Dooley would have to connect with the conductor of a brand new orchestra who would be working the Marco show. Following a dispute, the Opera House manager, Alfred Osborne Skinner, had recently dismissed the regular orchestra. The replacement orchestra was an eight-piece ensemble conducted by William C. Bowden who lived on Sydney Street, just around the corner from the Hotel Dufferin.

DAMAGE CONTROL

Repeating their experience in Yarmouth, Professor Dooley and the Houdinis had to spend five days in an unfamiliar city before opening their week-long stand. The fact that Dooley neglected to book dates for the week between Yarmouth and Saint John was a careless oversight. Transporting a troupe over long distances between shows was called a "jump." To cost-conscious managers, "jump" was their least favourite four-letter word.

Other theatrical companies would often pull off one-night stands en route from Yarmouth to Saint John to help shorten travel times and offset transportation costs. It was easy to cash in on the audiences in the prosperous Nova Scotia towns of Annapolis Royal and Digby. Both towns had theatres and were directly across the Bay of Fundy from Saint John. And the side-wheel steamer, *City of Monticello*, made daily trips to Saint John from both Digby and Annapolis Royal.

For some reason, however, Dooley chose to move his troupe all the way to Saint John without any potentially profitable stops. After arriving in Saint John, Dooley scrambled to find some late bookings in the nearby communities. But the smaller towns to the north and west were fairly well booked as the summer theatre season was off to an early start.

Rose Sydell and the London Belles were playing Chatham, Newcastle, and Sackville this week, effectively blocking Dooley from booking his Marco show into one of the smaller towns within easy range of Saint John. Instead, Dooley sent

Rose Sydell, the legendary leader of the London Belles, often wore breathtakingly elaborate costumes on stage. Rose, who once offered an act entitled "Pleasure and Plenty of Satan's Honeymoon," received much of her jewelry from her legions of male admirers.
(Billy Rose Theatre Division, The New York Public Library for the Performing Arts, Astor, Lenox and Tilden Foundations)

posters to St. Stephen, a town seventy miles to the west, opposite Calais, Maine, on the United States border. St. Stephen's *Saint Croix Courier* mentioned the planned shows: "Marco's variety troupe is billed to appear at St. Croix Hall at an early date."

The popular Markos Modern Miracles troupe had played Saint John in September and again over the Christmas holidays. Several articles mentioned the mistaken identity between Marco and the performer named Markos. The *Saint John Sun* of June 4, 1896, warned readers that Marco had been copied and one imitator "has gone so far as to take his name and pass himself as the original Marco." The *Daily Telegraph* of June 4, 1896, also championed Dooley as the real deal. "The magician who appears here is the only and original Marco, and must not be confounded with any other." But only five months earlier, the same paper had heaped praise on Dooley's nemesis, Markos. "For many years the magician has been known here and he never fails to maintain his reputation as an illusionist of the most eminent order."

Even with help from the Saint John press, Professor Dooley had an uphill battle ahead if he was to entice theatregoers to attend yet another show by a magician named Marco or Markos. Unlike Willis Skinner, a.k.a. Markos, who toured with an entourage of talented dancers, comedians, and musicians, Dooley was offering a pure magic show. It would take a super-human effort by the entire troupe to drum up interest in the upcoming shows.

Houdini planned to revive one of his publicity tactics from the American Gaiety Girls tour. His visits to a few New England police stations had earned him some free press in Massachusetts. Tomorrow, he would try to repeat his earlier handcuff success in Saint John. But if Houdini wanted some free publicity at the expense of the Saint John police department, he would have to earn it.

The front page of a Markos programme from the popular magician's 1895 appearance in Yarmouth, NS. (Tom Boldt Collection)

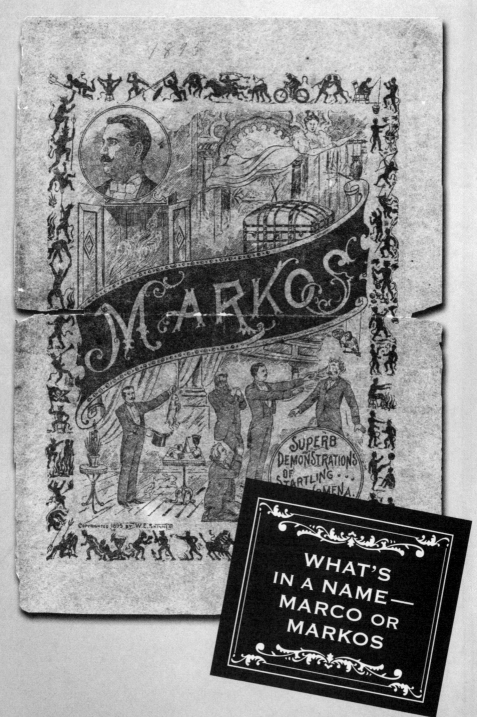

WHAT'S
IN A NAME—
MARCO OR
MARKOS

WHEN PROFESSOR DOOLEY began his Marco tour in May 1896, he knew a magician named Markos had already toured the Maritimes twice in the previous nine months. According to Dooley, this magician had stolen the name and had no right to use it.

A full year earlier, Dooley had started promoting a Maritime Marco tour that he abandoned for health reasons. Before he cancelled the 1895 summer tour, which featured a lady assistant named Miss Belmont, Dooley had forwarded his Marco posters and promotional material to theatres in Halifax, Yarmouth, and elsewhere. Dooley believed his Marco name was stolen by another magician who subtly changed it to Markos.

In the first of many attempts to distance himself from his supposed impersonator, Dooley asked the *Yarmouth Times* to clarify the difference between Marco and Markos with a press release stating: "Marco and Mlle Marco are billed for Yarmouth next Monday and Tuesday in a programme of mysteries. This company were [*sic*] billed through the provinces about a year ago, but Marco's illness caused the engagements all to be cancelled. Since then they claim other companies of similar name have been imposing inferior shows on the public on the strength of Marco's fame. This will be the genuine Marco's first visit here."

The suggestion that Markos was inferior to Marco was wishful thinking on Dooley's behalf. Markos was, in fact, an accomplished magician named Willis Skinner who had been performing professionally as Professor Skinner for over a decade. But Dooley might have been justified in hinting at some underhanded name stealing; there is no record that Willis Skinner ever performed using the name "Markos" before his Halifax stand in September 1895.

Harry Houdini supported Professor Dooley's identity theft theory, and even pointed an accusing finger at the unnamed individual who, in his opinion, masterminded the misdeed. In 1908 he wrote, "By some mischance [Dooley] was booked to open in the summer of 1895 and failed to appear; so management of

A Markos "Modern Miracles" advertisement and a Marco "Monarch of Mystery" programme are displayed side-by-side in this theatrical scrapbook. The outward similarity between the two companies is easily apparent. (New Brunswick Museum)

6 /95 (Cont.) /96   ⊙   '96 (Cont.)

Markos' Modern Miracles
Dec. 25/95 ~ Dec. 18/96

PART I.
Prof. West's Marionettes.
Life-like miniature actors, whose actions please young and old.

PART II.
Markos, the Magician.
Perplexing feats of prestidigitation. The floral illusion. How to cook an omelet. The wizard's supper. The superb hat trick and other marvels.

PART III.
Thomas Killeen, the well-known Irish Character Comedian, in a budget of wit.

PART IV.
Miss Nettie Sinclair
The young and beautiful exponent of mental telegraphy. During this act Miss Sinclair will describe various articles, while blindfolded, and perform other curious tests. This wonderful act has created a profound sensation in Washington, New York and other cities recently.

PART V.
Markos' Cabinet Phenomena.
The performance will conclude with the Celebrated Trunk Mystery, in which Markos himself will play the title role.

MARKOS' MODERN MIRACLES.
Mr. W. E. Skinner, ... Sole Proprietor
H. West, ... Special Agent.
CAUTION.—That part of the act of Miss Sinclair, technically known as "silent second sight," also the "newspaper test," are copyrighted by Markos, and will be protected to the full extent of the law.

... manch 10.
Thursday Evening—Banker's Daughter.
Friday Matinee—Peri.
Friday Evening—Camille.
Saturday Matinee—Fanchon.
Saturday Evening—Little Detective.

Evening Prices—10, 20 and 30 Cts.
Matinee Prices 10 Cts to all parts of the House. Seats on Sale.

Joe—Kelley & St. Claire—Alice
America's prime fun makers. Delineators of black face comedy and soft shoe and buck dancing. Special attention is called to the correct impersonation of the negro character by Miss St. Claire.

4—Decollete Swells—4
Burns, Booth, Price and Groff.

Thos.—Leo & Chapman—Jessie
In their new and original gymnastic sketch, "The Enchanted Farm."

6—Gaiety Girls—6
Groff, Line, Price, Burns, Booth, Evans. The emperors of German comedy.

Campbell and Shepp,
Originators of this style of comedy.

The Continuous Show.
Wild Rose	Alice St. Claire
Messenger	Lillian Price
Captain	Loura Groff
The Giddy Maid	Jessie Chapman
Little Trilby	Frankie Evans
A Guard	Irine Line
Secretary	Nellie Burns
King's Idol	Miss Booth
Master of Palace	John Sydell
Magistrate	Thomas Leo
King Bully Bo	Luke Cole
Court No-a-Count	Joe K. Kelley
Lord De Bum	Jos. Shep
	W.S. Campbell

Prince Ba Ba
—AND—
Wait for the HARRAH   ROSE SYD...

MARCO.
June 8 & 9

MONARCH OF MYSTERY. 13/96
In his latest Oriental, Egyptian and Modern Miracles, assisted by

MLLE. MARCO.
The World's Greatest Psychometric Artist, Clairvoyante and Exponent of Mental Occultism.

PART I.
The inimitable Marco in a bouquet of up-to-date experiments, baffling and mystifying the keenest observer, and calling the collective faculties into active service.
All nature's laws set aside. Laughter born of bewilderment and wonder, concluding with the
CONGRESS OF NATIONS.

PART II.
Marco's new and original conception of Du Maurier's
TRILBY.
OR THE MYSTERY OF L'HASSA
A reproduction of the most marvellous experiment of the Hindoo Yogis. A living breathing human being actually floats in space without any means of support.

CHARACTERS:
Svengali - . . . . Marco
Trilby - . . . . Mlle Marco

PART III.
Marco's Clever Conceit,
THE JACK OF CLUBS.
The Wonder of the 19th century. The Cabinet of Phantoms, or Fun with the Spirits, in which all the principal phenomena of the World's greatest mediums are duplicated in Full Light in an absolutely empty Cabinet, while Marco is seated outside the same, ten feet away.

PART IV.
The 20th century mystery, an original idea of
METAMORPHOSIS,
OR THE ASIATIC TRUNK MYSTERY.
Marco's Latest Theosophical Marvel,
THE VOODOU TEMPLE OF BRAHMA,
or the Astral Projection of a Human Body through Space. An original conception wonderfully startling in effect, and so nearly approaching the supernatural as to be almost miraculous. Affinity with chosen powers seems certain, and grave doubts are raised in the minds of thinking people by this strange production.

PART V.
NADIR SHAH,
The Hindoo Brahmin, in
THE MYSTERIES OF MAHOMET,
which baffles human belief. Comprising the greatest mysteries of the Oriental Necromancy. A grand, weird and wonderful exhibition of Oriental Necromancy and Oriental Necromancers, by which, in the far-famed Hindoo Jugglers and Oriental Necromancers, by which, in the darker ages, millions were held in subjection by the powerful Mahatmas, who, through its use, ruled as with a rod of Iron. The most incomprehensible and astonishing mysteries ever seen outside the Orient. Concluding with
"THE CREMATION OF FLORIBEL."
Who is apparently burned to ashes in full view of the audience. Suggested by the Cave Scene in Rider Haggard's powerful novel "SHE." The most startling miracle and weirdest conception of Egyptian occultism. Reserved with thunders of applause and pronounced by all the Actor of Mystery.

Programme subject to Change without Notice.

N.B. During the progress of the entertainment it will be necessary to borrow small articles, such as handkerchiefs, watches, coins, etc., which the audience is respectfully requested to furnish promptly. Otherwise, owing to the great length of the programme, the experiment will have to be omitted, if there is any delay in furnishing the articles called for.

EXECUTIVE STAFF FOR MARCO.
Manager	Stanley Orriss
Business Manager	Chas C. Bryant
Treasurer	J. M. McPherson
Stage Director	Harry Houdini
Mechanician	Burton Killy
Electrician	Budd Trout
Master of Properties	George M. Tur...

...ment will conclude with The Great Racing Scene.

"Dr. Carroll," . . . . Arthur

Polly Fletcher, Mr. Fletcher's niece, ... Agnes Muir
Nell, } Girls at the works, { . . . . Ella Warren Harmon
Cinders, } { . . . . Eva Westcott
Julia, maid at Knowlton's, ... Annie Marshall
— and —
Margaret Knowlton, a pearl that the toilers at the works have set . . . . ETHEL TUCKER

Gate Keeper, at De Rossum Ferry, ... George Nelson
Reuben Gray, seein' New York, b'gosh, ... Batley Andrews
Alice Denby, Gilbert Denby's daughter, ... Ella Cameron
Skip Hogan, a product of the Bowery, ... Mildred Hyland
Inez, one of the Bowery's unfortunates, ... Winnifred Greene
Grace Rankin, a child of the Bowery, ... Little Maude
— and —
EDDY HOGAN, ... JERE McAULIFFE
(With a pull in the Forth Ward)

one of the Halifax theatres engaged a bogus magician, whom they called Markos."[1]

It's entirely possible a manager liked what he saw in Dooley's Marco posters and tried to cash in on his futuristic superhero image. Perhaps Willis Skinner did agree to a stand using the Markos alias. If Houdini was correct about a Halifax theatre boss engineering such a Marco identity theft, the manager in question would have worked for Halifax's Orpheus Music Hall. This Granville Street hall was where Markos, a.k.a. Willis Skinner, was originally booked to perform in September 1895 before switching to the much larger Academy of Music.

The shift to the larger Halifax venue paid big dividends to Skinner. In his wildly successful September 1895 stand, Markos packed Halifax's biggest theatre for ten nights in a row, one of the most successful theatrical runs in the history of the city. Of course, it didn't hurt that Markos's assistant was a saucy showgirl named Mildred Franklyn whose racy dancing drew plenty of love-starved soldiers and sailors.

Following Halifax, Markos sold out houses in Truro, Amherst, and Saint John before closing his Maritime tour with three nights in Yarmouth. Like so many other American acts before him, Markos chose to end his Maritime tour in Yarmouth where he could hop a steamship back to Boston.

After holding the boards in Washington, DC, for almost a month, Markos returned again to the Maritimes for a whirlwind two-week Christmas tour. He opened in Saint John on Christmas Day and played for another week. This time, his audiences were much smaller. Markos returned to Yarmouth in January for a two-night stand before heading home.

It was then, only five months after Markos finished his second tour of the Maritimes, that Marco, a.k.a. Professor Dooley, showed up to play the very same halls and theatres.

He desperately reworked his promotions to read, "The original— The only—First time here, Marco, Man of Mystery." Maritime news-papers weren't overly sympathetic towards Dooley's dilemma, although the June 30, 1896, *Acadian Recorder* did offer a single sentence on his behalf: "He is not the Markos who was here last September although the names are somewhat similar."

Dooley wasn't the first magician who believed he had an imitator. During his illustrious fifty-year career, Signor Blitz tracked thirteen imposters, many leaving a trail of unpaid debts, forcing the real Blitz to fend off their bill collectors. Willis Skinner also claimed he had an impersonator and placed a sizeable ad in an 1895 edition of the *New York Clipper* that read: "This is to inform those who do not already know, that two years ago I changed my stage name from Prof. W.E. Skinner to Prof. Markos. The sleight of hand performer using the name of W.E. Skinner at present is not related to me."

Even the unknown Harry Houdini had three copycats in 1896; his brother Theo was still performing as Houdini, and so were his early partners from the Brothers Houdini, Jacob and Joseph Hyman. And Houdini would suffer many more imitators and imposters later in his career.

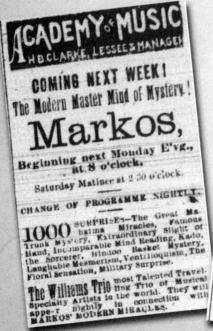

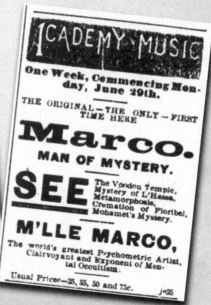

Professor Dooley's Marco ad *(right)*. When compared to the Markos ad *(left)*, from nine months earlier, it's easy to see why the public would think the two magicians were the same performer. (Nova Scotia Archives)

Marco was hardly a one-of-a-kind stage name like "Houdini" or "Signor Blitz." In fact, many performers had used the name before Professor Dooley. "Marco, the tattooed marvel" was a regular at the Boston dime museums. And then there were the circus contortionists who billed themselves as "Marco and Reto, The Living Knots."

Houdini never changed his mind about the Marco vs. Markos controversy, always backing Professor Dooley's side of the story. Despite smearing Skinner's name and reputation in print, Houdini conveniently forgot an ironic twist—in the late 1890s, when he operated his short-lived Professor Harry Houdini School of Magic, he actually promoted and sold a magic book penned by Willis Skinner.

Both Edward James Dooley and Willis Skinner abandoned their Marco / Markos personas shortly after their respective Maritime tours. Today, well over a century later, it's impossible to declare a winner in the Marco vs. Markos battle. Markos may have sold out theatres while Marco played to empty seats, but Marco won the battle for posterity. His hand-picked assistant is still recognized as one of the greatest performers in history—Harry Houdini.

This photograph of Markos showgirl Mildred Franklyn was retouched with silver paint for promotional purposes. In a curious footnote to the Marco vs. Markos story, Mildred married Joseph Hyman, who was Houdini's second partner in the Brothers Houdini act. The couple performed as Hayman and Franklyn in England.

(Billy Rose Theatre Division, The New York Public Library for the Performing Arts, Astor, Lenox and Tilden Foundations)

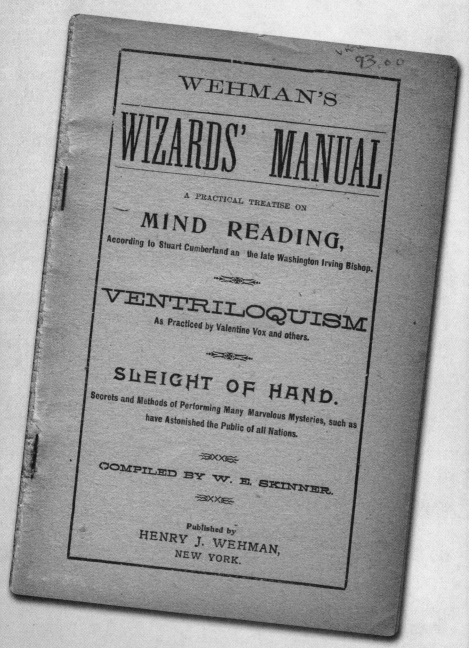

WEHMAN'S

WIZARDS' MANUAL

A PRACTICAL TREATISE ON

MIND READING,

According to Stuart Cumberland an the late Washington Irving Bishop.

VENTRILOQUISM

As Practiced by Valentine Vox and others.

SLEIGHT OF HAND.

Secrets and Methods of Performing Many Marvelous Mysteries, such as have Astonished the Public of all Nations.

COMPILED BY W. E. SKINNER.

Published by
HENRY J. WEHMAN,
NEW YORK.

Willis Skinner's 1891 book, *The Wizard's Manual*, still holds up as a valuable text offering insightful performance tips along with detailed explanations of innovative magic tricks. (Bruce MacNab Collection)

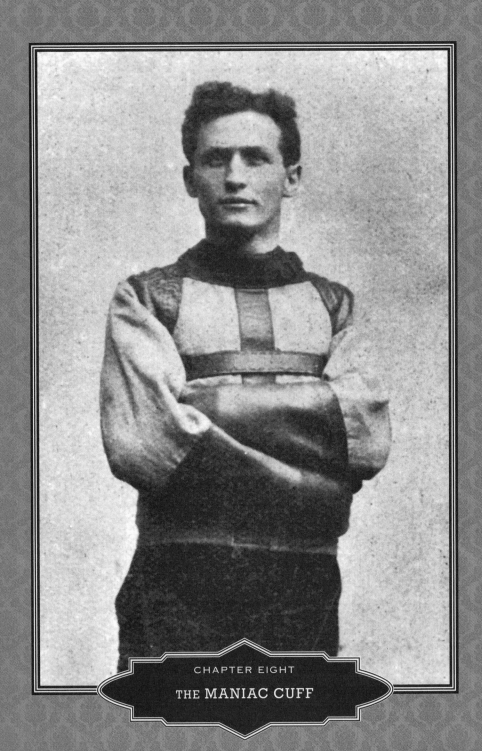

CHAPTER EIGHT

THE MANIAC CUFF

Saint John, New Brunswick
Thursday, June 4, 1896

"My brain is the key that sets me free."
—Harry Houdini's inscription on some of his autographed photographs

HARRY HOUDINI SET OUT from the Hotel Dufferin just before 7:30 on Tuesday night with Professor Dooley's assistant, Burton Kilby. The two young magicians strode confidently down the raised wooden sidewalks of King Street, Canada's steepest city street.

They were on their way to the Saint John central police station.

Harry Houdini had bragged to a reporter from the *Daily Telegraph* about his mastery of locks and handcuffs. The paper was happy to print on June 5, 1896, Houdini's challenge to the citizens of Saint John. "Mr. Houdini claims that there is not a handcuff in the city that he cannot get free from without breaking." In other towns, this boast could be met without a single raised eyebrow, but here in Saint John, Houdini's statement had captured the full attention of the top brass. At the police station, Houdini found Chief Clark and Captain Jenkins along with four newspaper reporters eagerly awaiting his arrival.

While no images of the infamous leather Maniac Cuff exist, Houdini would escape from many leather restraints like this sporty German number.

(Patrick Culliton Collection)

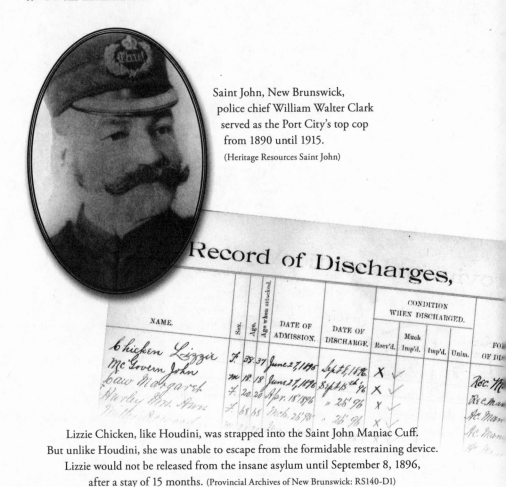

Saint John, New Brunswick,
police chief William Walter Clark
served as the Port City's top cop
from 1890 until 1915.

(Heritage Resources Saint John)

Lizzie Chicken, like Houdini, was strapped into the Saint John Maniac Cuff.
But unlike Houdini, she was unable to escape from the formidable restraining device.
Lizzie would not be released from the insane asylum until September 8, 1896,
after a stay of 15 months. (Provincial Archives of New Brunswick: RS140-D1)

Chief Clark and his men were hardly naïve small-town cops. Saint John was a rugged harbour town of forty thousand inhabitants and the police dealt constantly with a never-ending parade of shady characters made up of transient seamen and local drunks. Houdini's visit to the station found the police engaged in some typical work, planning to shut down a bawdy house and investigating a wife beating.

Captain Jenkins, who made a special trip from the south end division to see Houdini, didn't waste any time fastening a pair of modern regulation handcuffs on him. Houdini retired to Chief Clark's private office as the button was pressed on a stopwatch. After only nine seconds, the chief's door opened and Houdini stepped out with the unlocked handcuffs. Jenkins tried several more pairs of handcuffs on Houdini but he simply couldn't thwart the crafty magician.

Chief William Walker Clark offered the next challenge. The chief fastened a pair of padded leather wristlets on Houdini, and then wrapped a strap around the magician's wrists, behind his back. Well out of reach, the straps that bound Houdini's wrists were secured by a new patented Chicago lock. Houdini retired to Chief Clark's office where he managed to open the lock and take the rest of the restraint apart. Houdini once again emerged from the office a free man, but this test was obviously more difficult than Captain Jenkins's handcuffs. One of the reporters noted that Houdini "reappeared, streaming with perspiration."[1]

Houdini couldn't claim victory just yet. The Saint John police had an unusual apparatus reserved for securing violently insane prisoners. According to Chief Clark, the newly designed restraint was "almost perfect."[2]

Before Clark had taken delivery of the new device, insane prisoners were rolled up in carpet, bound with ropes and then transported to the asylum in this tubular form in the back of a wagon. Chief Clark was no fan of transporting prisoners as though they were giant helpless sausages; he had commented to the city's safety committee, "It seems to be cruel."[3]

The American-made restraint had been used for the first time less than a year earlier on a notorious Saint John character named Lizzie Chicken. After Lizzie was arrested on suspicion of being insane, the thirty-six-year-old woman snapped. Fearing for her safety, and their own, the policemen retrieved the brand new device and pressed it into service. A reporter working the police beat described the spectacle in the June 28, 1895, edition of the *Saint John Sun*. "She became very violent, and the wrist cuffs and waist strap were placed on her, and although she raved in a terrible manner she was unable to do herself any injury. She was examined by Dr. D.E. Berryman, who recommended that she be sent to the asylum."

Now, the very same device that subdued Lizzie Chicken was introduced to an unsuspecting Harry Houdini. With a throng of reporters, policemen, and other spectators looking on, the young showman had no option other than to submit to the chief's challenge. Refusing the test would make headlines in the newspapers and hurt the Marco Magic Company's chances for a successful stand in Saint John.

At the start, both of Houdini's hands were placed in a stiff leather glove. Chief Clark then strapped Houdini's forearms tightly together. Clark wrapped yet another belt around Houdini's arms. The belt was then wrapped around his waist and was tightly cinched and fastened at his back.

Houdini was trapped in the dreaded Saint John Maniac Cuff!

Houdini entered the chief's office so well fettered he couldn't close the door without help. One reporter wrote, "Everybody believed it impossible for a human being to throw off the gloves."[4] However, in a few minutes, Houdini exited the room free from his restraint.

As a compliment to Chief Clark, Houdini conceded to a reporter that the apparatus was "the hardest test to which he had ever been subjected in his life."[5] One of Clark's men, Officer Killen, returned the compliment to Houdini when he stated, "If Houdini is ever placed in my charge, I will not trust handcuffs but I'll stand over him with a shillelagh,"[6] referencing the Irish version of a policeman's billy club used for cracking skulls at Ireland's infamous Donnybrook Fair.

Despite his exhausting escape work, Houdini produced a deck of playing cards and entertained his police station audience with several tricks. Houdini was no slouch with cards in his early years thanks to countless hours of practice. "For years I took a pack of cards in my hands at ten o'clock in the morning, and until ten o'clock at night they were constantly being mixed, shuffled and manipulated."[7] As a finale to the evening, he asked a newspaper reporter to pick a card at random from the deck. A policeman with a note was dispatched to the nearby Hotel Stanley on King Street where Bessie Houdini, as Mademoiselle Marco, correctly identified the card.

A PUBLICITY MACHINE IS BORN

The Friday papers reported heavily on Houdini's visit to the police station.

The *Saint John Gazette* review of Houdini's escape work was colourfully entitled "Spirits in Chains," and read:

> A most novel séance was given in Chief of Police Clark's office at the police station last evening by Harry Houdini, a pupil of the wonderful Marcos [*sic*], who opens at the Opera House on Monday.
>
> The mysterious stranger showed himself very clever in palmistry and slight [*sic*] of hand as well as at mind reading in conjunction with Mme Marco who remained at the Hotel Stanley, yet told a selected card picked out at the police court.

The Saint John police station as it
looked during Houdini's visit.
(Heritage Resources Saint John)

Perhaps the most wonderful exhibition of the night was Houdini's handcuff trick. Several pairs of wrist cuffs, including the wonderful maniac cuff and belt, which Chief Clark is trying to persuade the city to adopt, were tried on the young man, and each in turn were as easy to open as though they were never locked.

This can be said of all the cuffs with the exception of the maniac cuff which proved the best test though they were finally opened.

Houdini scored some gems for his growing collection of press clippings. No fewer than four Saint John papers reported on his escapes at the police station. He cut out all the reports and pasted them in his press book. In addition, he meticulously clipped and pasted the name of each paper and the date for each of the clippings.

There was little mention of the rest of the Marco Magic Company other than in the *Saint John Globe* on June 5, 1896, that speculated, "If the other performers compare with Houdini, the public will enjoy a wonderful entertainment."

Having bested the Maniac Cuff, Houdini was set to visit a hospital where the father-in-law of Chief Clark's daughter was the long-time superintendent.

Houdini didn't realize it at the time, but this visit would one day give him more free publicity than any magician who came before him — or any magician who has since followed him.

CHAPTER NINE

A HOUSEHOLD OF
WRECKED MINDS

Saint John, New Brunswick
ca. Friday, June 5, 1896

"It is a Christian and generous feeling to turn from the dazzle and bustle of
daily life to seek the unfortunate objects removed from the world's mirror;
and where is there a better or rarer opportunity for cultivating it, than in
a visit to an asylum for the insane, to behold humanity in its saddest
garb—a household of wrecked minds, of all ages and sexes?"
—Signor Blitz, magician, on performing for the insane, 1872,
from *Fifty Years in the Magic Circle*

GIVEN THAT HARRY HOUDINI studied illusions, he would have been awestruck
by what he saw next to the New Brunswick Provincial Lunatic Asylum. The asylum
was built on top of one of the earth's greatest illusions—the Reversing Falls. Twice
a day, the rising tide meets the mouth of the mighty Saint John River, appearing to
reverse the flow of the waterway. An early explorer, Samuel de Champlain, wrote
that the very sight of the reversing falls frightened his seasoned crew.

The falls not only mark the collision of the river and the ocean but also the
collision of two ancient continents. One side of the river cliffs exposes dark ledge
rock while the other side is almost white in appearance.

    At the time Harry Houdini visited the New Brunswick Provincial Lunatic Asylum,
the building contained fifteen wards that could accommodate hundreds of patients.
(Heritage Resources Saint John)

Fittingly, it would be at this extraordinary confluence of water, stone, and humanity that Houdini's present life as a magician would collide with his future as an escape artist.

The insane asylum stood high above the falls on the west side of the river, a good forty-five-minute walk from the Marco Magic Company's lodgings at the Hotel Dufferin. Houdini had to cross a suspension bridge high over the dangerous rapids, offering him a chance to stop and watch the tumultuous falls below. And Houdini was fascinated by the power of rushing water. In 1897, while performing in Niagara Falls, New York, he noted in his diary that he watched the falls "every day and night."

After Houdini crossed the bridge, he had to make his way up the hill to the Provincial Lunatic Asylum. From here, he could take in a virtual panoramic view of the river, harbour, and surrounding countryside. From the asylum, the brick buildings of uptown Saint John were visible no more than two miles in the distance.

The asylum was an impressive complex that housed more than six hundred patients, a population almost evenly split between men and women. The overwhelming majority of patients were labourers and farmers. However, the hospital also claimed doctors, policemen, teachers, and engineers as inmates.

Staff at the asylum diagnosed dozens of diseases among its patients. The leading diagnosis was acute mania. Other inmates were listed as having melancholia, kleptomania, dementia, religious excitement, hysteria, over-anxiety, misplaced confidence, fright with heredity, and unrestricted evil affinities.

Once Houdini entered the Provincial Lunatic Asylum, he had to dodge inmates who were hard at work on their knees, happily scraping and refinishing the hardwood floors of the hospital. Others were busy painting, plastering, and making repairs that the superintendent described as "damages as are daily done in every Asylum for the Insane."[1]

As for what Houdini saw during that day in the Provincial Lunatic Asylum in Saint John is best left for the man himself to describe. Houdini wrote about his visit in the January 1908 edition of the *Conjurers' Monthly Magazine*.

> While in St. Johns [*sic*] I met a Dr. Steves [*sic*], who then was in charge of a large insane asylum, and received an invitation from him to visit his institution, which I accepted. After showing me the various wards, he eventually showed me the padded cells, in one of which, through the small bars of the cell door, I saw a maniac struggling on the canvas

Although the facility had no reading rooms or gymnasium
and the wards were poorly lit, it offered a spectacular view of the
suspension bridge and the harbour. (Heritage Resources Saint John)

padded floor, rolling about and straining each and every muscle in
a vain attempt to get his hands over his head and striving in every
conceivable manner to free himself from his canvas restraint, which
I later on learned was called a straitjacket.

Entranced, I watched the efforts of this man, whose struggles
caused the beads of perspiration to roll off from him, and from where
I stood, I noted that were he able to dislocate his arms at the shoulder
joint, he would have been able to cause his restraint to become slack
in certain parts and so allow him to free his arms. But as it was that
the straps were drawn tight, the more he struggled, the tighter his
restraint encircled him, and eventually he lay exhausted, panting and
powerless to move.

Since Houdini's experience at the hospital, some have questioned how a magician
could be allowed to enter such an institution. One explanation is astonishingly
simple: in the 1800s most of the large insane asylums throughout North America
regularly brought in entertainment—including the Provincial Lunatic Asylum in

The wards that housed the infirm may have been gloomy,
but the waiting areas of the Provincial Lunatic Asylum
were ornately trimmed. (Heritage Resources Saint John)

Saint John. The accountant kept a small budget for entertainment and staffers tried to host at least two shows a month.

The mental institution even had its own amusement hall that hosted regular concerts and performances for inmates. The auditorium was seen as a critical facility for the well-being and recovery of patients and was earmarked for much needed improvements because of its medical importance. That said, Dr. Steeves's staff was critical of the inconvenient access to the hall. Patients had to be supervised as they passed through the laundry, kitchen, and carpentry shop to get there.

The superintendent's 1896 year-end report made a point of thanking the performers, possibly including Houdini, who played to the inmates throughout the year. "I desire also most cheerfully to thank all the ladies and gentlemen who have from time to time furnished musical entertainments for the patients in the Institution. It may be gratifying to them to know that their efforts to amuse the patients were much enjoyed by them, and that I am firmly of the opinion these entertainments are beneficial to the patients."[2]

Magicians were among the most popular entertainers with insane asylum inmates everywhere. Signor Blitz played similar hospitals through his entire career, and he was well aware that his performances meant much more to the insane than to the regular theatre crowd. "Possessing the faculty of rendering the unfortunate happy, I improved it on every occasion, and my own heart was delighted in seeing how they could appreciate the most dexterous of my feats."[3]

Houdini knew all about Signor Blitz's career. Every serious magician of the day had read his memoirs, *Fifty Years in the Magic Circle*. And this day had offered Houdini the chance to find out for himself why the late, great Mr. Blitz found insane asylums and their patients so inspiring.

Houdini would visit many mental hospitals in his life. In November 1911, while chatting with a reporter from the *Pittsburgh Leader*, Houdini told a humorous story about an encounter with a doctor during one such visit:

> In the course of their conversation Houdini mentioned the fact that he had come with the intention of trying on the straitjackets and confidently declared that he could free himself from any in which the official of the institution cared to bind him. The doctor looked quizzically at Houdini and then said: "How are they treating you here? Do they give you plenty to eat? Let me see; stick out your tongue." Houdini wonderingly obeyed. The moment he was gone...it dawned upon Houdini that the doctor had mistaken him for a lunatic. He could not conceive that any man in his sane senses could hope to get out of his straitjacket.

Harry Houdini never found peace with the insane as Signor Blitz had. In 1925, after performing at two asylums in the same week, Houdini made a startling entry in his diary. "There ought to be a law to put them out of their misery. I would not do it myself, but some of the cases are terrible."

As young Harry Houdini walked back to uptown Saint John, his mind raced with possibilities. The vision of the struggling patient haunted Houdini's every thought, as he recalled years later.

> Previous to this incident I had seen and used various restraints such as insane restraint muffs, belts, bedstraps, etc., but this was the first

time I saw a straitjacket and it left so vivid an impression on my mind
that I hardly slept that night, and in such moments as I slept I saw
nothing but straitjackets, maniacs and padded cells! In the wakeful
part of the night I wondered what the effect would be to an audience
to have them see a man placed in a straitjacket and watch him force
himself free therefrom. The very next morning I obtained permission
to try to escape from one.[4]

It's possible that Houdini performed the straitjacket escape for the very first time
in Saint John. Surprisingly, Houdini's early performances of the straitjacket escape
were poorly received by audiences. Houdini blamed these early failures on the fact
that he did the escape behind the curtain and out of sight of the audience. He
recalled the days after discovering the straitjacket at the Provincial Lunatic Asylum.

During one entire week I practiced steadily and then presented it on
the stage, and made my escape there from behind a curtain. I pursued
this method for some time, but as it was so often repeated to me that
people seeing me emerge from the cabinet after my release, with hair
disheveled, countenance covered with perspiration, trousers covered
with dust and ofttimes even my clothes being torn, remarked, "Oh,
he is faking, it did not take all that effort to make his escape," that
eventually I determined to show to the audience exactly what means
I resorted to, to effect my release, and so did the straitjacket release
in full view of everybody.[5]

There, in Saint John, New Brunswick, in 1896, young Harry Houdini knew the
straitjacket was a fantastic discovery. But even Houdini couldn't have envisioned
that one day he would wriggle free from one of the restraints while suspended
upside down high above the streets of an American city, cheered on by over eighty
thousand spectators.

⊱—꞉•⟩•⟨⟩•⟨•꞉—⊰

DR. JAMES T. STEEVES had been the superintendent of the Provincial Lunatic Asylum for almost twenty years. The New Brunswick-born doctor, who studied medicine in Pennsylvania and New York, shunned treating the insane with drugs, suggesting, "Narcotics may be the instruments of doing harm." Neither did he allow his patients to languish inside the asylum. "Mostly all of the patients have not only been kept out of bed, but out of doors every day that the weather permitted,"[6] he wrote.

In his yearly government report for 1895, he commented that there had been fewer suicides in his twenty-year tenure at the hospital than most North American asylums had each and every year.

The doctor once explained why he was no fan of straitjackets: "To

Among the entertainers hired to give concerts at the asylum by Dr. Steeves Sr. (seated) and Dr. Steeves Jr. were the Carleton Coronet band and the Kingsville Band. (from microfilm, courtesy of New Brunswick Library)

STEEVES
VS.
STEEVES

allow patients with cerebral irritation to thrash about till they are fairly exhausted has not in many cases proved the best treatment in this house. Unwise or inaccurately executed methods of restraint might be still worse than undue freedom."[7]

But Dr. Steeves was no longer in control of the insane asylum during Houdini's visit. The father of nine had suffered a stroke in September 1895. He was still living in his apartment at the asylum, but his job had fallen to his assistant, his son, Dr. James A. Steeves. The junior Dr. Steeves didn't live up to his father's reputation for high standards of compassionate care and was accused of neglecting his patients. The press waged a ferocious campaign against the younger Dr. Steeves alleging, "We have time and time again shown that the management of our Provincial Lunatic Asylum at Saint John, for many years, has been a standing disgrace to our Christian civilization and that the public had lost all confidence in the institution except in that it provided a very comfortable, even luxurious home for the superintendent and his family, the inmates being only a secondary consideration."[3]

A week before Houdini arrived, the younger Dr. Steeves had been officially fired and ordered to leave the asylum by mid-August. An editorial about his dismissal in the *Fredericton Reporter* rejoiced, "A sigh of relief went up from thousands of sympathetic hearts when this announcement was made."

One of his first duties as a private physician was signing his father's death certificate when the elder doctor died at the age of sixty-nine in March 1897. The long-time asylum superintendent was buried at Fernhill Cemetery in Saint John, also the resting place of his brother William Henry Steeves, one of Canada's Fathers of Confederation.

In the autumn of 1903 the junior Dr. Steeves headed south for a wedding tour with his new bride. Their honeymoon ended six weeks later in Phoenix, Arizona, when the forty-two-year-old doctor died from tuberculosis.

With the death of Dr. James Steeves Jr. in 1903, his brother, dentist William Steeves, was the only Dr. Steeves who lived to hear about Harry Houdini's later straitjacket exploits. Ironically, it was the dentist's father-in-law, Chief Clark, who had strapped

Houdini into the Maniac Cuff at the Saint John police station back in June 1896.

It's quite possible that William Steeves introduced the magician to his brother, Dr. James Steeves Jr. In 1896 the young dentist was making headlines in Saint John for partnering with an electrician from the street railway in an attempt to build a hand-held X-ray device. The press dubbed him the "Saint John Experimenter" during Houdini's visit. Considering the rising vaudeville popularity of X-ray—a brand new technology in 1896—it's easy to imagine Houdini visiting the dentist, curious about his research.

William Steeves moved his dentist practice to Fredericton from Saint John during his family's scandal-plagued summer of 1896. The dentist kept a low profile in the New Brunswick capital, although there is proof he had an interest in show business. In 1908, at a packed Fredericton rink, Dr. William Steeves appeared on stage and locked three pairs of handcuffs on an American escape artist billed as "Karland the Handcuff King".

Dr. William Steeves died in 1953 and his father-in-law, Police Chief Clark, died in 1930. In a curious twist of history, both men died in the same house on Lansdowne Street in Fredericton.

(above) William Steeves often ran his advertisements next to those of visiting theatrical troupes, like this one announcing a performance by the widow of Tom Thumb.
(Image courtesy of Harriet Irving Library, UNB)

(left) The Opera House was located on the second floor of Fredericton City Hall.
(Provincial Archives of New Brunswick: P5-344A)

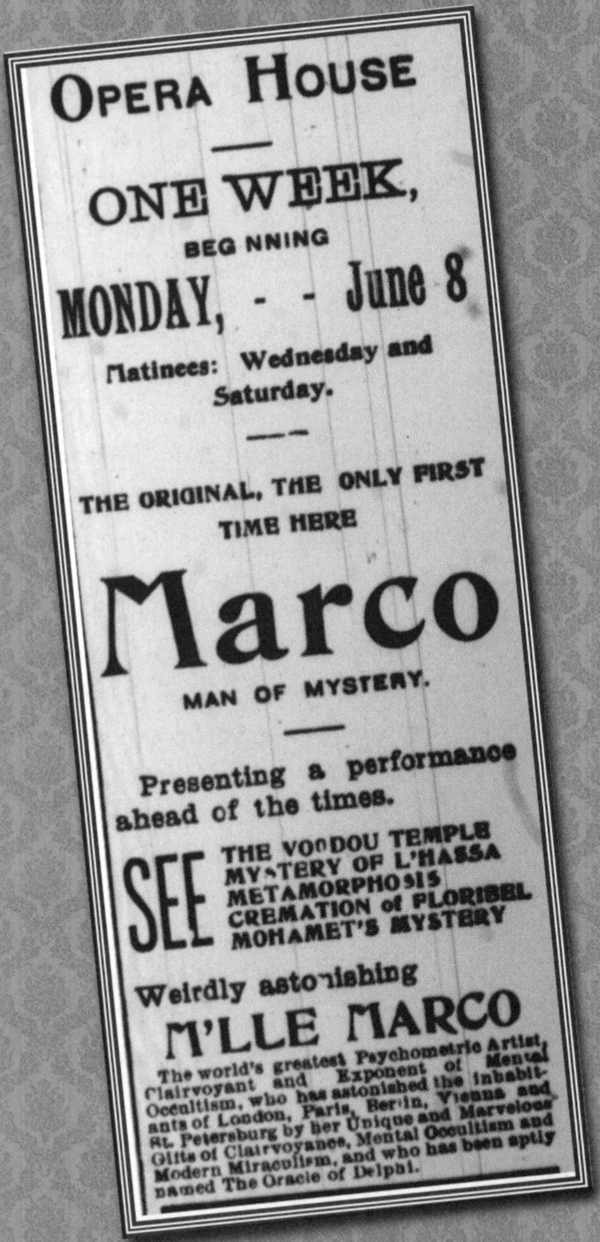

OPERA HOUSE

—

ONE WEEK,

BEG NNING

MONDAY, - - June 8

Matinees: Wednesday and
Saturday.

———

THE ORIGINAL, THE ONLY FIRST
TIME HERE

Marco

MAN OF MYSTERY.

—

Presenting a performance
ahead of the times.

SEE THE VOODOU TEMPLE
MYSTERY OF L'HASSA
METAMORPHOSIS
CREMATION of FLORIBEL
MOHAMET'S MYSTERY

Weirdly astonishing

M'LLE MARCO

The world's greatest Psychometric Artist,
Clairvoyant and Exponent of Mental
Occultism, who has astonished the inhabit-
ants of London, Paris, Ber·in, Vienna and
St. Petersburg by her Unique and Marvelous
Gifts of Clairvoyance, Mental Occultism and
Modern Miraculism, and who has been aptly
named The Oracle of Delphi.

CHAPTER TEN

PORT CITY PROBLEMS

Saint John, New Brunswick
Monday, June 8, 1896

"The basis of it all is that we attract your attention to something
and then do exactly the opposite from what you expect us to do."
—Harry Houdini, *Cleveland Leader*, October 20, 1916

PROFESSOR DOOLEY HAD HIGH HOPES for Monday night's opening. He had spared no expense on advertising in the Saint John newspapers, and Harry Houdini had generated some free press with his visit to the police station on Thursday evening.

For Houdini, the Saint John Opera House was a perfect example of the big-time venue he had always dreamed of playing. And the world-class theatre offered a perfect opportunity to work on his voice projection. Houdini would become a legend in theatrical circles for his commanding stage voice that could often be heard in the outer lobby. He once wrote about his early years in a magazine published by the Society of American Magicians, describing how he developed his powerful performance speech.

The first Marco advertisement that appeared in a Saint John newspaper. Although Bessie Houdini, a.k.a. Mademoiselle Marco, was on her first trip outside America the fine print claims she had "astonished the inhabitants of London, Paris, Berlin, Vienna and St. Petersburg." (Provincial Archives of New Brunswick; SJ *Daily Telegraph*, June 3, 1896, 3)

When I had an engagement at an extensive place where I was afraid my voice would not carry, I would actually go in training for that place. I would run around the block early in the morning at a dog trot, and get my lungs in good condition, for it is a fact that in my work I required wonderful lungs to use in my physical manifestations before an audience. I would also take long walks, away from habitation, and address an imaginary audience. I was at that time called the "Syllable-Accenting American," because I would spell my words, figuratively, that they should be carried to the gallery. I never spoke to the first row. I would walk down to the footlights, actually put one foot over the electric globes as if I were going to spring among the people and then hurl my voice, saying, "Ladies and Gentlemen." When you can make the men in the gallery hear each syllable, the audience in front, or downstairs, are also most effectually served.[1]

For all his limitations as an amateur magician trying to punch through to the professional ranks, Professor Dooley must have been a great mentor for Houdini, at least when it came to elocution. Early in Houdini's career, he was scolded by a theatre manager for uttering loutish words like "youse" and "ain't" during his performances. By 1896 it appears Houdini had corrected much of his early dialogue, which was an unholy amalgam of Manhattan street slang infused with the remnants of an eastern European accent. Only one recording of Houdini's voice has surfaced, revealing speech that is refined, but deliberately slow and accented.

After five days preparing their voices and prepping the Opera House stage, opening night finally arrived. But there was some serious competition for the Marco Magic Company. The national election campaign was heating up as Nova Scotia's Sir Charles Tupper was fighting a losing battle to remain prime minister of Canada. As Dooley prepared to raise the curtain for the first time in Saint John, many of the city's meeting halls were hosting political rallies. Both Glad Tidings Hall and the Temperance Hall were packed to overflowing on Monday evening, while the biggest gathering was happening at the commodious Mechanics Hall.

Politics aside, Dooley promised the Saint John press that Marco would transform the Opera House into a "Temple of Mystery." As Dooley readied to open the show on Monday, he peeked out and saw over a thousand empty seats in his

"Temple." Only 181 people showed up. The theatre looked even less full because the audience was spread out among the orchestra, dress circle, balcony, and gallery seats.

Dooley had printed thousands of his Marco programmes on expensive pink paper, but only a handful was distributed on opening night. After reading the warning printed near the bottom of the programme, the small audience likely felt somewhat awkward, wondering if they would be targeted to participate in the show: "During the progress of the entertainment it will be necessary to borrow small articles, such as handkerchiefs, watches, coins, etc., which the audience is respectfully requested to furnish *promptly*. Otherwise, owing to the great length of the programme, the experiment will have to be omitted, if there is any delay in furnishing the articles called for."

SMOKE AND MIRRORS AND BLUNDERS

At eight o'clock, the house lights dimmed as Bowden and his orchestra made their debut. The talented ensemble opened the evening with a few well-performed numbers, earning them a positive review in the *Daily Telegraph*: "Bowden's orchestra made its first appearance and acquitted itself very creditably, the opening selection being loudly applauded."

Professor Dooley opened with his usual sleight-of-hand routine, manipulating playing cards, coins, and silk handkerchiefs with his skilled pianist's fingers. One of the Saint John reporters was impressed with Dooley's half-hour opening act and commented, "Articles appeared and disappeared by his deft fingers in a way that defied detection."[2]

Near the end of his opening set, Dooley introduced an illusion called the Growth of the Mango Tree, a conjuror's favourite dating back many years. The illusion starts with the magician watering a tree seemingly in its winter dormancy. Suddenly, the tree begins to sprout leaves and blossoms. Eventually fruit forms at the end of the branches right before the audience's eyes. The trick traditionally closed with the magician picking a fruit off of the tree and offering it to a female audience member to verify its authenticity.

Unfortunately for Dooley, the tree malfunctioned and he was unable to finish the illusion, prompting one reporter to write, "The growth of the mango tree did not come up to the expectation of the audience."[3]

Dooley's spoiled mango tree was soon forgotten when Bessie and Harry Houdini performed their Metamorphosis trunk act. Although it took the Houdinis six seconds to perform the Metamorphosis exchange instead of their usual blistering time of three seconds, the couple executed the illusion so perfectly that the same reporter who panned Dooley's failed tree trick gushed, "The trunk mystery was splendidly executed and made the hit of the evening. The rapidity with which Houdini and Mlle. Marco changed places was simply astounding."[4]

Dooley returned to the stage to perform Cremation of Floribel. The audience who read the description in Marco's pink programme had to believe they were about to witness something unforgettable. It described the unfortunate Floribel, "[w]ho is apparently burned to ashes in full sight of the audience. Suggested by the cave scene in Rider Haggard's powerful novel 'SHE.' The most startling miracle and weirdest conception of Egyptian occultism. Received with thunders of applause and pronounced by all the Acme of Mysticism."

Cremation of Floribel was an illusion Professor Dooley had developed from an article in the July 2, 1892, issue of *Scientific American*. He even plagiarized some of the magazine's description word-for-word for his programme description.

The illusion opened with Bessie Houdini, as Floribel, standing on a small table while Dooley lowered a curtain from a round hoop suspended above her head. Once Bessie was curtained, Dooley lit a fire under the table. After a frightful column of dark smoke poured out from the tube-like crematorium, Dooley raised the curtain amid a shower of ashes to reveal Mademoiselle Marco had been reduced to a skull and a smouldering pile of bones.

From the theatre seats, the audience saw a table with four legs. What they were really seeing was two front legs of a table. The two rear legs were actually the reflection of the front legs in mirrors placed under the table. After the curtain dropped, Bessie simply had to step off the rear of the table and slip into a trap door that led to the space under the stage. All her movements were concealed by the mirrors. Once she was gone, a stagehand set up the skull and bones.

The cremation illusion was a relatively simple concept, but it required a great deal of knowledge in audience sightlines to achieve a convincing effect. Most importantly, the two mirrors under the table had to be butted together at perfect forty-five-degree angles, forming an arrow pointing at the audience. Dooley had to be mindful of the uncompromising law of reflection: the angle of incidence is equal to the angle of reflection. He had to remain within a "safe zone" so his reflection

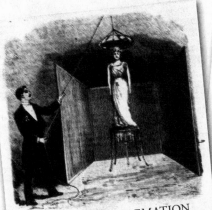

PREPARED FOR CREMATION

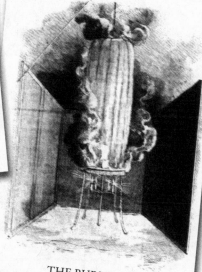

THE BURNING

THE ESCAPE

These sketches from the July 2, 1892 *Scientific American*, show how the Cremation of Floribel illusion was presented when Professor Dooley torched Bessie Houdini in Saint John.

(Courtesy of Harriet Irving Library, UNB)

THE FINISH

couldn't be seen from any of the seats. It would appear the Marco Magic Company lacked the know-how to pull off the illusion convincingly. Just like the mango tree, a newspaper reported that Professor Dooley and his crew fell well short of the mark while cremating Bessie Houdini.

At the end of the evening, Jack McKierney signed for the company's box office take. The total receipts for the night added up to $54.95. This cash was split fifty-fifty with the house, leaving $27.47 for Professor Dooley and his company.

As the troupe headed back to the Hotel Dufferin, they knew their show needed to improve. The failed illusions on opening night didn't set a hopeful tone for the remainder of the stand. But Dooley could take some comfort in the fact that a very small house saw the failed illusions. Still, they all knew that in show business, bad reports travelled infinitely faster than good ones.

Little did the Marco Magic Company realize that tomorrow one of their young troupe members would disappear — for real.

The Saint John Opera House, which was built in 1891, eventually became a movie theatre. The front portion of the building survived a 1959 fire and still stands in 2012. (Heritage Resources Saint John)

HOUDINI'S PUBLICITY WORK at the police station was great. But he was eclipsed by another performer who wasn't even in the country. The Friday papers carried a front-page report about Anna Eva Fay who had caused a sensation in Saint John the previous summer with her clairvoyant act. Under the heading, "A Fakir Exposed," the article explained in detail how Anna Eva Fay really produced her startling spirit manifestations and mind-reading effects that had thrilled so many citizens of Saint John.

The Anna Eva Fay story appeared right beside a short article about the

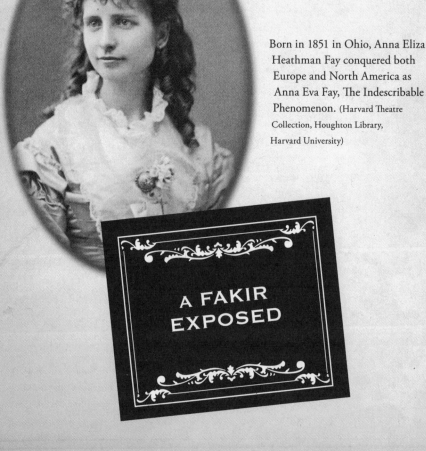

Born in 1851 in Ohio, Anna Eliza Heathman Fay conquered both Europe and North America as Anna Eva Fay, The Indescribable Phenomenon. (Harvard Theatre Collection, Houghton Library, Harvard University)

A FAKIR EXPOSED

Marco Magic Company's upcoming appearance. Unfortunately, the Fay article exposed much of the same trickery that Dooley and the Houdinis planned to use in their Monday opener at the Opera House.

Twenty-eight years later, on July 9, 1924, Houdini would pay a visit to an elderly Anna Eva Fay at her estate in Melrose, Massachusetts. Fay opened up to Houdini as he reported in his diary. "She spoke freely of all her methods. Never at any time did she pretend to believe in spiritualism." Houdini also wrote that he paid a cameraman named Moffitt to film the encounter. If the two hundred feet of film mentioned by Houdini still exists, it would be welcomed by magic historians with joy.

Anna Eva Fay might have crashed his party, but Houdini had set a personal best for publicity, all because of his handcuff act—an act that had been practically ignored by American reporters.

Harry Houdini and Anna Eva Fay pose next to a fountain on her estate in Melrose Massachusetts on July 9, 1924. Like Houdini, Fay suffered from horrible seasickness when she sailed from Boston to Nova Scotia in 1895. (Patrick Culliton Collection)

CHAPTER ELEVEN

MARCO LOSES HIS BUTTONS

Saint John, New Brunswick
Tuesday Afternoon, June 9, 1896

"We folks who do these hazardous feats know full well the danger,
and that is what they pay us for."
—Harry Houdini, April 19, 1918, discussing an accidental stage death
at the Hippodrome in a letter to Robert G. Shaw

THANKFULLY, THE SAINT JOHN PRESS wasn't totally unkind in their reviews of opening night. Although the *Saint John Sun* published a review that mentioned the poorly executed illusions, most of the papers chose to print falsely positive reviews rather than risk offending Dooley and losing his advertising dollars. The *Daily Telegraph* reported, "A very large audience was at the Opera House last night to greet Marco, who proved to be a master of his art and delighted as well as mystified his audience. The performance was the best of its kind that has ever been presented to the Saint John public."

The *Sun* offered an excuse for the botched performance of their big-spending advertiser. "Taken as a whole, the performance was interesting, if not brilliant,

Burton Kilby, aka Buttons, once told a *Saint John Daily Telegraph* reporter
he was Houdini's manager and he planned on taking the magician
on a tour of Europe. (Patrick Culliton Collection)

but much allowance must be made for a first night on a strange stage." Calling it a "strange stage" was a misleading comment considering the Marco Company had the stage all to themselves for five full days to prepare for their opening night. Furthermore, the Opera House stage was a magician's dream come true. During its construction five years earlier, the *Saint John Progress* reported, "Here and there are trap doors, but so snugly fitted that one would hardly know they existed, while men are sawing out others that bring to view a commodious apartment beneath the stage."

The *Saint John Globe* raved about the Houdinis' Metamorphosis illusion. "The trunk mystery beat every attempt ever made by other magicians in the past." The paper mentioned Harry three times in the complimentary write-up, but they misspelled his name as "Houdinion." Despite the spelling error, Houdini pasted the article, along with one other, into his press book.

Misspellings of the unknown name "Houdini" were common in the early years. Perhaps the worst error was Hunyadi, also a brand of laxative. Other misspellings were Houdenese, Houdins, and Houdni. Some of the misspellings help to support a long-held belief, quietly passed on through an elite fraternity of magicians. The insider's secret, privately relayed by eighty-three-year-old magician and Houdini

In an April 10, 1894 note, Jacob Hyman appeared to sell his share of the act. "Know ye, that I Jacob Hyman known as J.H. Houdini of the Bros. Houdini for value received do hereby agree to dissolve said firm." However, Jacob would continue to use the Houdini stage name in the years that followed.
(Patrick Culliton Collection)

biographer James Randi in 2011, conflicts with our conventional knowledge of Houdini's nineteenth-century career. The theory suggests that early on, including the Marco tour, Houdini sometimes pronounced his name as "who-din-eye" not "who-dee-nee."

Aside from praising "Houdinion's" Saint John debut, the press played along with Dooley's claim that Marco was vastly superior to Markos. All of the papers published reports such as, "This is the original Marco and must not be confused with the imitator who has been touring the country using the famous magician's name to impose on the public."[1] The *Saint John Gazette* really stretched the truth by stating, "Marco is not the 'Markos' who appeared here last September, he is a very superior magician in every way."

A REAL VANISHING ACT

By this time, the talk of Saint John wasn't the Marco Magic Company, but the big horse race scheduled for Wednesday afternoon at the Moosepath Trotting Park. The newspapers printed daily reports about the upcoming race while the city braced for an influx of visitors from Nova Scotia and New England.

With so many visitors flooding into Saint John for Wednesday's race, Professor Dooley had reason to expect a sizeable crowd for Tuesday, the second night of the troupe's engagement. But first, there was a lot of work to be done. Dooley had decided to include Houdini's handcuff act in the show for the rest of the week. Houdini was to make arrangements for a policeman to bring an assortment of handcuffs and leg irons to the evening's performance.

Meanwhile, Dooley and Burton Kilby, a.k.a. Buttons, had to spend the morning rehearsing a new illusion that had Buttons fly from the stage to a side balcony at the wave of a magic wand. The balcony trick was spectacular but a little risky. The carpenters had installed a spring trap, housed beneath the stage in a wooden box, the top of which was flush with the stage boards. When Dooley stepped on the trip lever, two enormous springs attached to a small platform were released. The springs ejected Kilby with terrific force toward a balcony just above the side of the stage.

Ultimately, it was up to Kilby to be properly positioned on the hidden ejector so that when he was launched, he would make it to the balcony. Professor Dooley and Kilby had tested the apparatus six times that morning and were confident the illusion would be a showstopper at the evening's performance. They had agreed to run through it a few more times that afternoon to be well prepared for an audience.

At the end of morning rehearsal, Dooley was summoned to Mr. Dockrill's office to discuss the dismal box office take from the previous night. After reviewing business with the accountant for some time, Dooley returned to the Hotel Dufferin.

Later in the day, Dooley was surprised when Kilby didn't meet him at the hotel for afternoon rehearsal. The teenager was dedicated to the company and had never once been late for a show or a rehearsal. Surprise turned to alarm when Kilby didn't arrive for the evening meal either. The rest of the troupe ordered their pre-show dinner and hoped a hungry Buttons would show up at the Hotel Dufferin dining room.

But Buttons didn't arrive.

Now, Dooley had a crisis on his hands. Kilby had to be found. Dooley dispatched the entire Marco Magic Company to scour Saint John looking for the stage boy.

One by one, the magic troupe returned to the Hotel Dufferin dining room. Dooley could tell by their long faces that Kilby was still missing. Now Dooley had plenty to worry about. A hardscrabble foreign harbour town like Saint John was no place for a young performer to go missing.

Nevertheless, with or without Buttons, the Marco Magic Company show would have to go on. Dooley would simply have to improvise to make up for Kilby's disappearance. Likewise, his assistants and stagehands couldn't miss a beat as the props and lighting still had to be prepared for the evening show.

Later, at the Opera House, Professor Dooley prepared to assume his Marco persona as Bowden's orchestra started arriving and found their seats in the pit. While Houdini practised addressing the gallery, Professor Dooley began testing the larger stage props. As he stepped on one of the stage levers, a terrifying scream rang out across the theatre.

Everybody stopped and watched in horror as Buttons smashed into the rigging above the stage and came crashing back to the floorboards.

In an instant, everybody realized what had happened—Kilby had been trapped in the ejector under the stage since the morning rehearsal!

Buttons struggled to his feet and grimaced in pain. In the *Saint John Gazette*, a witness described the anger-fuelled aftermath of Buttons's unexpected appearance. "After rubbing his bruises and regaining his breath, in wrathful fury he explained his absence." The report went on to mention, "He now vows that when that particular trick is working in future Marco will not be so absent minded or else he will have to get a new boy."

In the end the young performer calmed down and prepared for the evening's performance. The Saint John newspaperman who caught wind of the incident anointed Kilby with a new nickname — "The Boy Rocket" — in honour of his unplanned performance.

Outside, carriages were arriving at the theatre and the patrons lined up at the box office as the lobby lights were turned on. Now that Professor Dooley had found his Buttons, the Marco Magic Company was ready to step into the footlights for their second show in Saint John.

>─┤◆>─○─<◆┤─<

A New Array of Modern Miracles Scientific Illusions.

Parlor and Stage Entertainments. Wardrobe A 1.

Introducing the Occult Mysteries of of the Hindo-Brahmins.

Kilby
The
MAGICIAN.

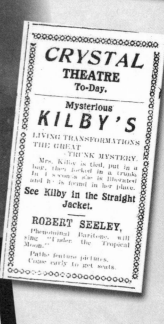

BUTTONS

AT SEVENTEEN, Burton Kilby was one of the youngest members of the Marco Magic Company. A reporter in New Brunswick described Kilby in the *Saint John Daily Telegraph*. "A bright and good-looking little chap, uniformed in a cadet regalia, has attracted considerable notice on the streets during the past few days."

The New Britain, Connecticut, boy, who normally worked in a box factory, went by the names Albert, Burton, or Bert. Inspired by Kilby's favourite outfit that featured three rows of shiny buttons, Professor Dooley chose an entirely new stage name for Kilby—Buttons.

After touring the Maritimes with Marco, Buttons worked in a brass factory by day, playing small-time clubs and fairs on the side. Dooley attended Buttons's wedding in 1900, writing Houdini afterwards, "Think of it—a kid like him getting married! He ought to be spanked and sent to bed."

In 1906 Buttons wanted to buy a piece of Harry Houdini's act. He wrote to Houdini promising, "I will try to make a success and be on top as Houdini #2." Houdini exchanged letters with Buttons throughout the next two years and even put him in touch with a New York manager.

Sadly, Buttons didn't become as famous as his former co-star, Houdini. But he did return to the Maritimes, headlining a tour with his wife, billing the couple as the "Mysterious Kilby's." On that tour, the man who once wanted to be Houdini #2 performed a Metamorphosis-style trunk act and a straitjacket escape between moving pictures at Maritime theatres.

(top) Burton Kilby posed in his multi-buttoned cadet uniform for his 1906 magician's letterhead which featured his wife and assistant, Nellie. (Harry Ransom Center, The University of Texas at Austin)

(right) In 1908, Burton "Buttons" Kilby toured the Maritimes with his own escape act. At the Crystal Theatre in Moncton, he escaped from a packing crate after its cover was securely nailed. (Provincial Archives of New Brunswick: *Moncton Transcript*, May 26, 1908, 5)

HARRY HOUDINI

KING OF CARDS

NATIONAL PR.& ENG. CO. CHICAGO

CHAPTER TWELVE

A CHANGE OF PROGRAMME

Saint John, New Brunswick
Tuesday Evening, June 9, 1896

"Did you ever think, that the greatest trick
is just being yourself at all times?"
—Harry Houdini, from Personal Interview Letter Series
by Joe Mitchell Chapple

HEAVY RAIN STARTED TO FALL as the Marco Magic Company prepared for its second performance in Saint John. Professor Dooley had to hope the rain might bolster attendance. But, realistically, even if the evening's baseball games were cancelled, sports fans would likely stay home instead of getting drenched heading to the Opera House.

Bowden's orchestra struck up their opening number at eight o'clock to open the show. The overture filled the theatre with an awkward resonance as it bounced off close to 1,100 empty seats. The poor attendance of 181 at Monday night's opener now looked like a great achievement. On this rainy night in Saint John, only 122 paying customers showed up for the performance.

The Opera House management was already looking past the fledgling Marco Magic Company and was focusing on a more professional outfit. Earlier in the day,

Houdini's transition from the "King of Cards" to the "Handcuff King" was in full flight when he reached Saint John in 1896. (Library of Congress)

work had begun for the return of the popular W.S. Harkins Company on June 24. The theatre's carpenter, William Hughes, had been to Halifax to oversee the Harkins's production of the play *War of Wealth* at the Academy of Music. Hughes and a scenic painter had now returned to Saint John and were busily preparing for the upcoming production in spite of Marco's ongoing stand at the theatre.

As usual, Professor Dooley opened Tuesday's performance with a half-hour set of traditional sleight of hand magic. And the organist-turned-magician must have felt right at home, because aside from Dooley's patter and the occasional applause from the tiny audience, the enormous theatre was as quiet as a church.

After Monday's embarrassing experience, the Growth of the Mango Tree was not repeated. And there was no further mention of the Cremation of Floribel. Professor Dooley wasn't entirely finished with Floribel, but he wouldn't attempt to incinerate her on this night, or any other night here in Saint John. A reporter with the *Saint John Sun* took note of the wisely deleted illusions and noted, "Marco made a number of changes in his programme."

As usual, Harry and Bessie impressed the small Tuesday night audience with another remarkable presentation of their Metamorphosis trunk trick. By now, it was obvious to all that the Houdinis' trunk exchange was the best illusion offered by the Marco Magic Company. Dooley made a point of explaining that his programme would change every night *except* for Metamorphosis.

Professor Dooley knew he had to generate some more interest in his show by cashing in on Houdini's popularity with the local press. With this goal in mind, Houdini agreed to attempt a challenge as an unannounced feature of Tuesday evening's programme. If all went well, his escape work would get a write-up in Wednesday's papers and hopefully inspire more citizens to come out to the show.

Although Houdini had allowed committees from the audience to tie him onstage many times before, it was typically only his hands and feet for Metamorphosis. He had also started visiting police stations in late 1895 doing handcuff escapes to generate publicity. But now in Saint John, he was combining the two by inviting the police to the theatre to appear onstage. To the audience, this completely removed the possibility that Houdini had planted confederates in the audience to tie him with trick knots or challenge him with gaffed handcuffs.

The Saint John police force was represented by Officer George Baxter. This was a well-earned break for the officer who had been assigned the unpleasant task of shooting a sick horse on Monday. And Baxter had worked a lively weekend shift, too. The officer—along with Captain Jenkins, whom Houdini met at the police station on Thursday—raided a Sheffield Street bawdy house on Sunday afternoon.

Several other well-known local citizens were also invited to bring ropes, chains, and shackles to Houdini's Tuesday night performance. Joining the policeman on stage was Arthur McGinley, listed in the 1896 city directory as a hairdresser, and the Hotel Dufferin manager, John McCafferty.

At first, the three local men decided to challenge Houdini with rope. However, the combined knot-tying skill of the three local men couldn't hold Houdini. Officer Baxter's handcuffs and shackles proved to be no match for Houdini's skills either.

In a final attempt to hold the showman, the men cuffed Houdini's hands behind his back and then secured his feet with leg irons. A final pair of handcuffs was used to connect the cuffs on his wrists to the leg shackles before Houdini was placed in a curtained enclosure. Mere seconds later, he emerged free from all of Baxter's prison jewellery. Houdini affected his escapes so quickly, the *Saint John Sun* reported that the policeman's finest shackles "only proved playthings to this mysterious magician." The *Sun* went on to suggest that Houdini's performance had crossed a line from the theatrical realm to the other side. "It is certainly a marvelous performance and many people last night avowed that he must certainly be in league with the spirits."

After Houdini retreated to the wings, Professor Dooley returned to the footlights. On this evening, he had much better luck with his illusions. The Tuesday show was poorly attended, but at least it was a success on the stage. One reviewer who attended both nights' shows commented, "The performance was much smoother than the previous night."[1]

J.M. Whitehead signed for the company's meagre share of the box office receipts and collected a bounty of $16.80 on behalf of the Marco Magic Company.

At the close of the show, Houdini could look forward to meeting Samuel "Samri" Baldwin, a legendary entertainer who would be arriving in Saint John as a guest of Professor Dooley. This veteran performer, who dominated so many stages in the nineteenth century, would meet the young man named Houdini who would dominate the same stages in the twentieth century.

Wednesday, June 10, at the Hotel Dufferin, the torch would be passed.

>⊷⟨⊷⊶⊙⊷⟨⟩⊷⊢⋖

In 1907, Houdini published an article claiming he invented the "challenge" element of the handcuff act. But in the same write-up, Houdini conceded, "I do not claim to have conceived and originated the simple handcuff escape, as every novice in this line knows that it has been done for years." (Library of Congress)

THE
ART OF
SUSPENSE

YEARS BEFORE Houdini played Saint John, a performer named Professor Barrael had introduced both rope and handcuff escapes to the city. Working with a boy assistant, he also did an act called the Striboff Mystery that was almost identical to the Houdinis' Metamorphosis illusion.

An 1891 *Saint John Globe* review of Professor Barrael's performance raises questions about the origins and originality of Harry Houdini's preamble to the Metamorphosis illusion. "Professor Barrael is without doubt one of the cleverest performers seen in this city. His exchanging of coats while in the spirit cabinet was done in the twinkling of an eye, the mystery being how he got his hands, which were securely tied, and in addition handcuffed, free to take his coat off, and even if he did how he put them back again."

Barrael and Houdini were both lightning quick escape artists. But Houdini would eventually learn that staying concealed for a longer time actually built tension, making a more entertaining act. Later in his career, he was plunged headfirst into a vertical tank of water which was then securely locked. Audiences stared in horror at the curtain covering the "Chinese Water Torture Cell" for minutes on end. Houdini, of course, had escaped quickly and simply waited in the wings, often reading, while his audience grew more anxious.

During one such performance, the crowd, convinced the escape artist was drowning, was so quiet that a stagehand told Houdini to stop turning the pages of his newspaper because the rustling paper could be heard in the gallery.

(bottom) The Chinese Water Torture Cell. Behind the scenes Houdini called his invention the "U.S.D." or the "Upside Down." Before being lowered into the water-filled cell, Houdini invited the audience to hold their breath for as long as it took him to escape. (Library of Congress)

CHAPTER THIRTEEN

HOUDINI MEETS
THE WHITE MAHATMA

Saint John, New Brunswick
Wednesday, June 10, 1896

"I believe that Houdini was the very first man to call himself
a jailbreaker, but I used handcuff keys and got free from handcuffs
before he was born, and surely many years before he or any other
living man ever gave a handcuff trick."
— Samuel Spencer Baldwin in a letter to magician
James Harto, March 6, 1915

ON WEDNESDAY, JUNE 10, Samuel "Samri" Baldwin checked into the Hotel Dufferin as a guest of Professor Dooley. Mr. Baldwin was enjoying a break from his latest American tour. His itinerary included most of the largest American cities and closed with a two-week stand in Cleveland, Ohio, on May 30. Baldwin had opted to take the summer off and planned to resume the tour in Philadelphia on the last day of August.

The veteran showman was suffering from a serious medical problem — perhaps related to his recurring battle with throat hemorrhages. It's possible he was advised to travel to Saint John; American physicians of the day sometimes prescribed cool

Samuel "Samri" Baldwin posing as the White Mahatma. Baldwin
may have been the first performer to escape from handcuffs on
the theatrical stage. (Harry Ransom Center, The University of Texas at Austin)

135

salty air for their patients and recommended they head north to the Maritime provinces.

Oddly, for such a well-known star, Baldwin's arrival went virtually unnoticed in Saint John. The *Sun* was the only one of five city newspapers to report on his arrival; a very brief note in a social column stated, "S.S. Baldwin, the original White Mahatma, is at the Dufferin, being on a visit to Marcos [*sic*], who is playing at the Opera House. Mr. Baldwin has appeared in all the leading cities of Europe and America, and is recognized as the greatest in the profession."

Samuel Spencer Baldwin was born in Cincinnati, Ohio, in 1848. As a teenager, he fought in the Civil War and was wounded several times. In the years immediately following the war he worked as a journalist and a printer before entering show business. From the very beginning of his stage career, Baldwin was very much at home in the footlights. The smallish but sturdy performer was a confident humorist who could seamlessly blend comedy with forays into the darkest side of humanity.

Although Samuel Baldwin ranked as one of the most successful entertainers of the late-nineteenth century, he didn't succeed alone. His first and second wives, Clara and Kittie, were his co-stars.

The Baldwins' act featured music, mind reading, magic, fortune telling, séances, and a routine called Solmonancy. In this disturbing act, Mrs. Baldwin would go into a deep, deep trance. After a tense minute passed, she would scream out in terror and start describing her horrible visions that normally featured train wrecks, murders, and suicides.

While touring India, Baldwin had carefully studied Hindu culture. He started dressing in a turban and a traditional homespun Indian robe and billed himself as the White Mahatma. Back in America, the public were awestruck with his Mahatma character.

Almost immediately, Baldwin had to accept imitators of his Indian stage persona. Proving that imitation is the greatest form of flattery, Anna Eva Fay stole the White Mahatma title for herself. And it served her very well. The ninety-pound Fay exploited her Mahatma title and found even greater success than the Baldwins, doing an almost identical act. But Baldwin dismissed her act by explaining that Mahatma was a male-only title. "Might as well speak of a female bull," he huffed.[1]

One of Samri Baldwin's posters complete with black cat and owl.
(Library of Congress)

THE GRUESOME SECRETS OF MAHATMA LAND

At the Hotel Dufferin, Baldwin could regale Houdini for hours with stories that would leave the studious young magician spellbound. Baldwin had toured the world several times, often playing throughout Europe, North America, and the United Kingdom along with visiting such exotic locations as Gibraltar, Turkey, Morocco, Algiers, Egypt, South Africa, Zanzibar, India, Arabia, Siam, Singapore, China, and Japan.

A page from Baldwin's scrapbook showing a group of pirates
executed by beheading on a Koolong Beach near Hong Kong.
(Harry Ransom Center, The University of Texas at Austin)

Around the time he joined the Marco Magic Company, Houdini had started keeping a tiny pocket diary and a press book for newspaper clippings. But Baldwin travelled with a magnificent scrapbook that was packed with photos, reviews, programmes, and hand-painted drawings that he exhibited to theatre managers as proof of his drawing power.

Baldwin's scrapbooks revealed a dark side to the man. While world-famous magicians like Alexander Herrmann and Harry Kellar were offering illusions based on beheadings and cremations, Baldwin had actually witnessed the real thing in his travels to faraway lands. Photos in his scrapbook captured crucifixions in Burma, execution by elephant in India, cremations in Calcutta, and death by a thousand cuts in China.

One series of Baldwin's photos offers a rare insight into his unique interpretation of horror. The photos show a group of pirates kneeling in the sand, their hands tied behind their backs, awaiting execution by beheading. There are before and after photos but none of the actual act. Instead, the photos show the pirates' faces as they watch their comrades being executed. The look of horror on their faces inspires an image in the mind's eye much more horrific than can ever be produced by a photograph. This was the essence of Samuel Baldwin's showmanship: allow the audience to tap into their darkest fears and terrify themselves with their own imaginations. Houdini would employ the same tactic later in his career when he would let his anxious audience believe he was drowning in water behind a curtain while precious minutes ticked by.

Houdini eventually acquired Baldwin's 1890s scrapbook from the White Mahatma's daughter, Shadow, and it survives to this day in the Magicians Collection at the Harry Ransom Center in Austin, Texas.

In 1895 Baldwin published a book called *The Secrets of Mahatma Land Explained: Teaching and Explaining the Most Celebrated Oriental Mystery Makers and Magicians.* His highly entertaining book relates stories of his travels that brought him to every continent on Earth except Antarctica.

Houdini, along with every other studious magician, had his own copy of Baldwin's splendid book. Much of the book recounts his meeting with magicians and medicine men in Africa and India where he asked the locals to show him their very best deceptions.

In his book, Baldwin explained the difference between himself and a tribal magician. "My performances were given simply with the idea of entertaining the public. *His* deceptions were given purely with the view of making his tribal comrades have an implicit belief in his supernatural powers." In another passage he bluntly explains the consequences when an African Obi man fails to use his magic to produce rain in a timely fashion. "The inhabitants roast the man and eat him."

It's easy to speculate how Professor Dooley became acquainted with Samuel Baldwin. Although Baldwin spent much of his time living in New York City, his American address for his business affairs and fan mail was Hartford, Professor Dooley's home city.

Samuel Baldwin and Professor Edward James Dooley had something else in common aside from Hartford; they both had an eye for talent. Baldwin easily spotted the genius in Dooley's young assistant, the mysterious Harry Houdini.

FATHER
OF THE
HANDCUFF
ACT

Houdini shares a laugh with Baldwin. Both men would die within a few years of enjoying this compelling moment. (Harry Ransom Center, University of Texas at Austin)

THREE YEARS before Houdini was born, Samuel Baldwin added a unique feature to his act—handcuff escapes. Baldwin allowed his audience to handcuff him and then retreated to a large wooden cabinet where, out of view, he would liberate himself from the restraints. After his escape, he would show the audience the handcuffs linked through each other. Other times he locked the cuffs onto the handle of a china water pitcher.

The "marvelous handcuff test" was reported in no fewer than three New Orleans newspapers back in 1871. Baldwin kept the handcuffs in his act as he developed into a world-famous performer who could sell out theatres on almost every continent. In 1915, long after Houdini had become an international legend for his escape act, Baldwin wrote magician James Harto and took credit for debuting the act. "The first

According to legend, Samuel "Samri" Baldwin enlisted in the US Army at age thirteen and fought for the Union in the Civil War. (Harvard Theatre Collection, Houghton Library, Harvard University)

MISS KITTIE BALDWIN'S SOMNAMBUMISTIC VISIONS.

The violent visions of Samri Baldwin's wife, Kittie, kept the couple's audience on the edge of their seats. (Harry Ransom Center, The University of Texas at Austin)

public handcuff escape ever given in the United States and elsewhere so far as I have been able to discover was given by myself in 1871 in the city of New Orleans."

In the same letter, a feisty Baldwin appeared ready to defend his claim as the inventor of the famous handcuff act: "I will take a thousand dollars that I can prove all this and that any man who says he did the handcuff trick before I had done it for years, is a liar of the first water. I can prove all of this by the dated programmes, newspaper notices, house statements, letters from managers, etc. I did it all over the world and finally almost gave it up in order to work my clairvoyancy which was a greater sensation."

By the time Houdini was seriously pursuing the handcuff act in 1895, Baldwin had already been working his handcuff escapes for almost a quarter century. In the 1870s Baldwin offered a cash reward for anyone who could produce a pair of handcuffs that he couldn't escape from. And Baldwin was still offering the reward in the 1890s. During his record-breaking Canadian stand in Hamilton, Ontario, in March 1895, he offered

a thousand-dollar reward to anyone who could produce a set of handcuffs that could hold him for more than three minutes. Baldwin's cash challenge would become a hallmark of Houdini's later handcuff career.

Although Houdini would go on to publish many books and write extensively about his handcuff career, he would never mention his 1896 encounter with the father of the handcuff act, Samuel Spencer Baldwin, in Saint John, New Brunswick. However, there is evidence Houdini planned on writing about Baldwin.

In a letter to Baldwin's daughter following his death on March 10, 1924, Houdini wrote: "You ask me if I would like to have some of the clippings and scrapbooks? I would very much like to have them for my collection. Any of the clippings or material you give me will be carefully filed away for the future, any time I wish to write a further article upon the original Great White Mahatma." But the future article was never written. Within three years of Baldwin's death, Houdini would be gone, too.

OPERA HOUSE

—

Every Night This Week!

Only Matinee Saturday!

THE WONDERFUL

Marco

The entire press said best performance of magic ever presented in this city.

—

N. B.—Owing to the race today the management has decided not to play the matinee as announced

—

Ticketa 15c., 25c., 35c., and 50c.

Seats now on sale at the Opera House Box Office.

CHAPTER FOURTEEN

DECEPTION AT THE DUFFERIN

Saint John, New Brunswick
Wednesday Afternoon, June 10, 1896

"It is needless to say that women make the most patient
as well as the most dangerous pickpockets."
— Harry Houdini, from *The Right Way To Do Wrong*

SHORTLY AFTER HIS ARRIVAL in the foggy city, Samuel Baldwin and the Marco Magic Company gathered together for a late lunch at the Hotel Dufferin. For the time being, with the legendary White Mahatma as a guest at his table, Dooley could overlook the Marco Magic Company's most recent predicament; they weren't supposed to be sitting down for lunch. Instead, they should have been at the Opera House raising the curtain for the matinee performance. But obviously they weren't.

Dooley had cancelled his scheduled Wednesday matinee on account of a horse race being held at Moosepath Trotting Park. The popular race featured the top horses from Massachusetts, New Brunswick, and Nova Scotia who were running for a big money purse and bragging rights as the fastest horse in the east.

🢒 This advertisement for the Marco Company was run in the Saint John newspapers on Wednesday, June 10, 1896. As noted, Dooley cancelled his Wednesday matinee on account of the big horse race. The race was also cancelled due to rain.
(Provincial Archives of New Brunswick: SJ *Daily Telegraph*, June 10, 1896, 3)

Cancelling the matinee seemed like a sensible decision at the time. But then the word came early on Wednesday morning—the big race at Moosepath was cancelled because of the rain. Unfortunately for Professor Dooley, it was too late to pull the newspaper cancellation notices that announced, "Owing to the race today the management has decided not to play the matinee as announced."

The race postponement didn't slow the arrival of special race excursion trains and steamships that were still dumping hundreds of race fans in Saint John. Likewise, dozens of press agents were landing in Saint John to cover the race. Imagine if they had attended the Marco show. Just think about the great press coverage!

Professor Dooley now had reason to ponder whether this tour was somehow cursed. Here he was in Saint John, a city crowded with visitors and citizens who booked a day off work to see the year's biggest race. Now, all these race fans were looking for something to do with their afternoon. And he had cancelled the matinee!

He could only dream about the lost opportunity to fill the Opera House. And it was obvious there were far too many visitors in this city with nothing to do but spend their time and money getting drunk. Fuelled by liquid courage, one industrious pod of race fans passed their time by street fighting with a group of obliging sailors.

At least Professor Dooley could enjoy the press reviews of Tuesday evening's performance. The morning papers once again raved about the Houdinis' marvellous Metamorphosis illusion. The *Saint John Globe* offered a bit of intrigue when they reported that, "Mr. Houdini will repeat his handcuff feat every night, and all possessors of handcuffs are invited to bring them and test this young man's ability."

Professor Dooley exploited the good reviews of the Marco show by running a large advertisement in Wednesday's afternoon paper that proclaimed, "Did you read yesterday's papers? They all said Marco gave the best performance of magic ever seen here, Wonderful! Mysterious!"[1]

Dooley put aside his worries and entertained his entourage in the Dufferin Hotel dining room. The group of magic company members and a local reporter were laughing and telling jokes at a furious pace. The reporter described Dooley and his colleagues in the *Saint John Globe*. "As the fun went on he and his party became more jubilant and each joke that was perpetrated on the other was encouraged by hearty laughter."

Houdini and the rest of the show people at the table gained their composure long enough to order their supper—soup to be followed with fish—and then

Streetcars from all parts of Saint John passed by the Hotel Dufferin
every few minutes. (New Brunswick Museum, Saint John, NB)

continued with their good humour. Suddenly, a man seated at a nearby table put
an end to the hilarity.

"My watch! It's gone!" he shouted.

The chatter in the dining room stopped. In an instant, the only audible sound
was the rain beating against the north windows.

The man was adamant that he had had his watch with him when he entered the
dining room. Furthermore, the diner wanted the police summoned to the Charlotte
Street hotel to investigate his loss. Instead, the Hotel Dufferin proprietor, LeRoi
Willis, was called into the dining room to deal with the upset diner.

Mr. Willis already had his hands full today. His hotel was the epicentre of race
activity in Saint John. Aside from overseeing his guests and busy staff, he was also
managing the big race and even had one of his own horses entered in the contest.

The sombre diners watched as Mr. Willis interviewed his unhappy guest. This
was now becoming a serious matter. The victimized customer was genuinely and
publicly upset with the hotel manager. Any hotel that allows thieves to work its
dining room would quickly be ruined by word of mouth.

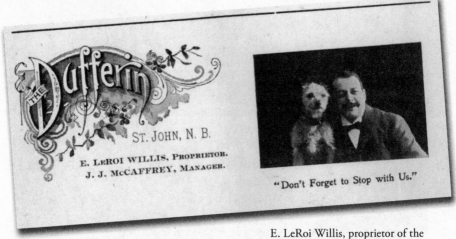

THE Dufferin

ST. JOHN, N. B.

E. LeROI WILLIS, PROPRIETOR.
J. J. McCAFFREY, MANAGER.

"Don't Forget to Stop with Us."

E. LeRoi Willis, proprietor of the
Hotel Dufferin
in Saint John, with a canine accomplice.
(New Brunswick Museum, Saint John, NB)

LeRoi Willis had worked tirelessly to improve his hotel's image by installing new marble floors and plate glass doors. Several odd promotions like having an orchestra perform in the hotel's lobby and exhibiting a live wild turkey had won favour with the public. Through Willis's hard work, his hotel and dining room were now considered among Saint John's finest.

One of Mr. Willis's favourite possessions was a recent handwritten endorsement from America's most well-known band leader that read, "During my stay in St. John [sic] I was delighted with the excellent management and attention I received while at the Hotel Dufferin. Sincerely yours, John Phillip Sousa."[2] And after today, Willis could boast that the great Samuel Baldwin had stayed at his hotel.

But now, in front of a full dining room, Mr. Willis was watching his reputation circling the drain. He had to use his best damage control tactics and resolve this embarrassing theft. Willis knew perfectly well that in the hospitality business your reputation signs your paycheque. And to add to his nightmare, he had a handful of eager reporters watching this whole scandal unfold right in front of their very eyes!

After questioning the watch-less man and the other diners, Mr. Willis determined the only possible thief could be the waiter because the victim was sitting alone at his table. The waiter was called out and cross-examined in front of the quiet diners. After enduring the humiliation of a "trial" in front of his customers, the waiter was allowed to return to his duties.

Although the customer had lost his watch, he hadn't lost his appetite and opted to continue with his now gratis meal. His main course of stuffed chicken arrived at his table in short order.

After cutting the chicken he yelled again.

Once more the dining room fell silent.

Inside his chicken, smothered with tasty dressing, were his watch and a small card. When the man flipped over the card it read, "Compliments of Marco."

The laughter resumed and the diners applauded Professor Dooley for the impromptu entertainment. The stunt was the talk of the hotel for days and kept the guests and staff busy trying to figure out how it was done.

Eventually the rain gave way to a fine Wednesday evening as showtime at the Opera House drew closer. The Tuesday night receipts weren't even close to being enough to cover costs. Professor Dooley knew he had to come up with a proven and practical means to fill the Opera House.

It was time to call on the services of an evil hypnotist.

CLOSE SHAVES

Houdini studies a set of manacles he discovered in Russia in 1903. This was one of a small number of special cuffs Bessie kept until her death. (Patrick Culliton Collection)

IF HOUDINI TOLD Mr. Baldwin about his close call with the Saint John Maniac Cuff, the veteran showman could offer some sage advice for when things went wrong. Not all of Baldwin's early escape challenges went smoothly either. At one show in Galveston, Texas, Baldwin broke his lock pick inside the sheriff's rusty old handcuffs. With a full theatre waiting, the showman had to think fast. Sure enough, he came up with a bizarre, but devilishly clever plan.

First, Baldwin took out his trusty pocketknife and slashed his wrist. Then he exited the spirit cabinet with the one cuff still closed and blood pouring freely from his wrist onto the stage boards. To the amazement of his audience, he announced that,

"The spirits have hit me a whack with a broken bell and have cut quite a gash in my wrist and I am bleeding severely. If the sheriff will please loan me his key until I open this cuff and let a doctor bandage my wrist I will later on do the handcuff experiment."[3]

Baldwin's inspired ruse worked perfectly. His spellbound spectators honestly believed that supernatural forces were doing their darnedest to keep him locked in the restraints. If Baldwin was willing to shed blood to pull off this caper, he would have certainly agreed to help Professor Dooley pull off an old-fashioned gag at the Hotel Dufferin dining room.

Besides, cutting chicken didn't hurt near as much as cutting your own wrist.

Harry Houdini's first partner Jacob Hyman performed as the "Great Houdini" at a Toronto theatre in November 1895. In later years, Jacob attempted to copy Harry Houdini's escape act.
(Patrick Culliton Collection)

Saint John, New Brunswick
Wednesday Evening, June 10, 1896

*"The Trilby romance is unhealthy in its action on most minds,
and it would be well for the world had it never been written."
—Lancaster Weekly Inquirer, May 4, 1895*

BESSIE HOUDINI STARTED her stage career as a singer in a Coney Island musical ensemble called the Floral Sisters. By all accounts, Bessie, who previously used the stage name Bessie Raymond, was a fine singer. This was a good thing—because in Saint John, she was going to have to sing for the people once again.

Professor Dooley needed a Trilby and Bessie filled the bill perfectly.

Trilby, a novel by George du Maurier, was one of the most popular books of the day. The early editions of this gothic horror story featured a cover laden with dark symbolism. The artwork set the tone for the book with a winged golden heart trapped in the centre of a spider's web while a sinister black arachnid moves in for the kill.

The story follows its central character, Trilby O'Ferrall, as she rises from her humble life as a model in Paris, to the toast of Europe as a singer. Trilby, who

Images like this one from the 1895 edition of *Trilby* both horrified and fascinated the public. (Public domain)

153

poses nude — in the book, du Maurier coined the phrase "in the altogether" — is revered for her feet by an aspiring young artist named Little Billee. Svengali, an evil-hearted virtuoso with a dark goatee and long black hair steals the heart of Trilby, and then spends three years training the tone-deaf model to sing while she is under his hypnotic spell. The training pays off. Svengali and Trilby become famous stars in Europe, performing throughout the continent to sold-out houses in the finest theatres.

Du Maurier's *Trilby* was perfectly timed to piggyback on the public's increasing fascination with hypnotism. Hippolyte Bernheim, a French physician, was the world's leading expert on the subject and his recent writings and lectures had lent credibility to hypnotism as an authentic medical phenomenon.

Published in 1894, the story found its way to the stage in very short order. A full five-act stage production of Trilby appeared twice at the Saint John Opera House in April, just two months prior to the Marco Magic Company's visit. The production was so well-received, management brought the company back the following month for an additional four performances. The novel was also turned into a burlesque comedy called *Thrilby* with the evil Svengali transformed into a bumbling jackass named Spaghetti.

In 1895 the husband and wife team of Alexander and Adelaide Herrmann transformed *Trilby* into a full magic act featuring a dramatic levitation scene. Even with an outrageous top ticket price of $1.50, the Herrmann's week-long *Trilby* debut brought in more than twenty thousand to a Pittsburgh theatre, setting a record for the city. Others took notice of Herrmann's success, and by the summer of 1896 the Trilby levitation illusion was a staple for most magic companies.

Hoping to cash in on Trilby's ongoing popularity, Professor Dooley forwarded a fanciful press release to the *Saint John Sun* proclaiming the details of his "new" illusion. Conveniently, the article entitled "Marco's Trilby" didn't disclose the fact that he had performed the illusion in Yarmouth the previous week.

 (top) This sketch of Alexander and Adelaide Herrmann performing their popular Trilby illusion was published in a Halifax paper in July, 1896. (Nova Scotia Archives)

(bottom) This sketch accompanied an article in the August 8, 1896, edition of *Scientific American* exposing how Marco and others achieved their *Trilby* levitation illusion. (Courtesy of Harriet Irving Library, UNB)

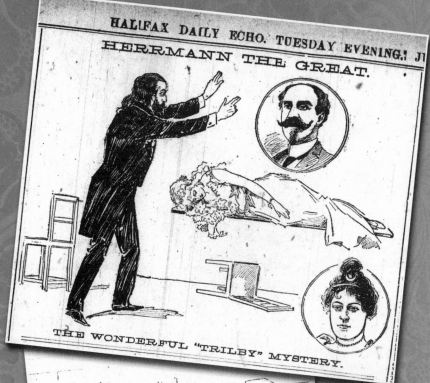

HERRMANN THE GREAT.

THE WONDERFUL "TRILBY" MYSTERY.

THE ILLUSION EXPLAINED.

One of the leading features to be offered by the original and only Marco will be his conception of du Maurier's *Trilby*, a beautiful sketch in one scene. Marco has been working on this feature for the last two years and has finally perfected it, and will introduce the illusion here for the first time on any stage. Marco will impersonate Svengali, Mlle Marco will appear as the beautiful Trilby and will sing the famous Ben Bolt. This conception differs from the novel or play, and effects are introduced which are not found in either.

The Houdinis were no strangers to Trilby. Bessie Houdini and the American Gaiety Girls performed a Trilby dance number during their winter tour. As a token tribute to Trilby's beautiful feet, Bessie and the other dancing girls performed barefooted. And during a brief hiatus from the American Gaiety Girls tour, Houdini performed as a hypnotist using the stage name Professor Morat.

Unfortunately, the *Trilby* novel had developed a cultist fanaticism with the mentally unstable. Several suicides were blamed on the novel, including one in Dooley's home city of Hartford. An eighteen-year-old named Norton Reed had obsessively read and reread *Trilby*. He was found dying from poison and claimed Svengali had hypnotized him. In his last living moments, he asked if he would see Trilby in heaven.

PROFESSOR DOOLEY, A.K.A. MARCO, A.K.A. SVENGALI

With his young troupe thoroughly rehearsed and the stage readied, Professor Dooley and Bessie Houdini transformed into Svengali and Trilby.

At the start of the act, Dooley, as Marco playing the part of the evil Svengali, invited his beautiful assistant, Bessie Houdini, onto the stage. Bessie, impersonating Mademoiselle Marco impersonating Trilby, was placed into a hypnotic trance by the Professor and sang a few bars of "Ben Bolt," a song prominent in the novel. Next, Dooley prepared a special couch for Bessie by placing a plank crosswise between two chairs and covering the lumber with a sheet. With the aid of a stepstool, Bessie laid down on the makeshift sofa holding a large bouquet of flowers. Professor

🐦 An elegant Beatrice Houdini. (Library of Congress)

Dooley continued to pass his hands over Bessie until he was satisfied the time was right for a miracle.

Upon command from "Svengali," Bessie began rising into the air while Dooley cautiously removed both chairs. A surprised audience applauded as Bessie remained floating in the air. Professor Dooley passed a sword under and over his Trilby, proving there were no wires or ropes helping to levitate her. After it was clear there was no means of support in use, Bessie was lowered as Dooley returned the chairs to their original position, supporting the plank. Dooley awakened Bessie from her hypnotic trance and helped her down from her couch.

In full view of the audience, Dooley removed the sheet, lifted up the plank off the chairs and dropped it, letting it crash to the stage floor. There was no question

Harry Kellar was among the world's top magicians in 1896 and incorporated aspects of the *Trilby* levitation illusion into his act.

(Library of Congress)

the piece of lumber that had moments before levitated so mysteriously with Bessie aboard was nothing but an ordinary joist from a sawmill.

While Dooley's *Trilby* illusion was mystifying and beautiful in its presentation, it required a hidden mechanical juggernaut to perform. Behind a black fabric backdrop was a frame with a block and tackle to help lift an extendable bar that slid up and down a vertical track. When Trilby was ready to levitate, one of Dooley's assistants extended the bar through the backdrop. The end of the iron bar was fitted with a two-inch-wide mouth that slipped onto the plank as easily as an open-ended wrench slips onto the head of a bolt.

Trilby's large bouquet of flowers helps hide any movement of the backdrop curtain and blocks the view of the bar from the theatre's balcony seats. As the chairs are removed, a stagehand working behind the backdrop can easily raise and lower Trilby by use of the block and tackle mechanism. The orchestra helps mask any errant squeaks and creaks that might come from the backstage mechanics. At the close of the illusion, a stagehand retracts the bar.

Thankfully for Professor Dooley, the mechanical contraption worked perfectly in Saint John. The one-act *Trilby* illusion went smoothly and won rave reviews in several newspapers, including one that singled out the act as "[a] sensational feature of the programme."[1]

Despite the success of Dooley's expensive and complicated *Trilby* illusion, the Houdinis' Metamorphosis still stole the show. According to the *Saint John Sun*, Metamorphosis was "the hit of the evening." At the close of Wednesday's performance, Dooley had a new worry on his plate. Ed Knupp, the press agent for the Walter L. Main Circus, had arrived in Saint John and was staying at the Hotel Victoria. Dooley knew that Mr. Knupp was taking over the city for the next two days as he set the stage for the arrival of the big show on Friday.

Circus aside, it was time to focus on Thursday's show. His week-long stand in Saint John was half-finished now. He needed a solid drawing card to seize the attention of Saint John. And he had one.

If all went well for Professor Dooley, Bessie Houdini would fall victim to a terrible catastrophe.

>⋅⟩⟨⋅⊙⋅⟩⟨⋅⟨

CHAPTER SIXTEEN

OFF WITH HER HEAD

Saint John, New Brunswick
Thursday, June 11, 1896

"She is superstitious to a degree that is abnormal even among the
superstitiously inclined people of her profession. If she hears that
anyone has whistled in a dressing room she will never enter that room.
Yellow she wouldn't wear under any condition."
— *Pittsburgh Post*, October 21, 1906, describing Bessie Houdini

PROFESSOR DOOLEY'S BUSINESS PARTNER, Jack McKierney, was
given the dubious and regrettable honour of signing the Opera House ledger for
Wednesday's box office receipts. It wasn't pretty. The company's share of the take
was only $11.32. For the third straight night, attendance had been ridiculously low
and Dooley was quickly running out of time to rescue his Saint John appearance.

As the sun came up on Thursday, Dooley had to focus on his next crisis. Today,
his latest trouble was approaching by rail in the form of the Walter L. Main Circus
train. Tomorrow was circus day in the Port City. It was almost impossible to generate
interest in anything else. The circus was advertising two shows: one in the afternoon
and one in the evening as direct competition for the Marco Magic Company.

Alexander Herrmann continues his executioner's spree. The detective
skeleton is back and pointing an accusing bony finger at the magician.
(Harvard Theatre Collection, Houghton Library, Harvard University)

Professor Dooley had one more concern to add to his ever-growing pile of worries. Harshaw Clarke, the manager of the Academy of Music theatre in Halifax, Nova Scotia, was in town. Manager Clarke had checked into the Royal Hotel and would be attending Marco's performance. After all, he had booked Marco into his big Halifax theatre for a week-long stand beginning June 22.

Tonight, Professor Dooley would debut a sensational act.

Inspired by Samuel Baldwin's sinister scrapbook pictures, Professor Dooley notified the newspapers and started promoting a new spectacle. When the citizens of Saint John cracked open their Thursday newspapers they were greeted by provocative advertisements that read, "Marco will cut off a woman's head in full view of the audience."

Professor Dooley outdid himself in writing his press release for the decapitation act, which included a fabricated story about performing the illusion in Germany. The *Saint John Daily Telegraph* was more than happy to print Dooley's outrageous article in the Thursday, June 11 edition.

> The principal feature of Marco's performance tonight will be an illusion of decapitation, which is the magical term for cutting one's head off. This illusion as it is worked by Marco is one of the most mysterious and sensational effects ever introduced. It has been marveled at by the public of Europe, where it created the most profound excitement of anything in Marco's repertoire. Tonight the wonderful magician will endeavor to get a lady from the audience to try the experiment and if he can not [sic] find one who is willing to have her head cut off, he will call to his assistance Mlle. Marco. She will walk on the stage in full view of the audience, and will be given a seat that will not be in a cabinet of any kind or hidden by curtains of any description. To convince the audience that she is a real live performer, she will talk, sing, etc., and at a dramatic point, Marco draws a sword across the throat severing the head completely from the body. So realistic is this illusion that women are carried fainting from the theatre at this apparently horrible sight. When Marco performed this illusion in Berlin, Germany, he was ordered by the officials to take it off after the first night. It has been so much talked of that Marco has had numerous requests to put it on, so he will try it tonight.

The decapitation illusion had been around for many years. Beginning with birds, magicians appeared to decapitate the little creatures with a knife. In reality, they simply tucked the bird's head under its wing and produced a fake bird head to show the audience. Then, the magician would "reattach" the head, letting the bird fly off to assistants waiting in the wings. But decapitating birds didn't satisfy the public's blood lust for an execution by beheading. Before long, sword-wielding magicians were decapitating their assistants on stage. Although performed by a German magician named Professor Vanek as early as 1873, the human decapitation act was made famous by Alexander Herrmann in the late 1880s. But one magician took the act to a whole new level when the great Harry Kellar stunned audiences by cutting off his very own head!

Houdini saw the decapitation act at a very young age in Milwaukee when his father took him to see the British magician, Dr. Lynn. In broadsides advertising his performance, Dr. Lynn promised to chop up a man at every performance. And he lived up to his promise on the day young Ehrich Weiss saw his show. Houdini never forgot the act, called Palingenisia, and later wrote, "I really believed that the man's arm, leg and head were cut off."[1]

And now it was Professor Dooley's turn to introduce the macabre illusion to a New Brunswick audience. The Saint John press were intrigued by the beheading

This large newspaper advertisement greeted citizens of Saint John on Thursday, June 11, 1896.
(Provincial Archives of New Brunswick: SJ *Daily Telegraph*, June 11, 1896, 3)

OPERA HOUSE

To Night
A Great
Wonderful
Sensation.

Marco

Will Cut
Off a
Woman's
Head
In Full View
Of the
Audience.

Alexander Herrmann decapitates yet another stage assistant. (Harvard Theatre Collection, Houghton Library, Harvard University)

act and offered up plenty of commentary on the upcoming event. The *Saint John Gazette* had a bit of fun with Dooley's promotion suggesting, "One can see how easy it is to occasionally dispense with one's head and leave it at home for repairs. This experiment should prove interesting to the man who has been out all night and who would gladly be rid of his head the next morning."

With all the extra support from the press, Professor Dooley would have had high hopes for a packed Opera House on Thursday night. But when he peeked out at the seats just before showtime, his heart sank. It was now obvious that Saint John residents were saving their money for the circus. Bessie Houdini would have to sacrifice her beautiful head for a mere 134 souls.

But the show must go on—and the head must come off.

Not surprisingly, when Professor Dooley, as Marco, asked for a female volunteer who would like her head chopped off, no ladies came forward. As promised, Mademoiselle Marco was summoned from the wings to bravely surrender to Marco's sword. Bessie strode confidently to the centre of the stage and awaited her executioner. The audience listened breathlessly as Marco explained the hideous display they were about to witness.

For someone about to be executed, Bessie seemed remarkably tranquil as Marco raised his instrument of death high above his head. The stage lights flashed off the sword's long curved blade as Marco made good on his promise. Most in the audience closed their eyes at the horrific instant the sword severed Bessie Houdini's head from her body.

When they opened their eyes again, the tiny audience gasped. There was Marco carrying Bessie's head like it was a sack of onions. There was no question that Bessie's head was real. She spoke to Marco and even sang a few lines of a song. After lurking about the stage with his executioner's prize, Marco put Bessie's pretty head back in its proper place on her shoulders.

Miraculously, Bessie seemed none the worse for wear after being so violently decapitated. Never one to hog the limelight, the elfin Bessie simply smiled and nonchalantly exited the stage. The *Saint John Gazette* commented on Bessie's casual reaction to her beheading and subsequent resurrection. "Mlle Marco's head was cut off and carried around the stage and finally restored to its trunk when the little lady walked away just as unconcerned as if a thing as being beheaded was the most trifling in her daily life."

A DRESS FOR SUCCESS

The decapitation act required Bessie Houdini to dress in black from the neck down. She would take her place on stage wearing a dress that had been carefully crafted for the illusion. The dress was described in the 1891 magic manual, *Leaves from Conjurers' Scrap Books*, as "a framework of light wire covered with a fine evening dress." At the moment of decapitation, Bessie slipped out of the rigid backless dress leaving it behind. To the audience only her head was visible because of her black body garment.

Sneaking around the stage in full body tights showed how much confidence Bessie Houdini had gained since starting her career as a magician's assistant. Fewer than two years earlier Bessie, who was deeply self-conscious about her girlish figure in an era that favoured buxom showgirls, had been horrified at the very thought of wearing tights and close-fitting clothing in front of an audience. "I was actually getting over my prejudice and beginning to look forward to my debut as a public performer, when one night Harry brought home a pair of tights and made it clear that I would be expected to appear in these before large audiences of

perfect strangers. Then my morale broke and I heartily wished myself home with my mother. For hours and hours I wept bitterly over those tights, but in the end Houdini's diplomacy and unfailing tenderness brought me round to a less desolate view of the inevitable."[2]

Ultimately, it was a seasoned vaudeville singer, nicknamed the Irish Queen, who helped Bessie with her stage image. During a stand at Tony Pastor's theatre in New York City, Maggie Cline noticed Bessie was poorly dressed and made up for the unforgiving stage lighting. After a quick tutorial in the thirty-seven-year-old's dressing room, Bessie emerged with flowers and bows pinned to her dress and wearing proper stage makeup. The next time Bessie would reconnect with her mentor, a few years afterwards, the Houdinis would be at the top of the bill and Maggie Cline would be one of their opening acts.

Now in Saint John, with her head firmly back on her shoulders, a confident Bessie Houdini and the Marco Magic Company made their way home to the Hotel Dufferin in the pouring rain. Elsewhere, deep in the New Brunswick hinterland, the Walter L. Main Circus train was chugging its way towards Saint John from the United States border.

Thirty-four-year-old Walter L. Main had assembled a major circus that made the entire Welsh Brothers Circus look like a small-time sideshow attraction. Travelling by railway, the Ohio-based three-ring circus was a collection of almost every form of entertainment available. Marching bands, horses, reptiles, camels, a hippopotamus, high-wire artists, a horse-riding lion, divers, and clowns were shuttled from town to town by seventeen rail cars.

A rare image of Maggie Cline, the vaudeville vocalist who helped Bessie refine and define her stage image. Maggie often performed dressed head-to-toe in green, earning her the title "The Irish Queen."
(Harvard Theatre Collection, Houghton Library, Harvard University)

THE BLACK ART was an accidental discovery. At a Berlin performance in the mid-1800s, the audience couldn't see an actor dressed in black and wearing black face makeup. The player was invisible to the audience because of the lighting and the black background curtains. The effect spoiled the scene but inspired magicians to explore the stage phenomenon further.

The black art required that the background, sides, and floor be covered in black velvet or felt. This could be done within a specially constructed room or cabinet or across an entire stage depending on the scale and budget of the performance. When done properly, black objects were invisible to the audience. Black threads could be used to levitate small objects and black cloths could be used to hide objects. Assistants clad head to toe in black were also invisible to the audience.

One of the keys to producing a successful black art performance was a row of gas lights placed at the front of the stage. The lights had to be adjusted perfectly to create a shadowed stage while partly blinding the audience. In his 1891 book, *Leaves from Conjurers' Scrap Books*, H.J. Burlingame described the lighting when it was properly executed. "The effect of this arrangement of light and shadow throws the stage into impenetrable gloom."

Houdini's stint with the Marco Magic Company gave him a chance to observe the black art first-hand. However, Houdini's career would never depend on trick lighting and black fabric, but instead on very real and daring escapes.

(top) Harry Kellar's brilliant Self-decapitation poster. (Library of Congress)

(bottom) A black art decapitation sketch from H.J. Burlingame's 1891 book *Leaves From Conjurer's Scrap Books*. This magical marvel offered a detailed description of how to chop off a human head without any lingering damage to the victim.
(Courtesy of the Trustees of the Boston Public Library / Rare Books)

THE MYSTERIOUS
THE MYSTIFYING

HOUDINI

THE MARVELOUS MAGICIAN,
PREMIER CARD MANIPULATOR OF THE WORLD.

KING OF HANDCUFFS

POLICE CAPTAINS, SHERIFFS, OFFICERS, DETECTIVES, ETC. STAND POWERLESS
AND NONPLUSSED AT HIS MARVELOUS, INEXPLICABLE ESCAPE
FROM ALL HANDCUFFS.

ASSISTED
BY

...MLLE. BEATRICE HOUDINI...

PRESENTING THE

Miraculous Metamorphosis

GREATEST MYSTIFYING ACT IN THE WORLD.

YOU CANNOT BOOK AN ACT SUPERIOR IN OUR LINE.
WILL MAKE GOOD ANYWHERE

Chi. 4/4 1900

My dear Dr. Waitt.
I dont know if you owe me a letter or if I owe it to you so any way I will write just to let you know our thoughts stray towards Boston + our friend Waitt. My wife has been sick last two weeks but has now recovered. We are taking a weeks rest as we have been working pretty steady of late. Nothing new of any consequence only I hear we stand a good chance of coming to Boston

(over)

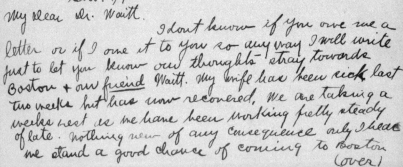

CHAPTER SEVENTEEN

RIDERS IN THE STORM

Saint John, New Brunswick
Friday, June 12, 1896

"I'm not an advertiser, I'm news."
—Harry Houdini addressing the Advertising Club of Boston
on September 21, 1926, *Boston Daily Globe*, September, 22, 1926

ON FRIDAY, JUNE 12, the rain fell, and then fell some more.

Across town at the Shamrock Grounds, an army of circus men were wallowing in mud as they struggled to set up their tents and cages. Bessie and Harry Houdini thanked their lucky stars they were no longer working the circus circuit on this miserable day. From their comfortable room in the Hotel Dufferin, the young couple could safely reminisce about their time with the Welsh Brothers when nasty summer storms would blow down their tents.

By evening, the storm clouds had passed and a standing-room-only crowd gathered under Walter Main's big top. At the end of the night's performance a dozen streetcars waited to take circus spectators home. As the crowd dispersed, hundreds of workers began breaking down the tents and loading the trains to repeat the show in Moncton the following day.

By 1900, Houdini was starting to give his escape act top-billing above Metamorphosis. Within six weeks of writing this letter, Houdini would sail for England where he would be catapulted to world fame. (Harvard Theatre Collection, Houghton Library, Harvard University)

CIRCUS FALLOUT

Back uptown, Chas Bryant signed for the Marco Magic Company's Friday night receipts. In what might be the worst box office take in the history of the twelve hundred–seat theatre, only twenty-four people attended the show. Once the take was split fifty-fifty with the house, the company raked in a dismal $3.77. The deflated Marco Magic Company returned to the Hotel Dufferin for one last night's sleep before their matinee and evening performances on Saturday.

Hopefully, the Opera House would be overflowing with excited boys and girls at the children's matinee. After a week of filling Saint John papers with stories about decapitations and cremations, Professor Dooley now had to switch gears. He had to convince Saint John parents that it was suitable to bring their children to his matinee. It wasn't going to be easy, especially on the heels of a circus that just left town.

The Houdinis had spent many afternoons entertaining children last summer with the Welsh Brothers Show. Harry had even performed a Punch and Judy show with wooden puppets. The Welsh Brothers knew it took silly gimmicks to bring in the children. For one Saturday matinee in Lebanon, Pennsylvania, they promised to give away three thousand pennies that one of the circus men would throw down from the centre pole into the circus ring. To sweeten the deal even more, the Welsh Brothers dropped admission from ten cents to five cents. The promotion worked like a charm, filling the big top with kids on a day threatening rain. The penny toss was the hit of the season, prompting the *Lebanon Daily News* to report "How those children and even some older folks did scramble to get them!"

Like the Welsh Brothers, magicians often dangled a cash prize or trinket giveaway—anything to entice children to pester their parents to take them to the matinee. When the Swedish magician Balabrega toured the Maritimes, he offered a five-dollar prize to the child who could create the most words from the letters found in the words, "Balabrega's Miracles." The word contest was a decided hit in Nova Scotia, filling the province's biggest theatre for a profitable Saturday matinee where a girl from the Sacred Heart Academy in Halifax claimed the cash prize with a list of 1,194 words.

Sadly, Professor Dooley simply didn't possess the promotional savvy of a top-shelf magician like Balabrega or the advertising experience of the Welsh Brothers. Instead he had the papers publish his almost pointless press release that stated,

Box office statement from Marco's Friday, June 12, 1896 performance shows only twenty-four paying customers. Main's Circus was noted to be opposition for the Marco Magic Company.

(New Brunswick Museum)

"The Opera House will be crowded with little folks who will be entertained by Marco's magic wand."[1]

At least Professor Dooley had enough sense to reduce the tickets for the Saturday matinee to twenty-five cents for adults and fifteen cents for children under fifteen. And the tickets were good to any part of the house. One thing that wasn't good was the attendance. The matinee drew only fifty-one adults and sixty-seven children.

Professor Dooley hatched one final desperate plan to fill the Opera House on Saturday evening.

He was going to show the audience how his tricks were done.

THE WALTER L. MAIN Circus train was a famous act that featured hundreds of animals, dozens of circus wagons, and scores of workers.

Aided by mechanical stake drivers, the canvas men erected the big top and ten smaller sideshow tents on the Shamrock Grounds while the circus animals were tended to. In many ways, the all-important creatures were treated better than their human co-stars. To make certain the meat-eating animals were well fed, the circus had its own butcher.

At noon, a mile-long parade left the Shamrock Grounds and started

(above) The 1896 advertising car for Walter L. Main's circus.

(right) Rain and muddy grounds always presented the circus with challenges. In Saint John, one of the biggest circus wagons sank to its axles in the miserable mire. A team of four horses was unable to budge the stubborn wagon so the circus men coaxed an elephant into pulling the cart out of its swampy predicament. (Provincial Archives of New Brunswick: P350-656, P350-755)

THE CIRCUS TRAIN

down Main Street. Word spread like wildfire throughout Saint John, and the parade route from Douglas Avenue to Paradise Row was soon lined with ten thousand spectators.

The parade featured over eighty-five horses and ponies that kept pace with several marching bands and a loud steam organ. Camels accompanied the cages containing bears, leopards, and lions. The circus lioness was featured prominently with a special perch on top of one of the wagons. The elephants marched as a group with the biggest pachyderm bringing up the rear and pulling a wagon. Clowns worked constantly to entertain the children who pushed their way to the front line of spectators at the curb.

One of the most popular wagons was the serpent wagon. An alluring young lady in exotic gypsy dress posed in the gilded cage with a huge snake coiled around her neck while dozens of smaller snakes writhed at her feet.

After winding through uptown Saint John, the circus parade returned to the soggy Shamrock Grounds. The wagons holding the exotic animals were parked while canvas men curtained the outer sides of the wagons, restricting the view of the animals from cheapskates who hadn't bought tickets to enter the tents.

The sideshow offered cheap entertainment as a hook to entice more customers to pay to enter the main tent. Pierre Perrier, the high diver, dove headfirst into a shallow trough of water. The strong jawed man, John Jennings, demonstrated seemingly non-human feats of strength such as lifting a five-hundred-pound cask of water with his teeth. And Miss Fatima entertained with her mysterious mind-reading demonstrations. During the afternoon show inside the main tent, Wallace the lion jumped on the back of a horse and did several laps of the outer track, winning loud cheers from the crowd as he jumped through suspended hoops of fire.

Clowns worked the crowd while jugglers, tumblers, and bareback riders offered simultaneous non-stop action in the rings. Inside a caged arena, trained animals formed pyramids and jumped through walls of fire. The grand finale following the daring trapeze act was a hilarious horse race with monkey jockeys.

Do Spirits Return?

HOUDINI

SAYS NO - AND PROVES IT

3 SHOWS IN ONE

MAGIC-ILLUSIONS-ESCAPES = FRAUD MEDIUMS EXPOSED

LYCEUM THEATRE

PATERSON

THURS. FRI. SAT. SEPT. 2·3·4

MATINEE SATURDAY

CHAPTER EIGHTEEN

SECRETS FOR SALE

Saint John, New Brunswick
Saturday, June 13, 1896

"You are advertised as if you intended to expose some evil in astrology,
clairvoyance, mediumship, etc. You may be clever in your tricks,
but silly to meddle with forces you know little or nothing about."
—A.F. Hill, letter to Houdini, April 11, 1906

ON SATURDAY AFTERNOON, the city's leading theatrical paper, the *Saint John Progress* was published. The weekly newspaper, which had always praised Dooley's nemesis Markos, refused to offer a single word about the Marco Magic Company; although, they did offer a neutral comment on Bowden's orchestra. "The new orchestra at the Opera House has been on duty since last Monday evening. They have yet to experience dramatic productions."

In the other local newspapers, Professor Dooley promised something special for Saturday evening's final performance in Saint John: "Marco, the magician, who has studied the methods of clairvoyance, mind reading and spiritualism, gives his last performance at the Opera House this evening. He will show how it is possible to answer questions about missing relatives and lost articles, how to read sealed letters,

Houdini would fill theatres in the 1920s by exposing fraudulent mediums on stage. His first experience with this form of stage show was in Saint John as a member of the Marco Magic Company on June 13, 1896. (Library of Congress)

describe articles in the pockets of the audience, give the numbers on bank notes, how messages are written on slates, and perform many other tests of his powers."[1]

Two Saint John reporters interviewed Professor Dooley on June 13 to find out if he really did plan on exposing the secrets of his trade. After fibbing to a representative of the *Telegraph* that he worked as a stage spiritualist in Europe for fifteen years, Dooley offered his thoughts about Anna Eva Fay and other spiritualistic mediums who had recently played the Opera House. "Since I have been in Saint John, I have been told by quite a few people that they knew how mediums that have been here lately accomplished what little they really did do, and some of them are very correct in their ideas."

The Catholic church organist-turned-magician then prattled on to a *Saint John Sun* reporter—at great length—about exposing spiritualism as a fraudulent practice. "My object in making these exposures tonight is to try and rid the country of the hundreds of fakirs who are going about doing this business in a way that has made it impossible for any of the old time and talented men in the line to make it a paying business," the professor explained, "Tonight I will show how this information is given. I will also expose the methods of mind reading—how a blind person on the stage tells articles in the pockets of the audience, numbers of bills and other tests that are made."[2]

A magician revealing secrets to his audience had been done before. At one closing performance in Shanghai, China, Samri Baldwin explained in detail how he escaped from handcuffs. And in Saint John, Balabrega closed his week-long stand on October 22, 1887, by explaining how his elaborate stage illusions operated.

While exposing magic onstage was somewhat rare, exposing spiritualism onstage was an industry in itself.

Dooley had also brought along a spirit cabinet on the Marco tour that he used in an act called Cabinet of Phantoms. On Thursday evening he had presented his take on the classic cabinet routine just before he decapitated Bessie Houdini. The *Gazette* review of Dooley's cabinet performance offers a detailed account of his act that he would be exposing on stage Saturday evening. "Marco was securely tied in the cabinet, his hands and wrists protruding through its sides and securely tied to chairs on each side of the stage. While his hands and face were visible to the audience all the time the usual spiritual manifestations were produced, bells rang, tambourines rattled, spirit hands appeared, messages were written and the spirits had lots of fun with Marco, concluding the séance by burying him under an avalanche of snow."

CITY HALL.

Monday and Tuesday,

June 15 and 16.

Marco,

—THE—

MONARCH OF MYSTERY!

In his New, Sensational, Original and Marvelous Entertainment of

ORIENTAL, EGYPTIAN, HINDOO AND MODERN . . .

Marvels . .

—AND—

. . Miracles

Surpassing the Wonderful Feats of the Mahatmas and Yoghis of India.

ALL NATURE'S LAWS SET ASIDE.

THE INIMITABLE MARCO

Will introduce an entirely New, Mystifying and Mirthful array of wonderful effects, and a series of Phenomena so nearly approaching the Supernatural as to be almost Miraculous.

Prices, 25, 35 and 50 cents. Seats at Fenety's

👉 Harry Houdini and the Marco Magic Company were booked to perform at Fredericton City Hall, but the shows were cancelled. (Image courtesy of Harriet Irving Library, UNB)

👈 Marco's final Saint John advertisement. (Provincial Archives of New Brunswick: SJ *Daily Telegraph*, June 13, 1896, 3)

OPERA HOUSE

—

TODAY,
SPECIAL MATINEE,
LADIES and CHILDREN,
TO ANY SEAT IN
THE THEATRE,
CHILDREN 10c,
ADULTS 25c.

Marco

WILL WORK WONDERS
TONIGHT.
MIND READING,
SPIRITUALISM,
CLAIRVOYANCE, ETC.,
EXPOSED.
MARCO WILL
SHOW HOW IT
IS DONE.

Professor Dooley and other magicians knew that spiritualism exposés cast a wide net for audience members because the religious types, who would never dare set foot in a theatre for magic, would gladly pay to see spiritualism discredited. Just to make sure everybody knew about his closing night's programme, Dooley paid for one more large advertisement that appeared in the Saturday afternoon newspapers. In large type the ad proclaimed, "Marco will work wonders tonight. Mind reading, spiritualism, clairvoyance, etc., exposed. Marco will show how it is done."

As promised, Professor Dooley crusaded against fraudulent mediums at Saturday night's performance. But the good citizens of Saint John took a pass on learning the mischievous ways of spiritualists and their devious trickery. Only sixty-two people showed up for the exposé, resulting in a $9.72 take for the Marco Magic Company.

NEXT STOP: FREDERICTON?

After Saturday's closing in Saint John, the Marco Magic Company had to pack up for their Monday opening in Fredericton, New Brunswick, where they were booked to perform for two nights. Professor Dooley had already done some advance work in the provincial capital, seventy miles upriver from Saint John.

Large advertisements announcing the upcoming Marco shows ran in both the *Fredericton Daily Herald* and the *Daily Gleaner*. The ads first appeared in the Wednesday, June 10, editions and ran for six straight days. Dooley also forwarded a review of one of the Saint John shows that was run in both Fredericton papers.

Fredericton wasn't a regular stop for most of the big touring companies that visited Saint John. Instead, the locals typically had their choice between boxing matches or lectures, but so far this season, the eight-hundred-seat Opera House, located on the second floor of city hall, was seeing some first-class vaudeville entertainment grace its stage. Rose Sydell and the London Belles had a successful stand at the venue, and the city hall theatre was set to welcome Rufus Somerby and his monkeys for two nights in mid-July.

One of the best nights in the theatre's history came a year earlier when John Phillip Sousa and his orchestra rolled into Fredericton. However, even the famous Sousa was no match for magician Willis Skinner who, in his pre-Markos career, packed city hall with his Professor Skinner show for two nights in October 1891.

Aside from Skinner, Fredericton had been good to many other magicians in the past. In the old days, Signor Blitz was welcomed with full houses, including one night in 1840 when one of his Fredericton shows was attended by the former United States president John Q. Adams. Likewise, Balabrega and Zera Semon both had profitable stands in Fredericton. And now, it was Professor Dooley's turn.

Or was it?

On Monday, a Fredericton newspaper printed an update on the Marco shows. "Owing to severe and sudden illness, Marcos [sic], the worker of wonders, who was billed for City Hall tonight and tomorrow night, has been obliged to cancel his engagement for the present."[3]

Although Dooley was prone to illness and had cancelled his 1895 tour of the Maritimes due to ill health, it's more likely that his latest "ailment" was the fact that advance ticket sales did not foreshadow a successful stand in Fredericton.

If Professor Dooley wasn't truly sick, he had every reason to be thoroughly exhausted. Saint John had been a demoralizing two weeks for the church organist. Dooley had reinvented his act almost every night and threw everything he had at Saint John: *Trilby*, decapitations, cremations, spiritualism, children's entertainment, singing, Houdini's brilliant escapes, Metamorphosis, levitations, and Buttons's Rocket Boy act. But none of his efforts lit a fire under the citizens of Saint John.

The large Marco advertisements continued to run on both Monday and Tuesday, encouraging people who hadn't seen the tiny cancellation note to head to the empty theatre.

Following the cancelled shows in Fredericton, the Marco Magic Company was booked to perform at the Moncton Opera House on Wednesday and Thursday evenings. But both Moncton shows were also cancelled, giving the troupe another week off.

Rather than stay in New Brunswick, Professor Dooley decided to send his company on to Nova Scotia. If nothing else, the troupe would have a full seven days to promote their week-long Halifax stand that was to open on Monday, June 22.

A good stand in Halifax would help make up for the losses from Saint John and the cancelled shows in Fredericton and Moncton.

But as Professor Dooley would discover — more bad news was awaiting the Marco Magic Company in his old hometown of Halifax, Nova Scotia.

>─◦◇◦─○─◦◇◦─◦

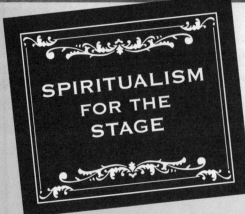

SPIRITUALISM
FOR THE
STAGE

Houdini shows a group of New York church ministers how "spirits" can ring bells under a table. Houdini was once observed in his dressing room tying and untying knots with his toes while he read. (Library of Congress)

THE RISE OF American spiritualism can be traced to the village of Hydesville, New York. In 1848 fifteen-year-old Margaret Fox and her twelve-year-old sister Catherine began communicating with a supposed spirit through a series of mystifying knocking sounds that seemed to be produced behind walls and above ceilings.

The Fox sisters claimed they were channelling the spirit of a peddler who had been murdered and then buried in the basement of the family's tiny wooden house. Within days, upwards of five hundred people made the pilgrimage to Hydesville to witness the eerie happenings for themselves.

The Fox sisters soon learned how to profit from their "powers" with the help of an older sister who taught music lessons in nearby Rochester. The sisters commanded up to $100 from the bereaved to channel the spirits of their dearly departed loved ones. Acting as a liaison between the earth and the great beyond, the girls became known as "mediums."

Once it became known that big money could be earned by simply knocking on tables for wealthy

Houdini poses in the spirit box he used to help expose a fake Boston medium named Margery. In spite of being well contained, Houdini was able to ring a bell inside the box on the table. (Library of Congress)

believers, the Fox sisters were widely imitated. Spiritualism soon found its way to the stage where mediums caused the "spirits" to ring bells and sound trumpets.

They were merely actors, but these theatrical mediums had one power that was very real—the ability to sell out theatres. The Fox sisters and their copycats couldn't keep up their charade for long. Scientists soon reported that the spirit knockings and communications with the dead were being cleverly faked. During a Rochester lecture in 1850, Dr. Potts removed his shoes and socks to demonstrate how the Fox sisters created knocking sounds by snapping their toes on table legs. The audience was delighted with the exposé and a new form of entertainment, spiritualism debunking, was created.

Although scientists had proven spiritualism was a massive fraud, the public was hooked on the new quasi-religion. Theatres were only too happy to offer entertainment by both spiritualists and spiritualist exposés.

Audiences soon displayed a marked preference for female spiritualists over males, giving women new opportunities to develop stage careers. But where women were seen as less corruptible than men, a child medium was seen as beyond reproach.

One such child, Laura Ellis, developed a successful theatre career thanks to a wooden box introduced by her carpenter father. To silence skeptics, Laura's hands and feet were tied to her chair in the cabinet with cotton bandages. And then bells and tambourines were placed in the cabinet before the doors were closed. After a few seconds, Laura managed to summon the spirits into her cabinet where they caused a ruckus with the musical instruments. Audiences bought the act and refused to believe that a small girl could untie her bonds, ring a few bells, and then retie the ropes before the cabinet doors were opened.

Thanks to Laura, allowing audience members to bind mediums with rope soon became standard practice. Consequently, the ability to escape from ropes inside cabinets became a standard skill for mediums. Thus was born the spiritualist's kindred performers—escape artists.

PART FOUR

HALIFAX, NOVA SCOTIA

The Carleton House, Halifax N. S.

ALBION HOTEL.
MONDAY—Geo Jacques, J E Hughson, Auburn; W C Hamilton, Grand Pre; F W Bell, Truro; John Douglass, Windsor; D Clough, Miss Clough, Lennox Ferry; Dr Whitford, Chester; W I Cowie, Liverpool; J D Douglas, Truro; John McMillan, Isaac's Harbor; E S McNutt, Yarmouth; S Hall, Annapolis; W C McKinton, Yarmouth; W M Alcorn, Annapolis.

REVERE HOUSE.
MONDAY—J S Chisholm, Lunenburg; H Morrell, Trowbridge; V Smyth, B Smyth, Wallace; Jos Couture, W E Webster, Quebec; Mrs J Clark, Bridgetown; Wm Bracker, Montreal; Miss McMaster, Ottawa; L W Dyer, Shelburne; J F Colwell, Truro; W J Peppett, Mount Uniacke.

CARLETON HOUSE.
MONDAY—Geo T Smith, Rockingham; B C Bent, Bridgetown; Harry Houdini and wife, J M Whitehead, New York.

CHAPTER NINETEEN

HOODWINKED IN HALIFAX

Halifax, Nova Scotia
Monday, June 15, to Sunday, June 21, 1896

"Some say I do it this way, others say I do it that way,
but I say I do it the other way."
— Harry Houdini, *Pittsburgh Leader*, March 1, 1908

IN THE MIDST OF A POUNDING rain storm on Monday, June 15, Harry and Bessie Houdini arrived in Halifax, Nova Scotia. From the North Street train station, the Marco Magic Company found their way downtown where city buildings crowded the steep hillside from the harbour up to the town clock at the base of Citadel Hill. High atop the Citadel, cannons and a star-shaped fort stood watch over the busy harbour while the heavy rain tried in vain to cleanse Halifax of its chronic coating of soot.

(top) The Carleton House was home to Harry and Beatrice Houdini for almost three weeks. The Argyle Street building still stands in 2012 but additional floors have been added. (Bruce MacNab Collection)

(bottom) The Halifax newspapers published lists of hotel guest registers. Here it's noted "Harry Houdini and wife" have checked into the Carleton House on Monday, June 15, 1896. (Nova Scotia Archives)

The grey skies, dreary fog, and relentless rain helped explain why Halifax wasn't a favourite stop for American theatre companies. In the *New York Mirror*, an actor with the King-Handley Company once wrote, "On this round globe of ours, we fondly hope and steadfastly believe there is no other such dull, unprogressive, dormouse of a town as Halifax, Nova Scotia."[1] Actors railed against dreadful food, unobliging women, and belligerent drunks taking up space on the streets and in theatre galleries. After enduring one torturous stand in Halifax, an American actor compared Halifax with Hades, the mythical realm of the dead.

Budd Trout, John Kenney, Bert Kilby, and Chas Bryant checked in to the Queen Hotel on Hollis Street while the Houdinis and Marco's treasurer, J.M. "the Irishman" Whitehead registered at the Carleton House Hotel on the corner of Prince and Argyle Streets. Professor Dooley didn't stay in a hotel with his assistants and stagehands, most likely opting to bunk with members of his Halifax family.

The Carleton House, which still stands in 2012, promoted itself as "homelike and desirable," not surprising for a hotel that was once a magnificent mansion. The liquor-free Carleton, with rooms priced from a dollar a day, was the hotel of choice for most of the small-time theatre companies that visited Halifax. The more successful troupes opted for the resplendent Halifax Hotel.

Right away, Professor Dooley got hit with bad news in Halifax—the Marco Company had a full two weeks, instead of one, to await their opening night. Dooley had been bumped from his June 22-27 week-long booking at the Academy of Music by Rose Sydell and the London Belles. Apparently, Manager Harshaw Clarke was suitably unimpressed with the Marco Magic Company's poor showing in Saint John.

BIG TOP ON THE COMMON

On Monday, Walter L. Main's circus parade wound through the streets of Halifax. The circus had arrived on time the previous evening at the cotton factory siding. At midnight, workers started unloading cars and pitching tents on the Halifax Common. At ten o'clock Monday morning, the parade left the circus grounds and headed downtown. The procession passed right in front of the Carleton House Hotel as it clamoured through the city streets before returning to the Halifax Common. In spite of the heavy rain and chilly air, an estimated twenty-one thousand people lined the streets to watch the parade.

Haligonians chuckled when they noticed police officers stationed outside every bank in the city. The Halifax police learned a valuable lesson years earlier when a circus came to town. Like a magician using misdirection to distract an audience, clever thieves had robbed a downtown bank while the parade created a perfect diversion.

The Walter L. Main parade was entirely trouble-free in Halifax — a sharp contrast to what happened in Saint John where the parade was sullied by drunken rowdiness, bloody fist fights, and children run over by circus wagons and streetcars. Halifax police kept a tight rein on troublemakers, both at the parade and on the Common where six thousand paying customers attended the afternoon show. Walter Main asked the *Chronicle* to publicly thank Chief of Police John O'Sullivan for a superb policing effort. The newspaper reported on June 16, 1896, that Walter Main believed the Halifax police were "more satisfactory than that of any force in any city that they have as yet visited."

While Bessie and Harry Houdini turned in at the Carleton House after their first day in Halifax, the harbour city's notorious underworld emerged from the darkness. One of the workers striking down the circus on the Common was attacked and brutally beaten by Halifax thugs. He was found bloodied, his head badly gashed, and was rushed to a surgeon.

Nobody would deny that Halifax had plenty of ruthless thieves and shifty characters. Tomorrow, one of them would provide brilliant inspiration for Houdini.

A REAL ESCAPE ARTIST

Tuesday morning, Haligonians awoke to the heartening sight of the sun creeping over the horizon. Summer was in the offing and Halifax was coming alive as the gloomy chill of spring burned away along with the oppressive harbour fog. One sure sign of summer was the arrival of "coloured" bootblacks from the Boston States, who were now in the city doing steady business shining shoes for Halifax businessmen.

Lately, the city was plagued with accidents as horses and buggies competed for space on the crowded streets with the newly installed streetcar system. Adding to the fray were bicyclists with their custom of "scorching" down the steep city streets at terrifying speeds. Making the city even more treacherous was the ongoing installation of underground gas pipes that found the streets trenched and piled high with excavated rock. Not far from the Academy of Music, more work was under way with the construction of the Keith furniture building on Barrington Street.

Officer Neil Ross was walking his regular downtown beat as the bootblacks and others settled into another workday, when suddenly, he recognized a fugitive who had escaped from the city prison two weeks before.

Walter Townsend was a twenty-four-year-old petty thief and troublemaker. Several months earlier, this long-time loser had been sentenced to four months at Rockhead Prison — the city's penal complex perched on a hill above Bedford Basin — for the cowardly crime of stealing five dollars from a little girl. Charges against Townsend had also been filed by his own family after he went on a drunken rampage, destroying windows and furniture at his father's Robie Street home. After serving forty-one days of his sentence, Townsend broke out of prison and had been on the lam ever since.

Officer Ross first observed Townsend on Granville Street and casually continued in the direction of his quarry. The policeman thought he had the advantage on the unsuspecting criminal. But at the last instant, Townsend looked up and noticed the blue-coated policeman. By now Officer Ross was so close that Townsend could count the lawman's brass buttons.

The chase was on.

Townsend bolted down Granville Street with Officer Ross hot on his heels. For two full blocks Townsend tried desperately to outrun his pursuer and keep his freedom. Out of frustration, Townsend attempted to shake his unwanted running companion by powering up the steep grade of Blowers Street. It was no use. Officer Ross was up to the task and followed the fleet-footed fugitive without falling behind a single stride.

Townsend had enough of the steep street and turned onto the cobblestones of Barrington Street. On the level street, Officer Ross quickly caught up to his prey and tackled the runaway to the ground. Excited onlookers poured out of the shops and diners ran out of restaurants to catch a glimpse of the captured fugitive, who was now sporting a pair of the Halifax police department's finest handcuffs.

Halifax was positively abuzz as word spread about the chase that happened in full view in the heart of the city. Townsend was arraigned in a packed police court the following day, and all the local newspapers sent reporters to follow the proceedings.

Houdini had seen all he needed. The public interest in this escapee inspired him to plot a new publicity stunt. This stunt, to be introduced in Halifax a week from now, would start Houdini on the path to a new career — as a jailbreaker.

ELECTION FEVER

The Houdinis' first week in Halifax was a busy one for the harbour city because of intense interest in the national election. A born-and-raised Nova Scotian, Sir Charles Tupper, was the sitting prime minister of Canada vying for re-election on June 23.

Every night, boisterous rallies were held at the Grand Parade, a stone's throw from the Houdinis' hotel. One liquor-fuelled rally was widely condemned; the *Halifax Herald* reported, "A prominent Conservative became disgusted at the manner in which whiskey was being dished out."[2]

Election gatherings were happening everywhere, including across the harbour in the town of Dartmouth where St. Peter's Hall was literally filled to overflowing for an all-candidates election debate that saw hundreds unable to squeeze into the building. Instead, the Dartmouthians congregated outside and listened to speakers that included a future prime minister, Robert Laird Borden.

Near the end of the week, a novel theatre advertisement attempted to bully some attention away from the electioneering. Two young men, driving the high bicycles of the day, carried a long wooden pole between them. Suspended from the pole was a large six-by-eight-foot frame that carried a flag promoting the Webling Sisters at Orpheus Hall.

In recent weeks, downtown Halifax was a tough place to promote the theatre or anything else. Every day, the downtown was rocked by explosions that rumbled through the streets and shook buildings. The gas lines were being installed in deep trenches that had to be blasted to remove ledge rock. The dynamiting was carried out carelessly, and there were several close calls with flying rocks breaking windows and pelting people and horses.

Sunday was a day of rest when the city finally shut down and citizens took a breather, and Monday, June 22, was Natal Day, a special holiday to celebrate the founding of Halifax in 1749. Monday was also a very special day for two visitors to the city—Bessie and Harry Houdini.

LIST OR MANIFEST OF ALIEN IMMIGRANTS FOR THE COMMISSIONER OF IMMIGRATION.

List No. 371

Required by the regulations of the Secretary of the Treasury of the United States, under act of Congress approved March 3, 1893, to be delivered to the Commissioner of Immigration by the Commanding Officer of any vessel having such passengers on board, upon arrival at a port in the United States.

S.S. "*Halifa*", sailing from *Halifa N.S.* *June 27 1896*, arriving at Port of *Boston*, *June 29, 1896* 36

No.	Name in full	Age Yrs. Mos.	Sex	Married or single	Calling occupation	Able to read	Able to write	Nationality	Last residence	Seaport for landing in the United States	Final destination in the United States (State, City, or Town)	Whether having a ticket to such final destination	By whom was passage paid	Whether in possession of money...	Whether going to join a relative...	Whether ever before in the United States and if so, when and where	Condition of health	Whether deformed or crippled	Condition of...
1	B. S. Courtney	24	m	s	Tourist	Yes	U.S.A.		Boston	Boston	Boston	Yes	self	more	Yes	Home	No	No	No	Goo
2	W. C. Hale	48	"	m	"	"	"		New York					"	"	"				
3	Dr. J. B. Beard	39	"	"	"	"	"		"					"	"	"				
4	T. H. Carins	50	"	"	"	"	Canada		Toronto					"	"	passing through				
5	Miss M. E. Parker	39	F	s	"	"	U.S.A.		New York					"	"	Home				
6	" C. H. Watts	40	"	"	"	"	"		"					"	"	"				
7	S. M. Brookfield	52	m	m	"	"	Canada		Halifax					"	"	on a visit				
8	Mrs. Thompson	73	"	"	"	"	"		"					"	"	"				
9	Jack Sydell	40																		
10	Mrs. do do	32																		
11	J. H. Barnes	30			"London Belles'															
12	W. S. Campbell	42			Theatrical Company								Returning							
13	Nellie Burns	21																		
14	Frankie Evans	20												Home						
15	V. A. Gelate	36			of New York															
16	Jos. Schepp	32																		
17	Con Bayer	24																		
18	Thos. Leo	37																		
19	Mrs. do do	24																		
20	Rose Sydell	27																		
21	May Booth	19																		
22	Jos. Kelly	37																		
23	Mrs. do do	30																		
24	Laura Graff	23																		
25	Lily Alice	20																		
26	W. Hoar	72	m	s	Tourist	Yes	Canada		Halifax					more	Yes	on a visit				
27	Mrs. Crocker	42	F	m	"	"	"		"					"	"	"				
28	Earle do	5	m	s	"	"	No		"					"	No	"				
29	Chas. Nickinson	46	n	m	"	Yes	"		"					"	Yes	"				
30	Gustave Gustavin	39	"	s	Seaman	"	Norway		"					"	"	Seek'g life				

UNITED STATES OF AMERICA, State of _____ S.S. County of _____

I, _____, Master of the Steamship _____, ... the foregoing is a full ...

report of alien immigrants arrived by said vessel at the port of _____ ... day of _____ ... of _____.

... e, and ...

Immigrant...

THE LONDON BELLES

511 ROSE SYDELL.

Ogden's Guinea Gold Cigarettes.

WHEN THE LONDON BELLES bumped the Marco Magic Company from their scheduled one-week stand in Halifax, it was business as usual for Harry and Bessie Houdini. Only ten weeks earlier, the London Belles and the Houdini's American Gaiety Girls were booked back-to-back when their burlesque tours collided at the Music Hall in Lynn, Massachusetts. This time, the Houdinis didn't have to look far to find the eighteen-member London Belles troupe—they were also staying at the Carleton House Hotel in Halifax.

In many Maritime towns, burlesque was restricted to male-only audiences. But in Chatham, New Brunswick, some ladies were admitted, covertly, to the London Belles through the back door of the hall and watched discreetly from the rear of the stage. Other than the antics of their men, the women found nothing offensive about the show whatsoever. The *Chatham World* commented: "The scantiest dresses worn by the chorus girls were similar to those worn by the female trapeze performers whom all the ladies look at unabashed at the circus."[1]

The London Belles, managed by the Kentucky-born brother and sister team of John and Rose Sydell, were active from 1890 until Rose retired in 1919. While swimming at Atlantic City in 1913, John Sydell, trying to rescue a friend, was caught in the undertow and drowned. In her later years, Rose offered the sanctuary of her Brooklyn home to showgirls who found themselves, "out of work and funds." In 1941 Rose Sydell died at the age of seventy-six.

(top) After their Halifax stand, the London Belles hopped aboard a steamship bound for Boston. The troupe is highlighted here in the steamship manifest. (National Archives and Records Administration)

(bottom) Known as the Queen of Burlesque, Rose Sydell enjoys a smoke and a shot. During the 1896 Maritime tour, Rose's brother John married one of the Belles in a lavish wedding held in Sussex, New Brunswick, on May 31, 1896. (Imperial Tobacco Group Plc.)

CHAPTER TWENTY

ANNIVERSARIES
AND ADVERSITIES

Halifax, Nova Scotia
Monday, June 22, to Thursday, June 25, 1896

"We have had our little tiffs, but your sunny smile
and my good (?) sense always robbed them of bitterness.
I love you, love you dearest, and I know you love me.
Your very touch, your care of me, dearest,
and the laughter in my heart
when you put your arms around me prove it."
—Anniversary letter (excerpt) from Harry Houdini to Bessie Houdini,
San Francisco, June 22, 1919

MONDAY, JUNE 22, 1896, was Bessie and Harry Houdini's second wedding anniversary. At daybreak it seemed a fierce thunderstorm would play spoiler with the couple's special day. But the morning squall cleared, giving way to a marvelous sunny afternoon.

In Halifax, Harry had to make up for the couple's first anniversary the previous summer when they had found themselves in Mount Carmel, Pennsylvania, on tour with the Welsh Brothers Show. Bessie was still smarting from her memories of that anniversary:

Harry and Bessie caught on camera in a playful moment. This photo offers a rare glimpse of Bessie's teeth. (from the collection of Dr. Bruce Averbook, Cleveland, Ohio)

Each night after the show the whole company would hunt up some lunch room and put in a substantial extra meal of whatever they could get. On the night of our wedding anniversary I asked all the circus folk to have coffee with us—we could hardly afford a larger treat—but by the time we got to the village all the places were closed.

Angry and disappointed, I berated Houdini soundly for not making advance arrangements. As we straggled back, I flounced into our cubbyhole, threw back the sheet of our cot, and discovered, hidden beneath it, a wonderful chicken dinner cooked to a turn. That day Houdini had been talking with a local clergyman and his wife. In the course of the conversation he had told the story of our elopement, and as a result the clergyman's wife had cooked this delightful dinner for us. I ate that dinner with tears streaming down my cheeks, but Houdini had no word of reproach for my outburst of temper.[1]

Thanks to Natal Day, Bessie and Harry had their choice of entertainment and activities on this beautiful summer day in Halifax. The couple could find concerts and parties in full swing across the entire city. Boats shunted citizens to picnic grounds on the Bedford Basin and the Northwest Arm while the Wanderers Grounds were packed with citizens enjoying baseball games and cycle races.

Harry and Bessie might have joined the locals lining up at the city's ice cream parlours for strawberries and cream. The first lot of strawberries had just arrived from the Annapolis Valley and the restauranteurs were doing a booming business selling this Nova Scotia favourite for ten cents a saucer.

The Houdinis could also celebrate their anniversary by taking in the opening show of Rose Sydell and the London Belles. The Natal Day holiday allowed the Belles to open their one-week stand with a packed matinee at the Academy of Music and follow it up with a full house for the evening show.

As Halifax waved farewell to Natal Day for another year, attention shifted to Tuesday's big event—election day.

As soon as the polls closed at five o'clock on election day, citizens gathered in large numbers on Hollis Street outside the Nova Scotia legislative building to await results. Early on, it became clear that Nova Scotia's Sir Charles Tupper would be easily defeated by the challenger from Quebec, Wilfrid Laurier.

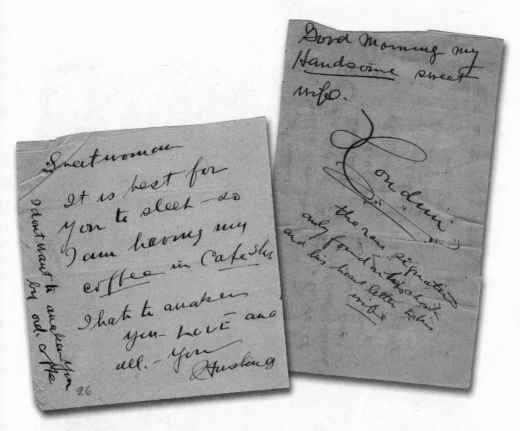

Even in his love notes to Bessie, Houdini signed his stage name. Years after Houdini died Bessie inscribed one of the notes with: "Every morning I would find a dear funny little message like these, on my pillow, and how I miss them dearheart."

(Harry Ransom Center, The University of Texas at Austin)

At the Academy of Music, Manager Clarke had taken a page from American theatres and arranged for a special wire to keep the audience up-to-date on the election results during the London Belles' performance. By the end of the evening, it was obvious that Sir Charles was no longer the prime minister of Canada.

With the election over, the Marco Magic Company could more easily promote their upcoming week-long stand at the Academy of Music. Professor Dooley had his hopes pinned high on his star assistant, Harry Houdini, to get the ball rolling.

And Houdini had an extraordinary publicity stunt planned for city hall.

Harry and Bessie celebrate Houdini's birthday with Joe and Mildred Hyman.
Joe Hyman was present the night Harry first met Bessie at Coney Island. The dog seen in
front is Houdini's dog Bobby, the Handcuff Dog. Houdini had miniature handcuffs and
straitjackets made for Bobby and trained him to escape from them. Bobby once performed
his escape act at the prestigious Annual Dinner of the Society of American Magicians.

(Patrick Culliton Collection)

HOUDINI HOLDS COURT AT CITY HALL

Late Thursday morning, Harry Houdini exited the Carleton House Hotel and walked past St. Paul's Church to the Grand Parade. Thanks to the Moirs candy factory, a looming brick structure occupying an Argyle Street block at Duke Street, the air was thick, as always, with the drool-inducing aroma of caramel and chocolate. At the steep George Street, across from a mortuary that would one day be overwhelmed with bodies from the sinking of the *Titanic*, Houdini descended a flight of stairs from Argyle Street onto the parade square. On the north end of the square stood the marble and stone-veneered Halifax City Hall.

Crossing the Grand Parade, Houdini honed in on the busy Halifax police department that operated out of the lower floor of city hall. Upon entering the eight-year-old building, Houdini was welcomed by Chief John O'Sullivan along with policemen McNally, Nickerson, and Fitzpatrick. The police station was stifling hot this day; more than a century later, sweat droplets from the policemen making their shift comments are still visible on the June 25, 1896, page of the station patrol book.

Besides serving as police headquarters, the station housed the police court, which dealt with lesser charges related to public drunkenness, prostitution, and petty thievery. The police court and the council chamber upstairs offered plenty of fodder for Halifax reporters on the prowl for city news. Houdini could count on finding a handful of reporters to watch him challenge the police department's handcuffs. Of course, he still had to get permission from the chief of police for his demonstration.

Luckily for Houdini, fifty-four-year-old Chief O'Sullivan had an interest in the theatre arts and personally kept a watchful eye on the Academy of Music, concerning himself with the safety of its patrons. The chief's lookout earned him a series of threatening letters, thanks to his habit of harassing liquor saloons in the vicinity of the theatre. The anonymous letter writer warned the chief that his activity could become "dangerous" and a "punching" could result if he kept up his vigilance. The letters hardly rattled the tall, capable chief. He actually stepped up his efforts near the academy and personally visited the saloons, inquiring about just where and when he could look forward to receiving his "punching."

The fearless Chief O'Sullivan offered his respectful station guest, Harry Houdini, the first challenge. The chief went easy on Houdini, testing him with a single pair of regulation handcuffs. Houdini shed them in thirty-two seconds. The chief then snapped three pairs of handcuffs on Houdini's wrists and reached for a fourth set. If Houdini planned to slide the cuffs off one at a time, he was out of luck. O'Sullivan carefully attached the fourth pair to connect the first three together. Seemingly undaunted, Houdini retired to the chief's office that overlooked the Grand Parade and returned two minutes later with all four of the restraints unlocked.

Chief O'Sullivan wasn't finished with Houdini yet. The Irish-born chief produced an ancient pair of British naval irons that immediately caught the full attention of the curly-haired magician. A *Halifax Herald* reporter described the vintage irons as "the old ones used in days long ago." Houdini had never seen anything like these restraints in the United States, but Halifax was a Commonwealth naval base, so it's no surprise the police department had a pair of British manacles.

Houdini had defeated vintage locks before. At the Gloucester, Massachusetts, police station, back in October, he escaped from what one reporter called "all the old-time bracelets." And in November 1895 he easily escaped from a variety of outmoded handcuffs at the police station in Springfield, Massachusetts. So, he might have felt overly confident about escaping from the aged irons here in Halifax. Normally, Houdini would study unfamiliar locks well in advance and seek help from his advisors, Gus Roterberg or W.D. LeRoy. But now, in a foreign country with Halifax reporters watching, he had little choice than to let the chief lock him in the foreign irons. Once O'Sullivan clicked the archaic restraints closed on Houdini, there was no turning back. Today in Halifax, he would have to improvise on the fly. The young magician retreated to the chief's office and the struggle began.

Houdini was in trouble.

He would have to draw on all his accumulated skills and knowledge to decipher these locks. Some of the overseas restraints had sophisticated double locks that required the key to turn halfway before plunging further into the keyway. The complicated locks could be tricky to open even for somebody who had the manufacturer's key.

Houdini fought with the puzzling irons for almost five minutes before he finally managed to crack the stubborn mechanism. The *Morning Chronicle* reported that the challenge "bothered him considerably." Even Houdini admitted that the chief's antique irons had baffled him, prompting the *Acadian Recorder* to mention, "Houdini said he was never so badly shackled before."

While Houdini watched attentively, Chief O'Sullivan showed him how the locks opened with a proper key. Houdini was a quick study. After seeing the shape of the key and the direction it turned in the lock, he asked to repeat the challenge. This time, he was free in two and a half minutes.

After the close call with Chief O'Sullivan's antique device, Houdini took a break from his escape work and produced a deck of cards, allowing a policeman to select a card at random. Houdini declared that back at the Carleton House Hotel, Mademoiselle Marco (Bessie Houdini) would be able to correctly identify the card by reading the policeman's mind. To test Houdini's outrageous claim, one of O'Sullivan's men was dispatched to the hotel to find this supposed clairvoyant with a note that read, "What card was thought of?" While they waited for Bessie's reply, Houdini entertained the onlookers with some card tricks that one reporter described as "marvelous...excelling any ever seen here, fairly mystifying all present."[2] Eventually, Houdini's impromptu show was interrupted when the policeman returned from the Carleton House; Mademoiselle Marco had indeed identified that the queen of hearts was the selected card.

Now it was time for Houdini to offer his grand finale.

CHAPTER TWENTY-ONE

I'M IN THE JAILHOUSE NOW

Halifax, Nova Scotia
Thursday, June 25, 1896

"Of course I have a secret method of picking locks, that's my business."
— Harry Houdini responding to a heckler at Keith's Theatre
New York Telegraph, February 3, 1906

A WEEK EARLIER, Halifax had been enthralled by the Rockhead Prison jailbreaker. Today, Houdini planned to piggyback on Walter Townsend's notoriety and break out of Chief John O'Sullivan's Halifax lock-up.

The Halifax police station hosted both male and female prisoners. The women's lock-up was located in the centre of the building, very close to the chief's office and adjacent to the police court. Two large windows helped warm the women's quarters with southern sun throughout the day. The female prisoners enjoyed a large common area with easy access to a spacious bathroom that was also lit by natural light through another south-facing window. Within the room were five small cells to isolate any "ladies" who became unruly during their incarceration. The women's jail was off-limits for Houdini's demonstration on this day because Mary Kate O'Connor was incarcerated, awaiting trial on theft charges.

A manacled and tightly-cuffed Houdini poses behind bars that were cleverly added by the illustrator. (Harry Ransom Center, University of Texas at Austin)

The women's lock-up was a charming and luxurious boudoir compared to the jail cells reserved for men. The fifteen men's cells were located on the shady Argyle Street side of the station. The cramped units measured four by seven feet. The cell walls were built using a double course of bricks, creating indestructible partitions almost a foot thick. Each cubicle welcomed its unlucky occupant through a narrow twenty-inch opening hung with an iron grated door. Even though the police station ceiling was a good ten feet high, the cell walls were less than seven feet tall. But no prisoner could hope to escape by climbing up and over the cell walls. Thick iron mesh was installed across the top of all the cells, preventing prisoners from even thinking about an upward stab at freedom.

With Halifax's steep grade, only the small upper windows illuminated the men's lock-up and they were too high above the cells' iron mesh ceiling for prisoners to enjoy any views of Argyle Street. Worsening the depressing basement ambience, the windows were covered with iron bars and set below the sidewalk in deep window wells, allowing only diffused daylight to cast glum shadows. And now, one of these dreary little jail cells in the basement of city hall would be Harry Houdini's new living quarters.

A SLIPPERY PRISONER

Houdini noticed several cells were already occupied by prisoners, temporary guests of Chief O'Sullivan. Coincidentally, one was occupied by the real escape artist, Walter Townsend, who was awaiting his afternoon trial. Several other prisoners were awaiting transfer to the federal penitentiary in Dorchester, New Brunswick.

Houdini started by stripping down to a bathing suit, proving he wasn't concealing any crowbars or heavy duty apparatus that could be used for busting out of O'Sullivan's lock-up. The officers handcuffed Houdini, escorted him into one of the brick cells, and clanged the heavy iron door shut behind him. After locking the door securely, the policemen locked Houdini's clothing in another cell.

The policemen returned to their work in the busy station, monitoring the police court proceedings and fielding the usual calls related to Halifax's less than industrious population of unruly drunks and prostitutes. In all the hustle and bustle, the police didn't notice their newest jailbird had left the station. But a phone call from a local hotel advised the station that their prisoner had escaped and, furthermore, was requesting the return of his clothes.

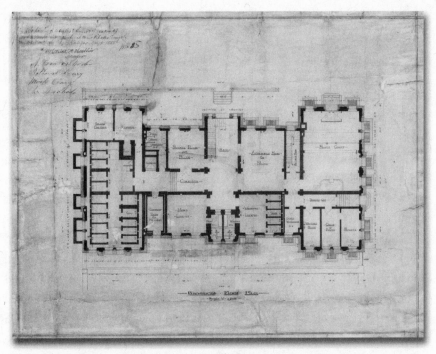

The original Halifax City Hall floor plan shows the locations of the basement jail cells.
City Hall still stands in 2012, but the police station has moved. (HRM Archives)

Later in his well-documented jailbreaking career, Houdini dispensed with the bathing suit and would strip stark naked before doing jail escapes. Just as he had done in Halifax, Houdini would offer a short sleight-of-hand demonstration as a preamble to his jail escape. But unlike Halifax, he did his card and coin warm-up in the nude. A Chicago reporter, who witnessed one of Houdini's nude exhibitions, commented that the less than bashful Houdini was "perfectly proportioned and splendidly muscled."[1]

As for the British naval irons, it seems Houdini took a pair home with him as a souvenir of Nova Scotia, perhaps a gift from Chief O'Sullivan. As late as 1908, Houdini's stage inventory included a set of restraints he called "the Nova Scotia Leg Irons." On his personal handcuff list, he noted the irons were "found by Houdini in Nova Scotia in 1895 [*sic*]. Key turns half way. Scarce."[2] Unfortunately, Houdini's Chicago lock associate, August Roterberg, lost the key to the rare apparatus after it was sent to him to make a duplicate. In a note to Houdini he wrote, "Nova Scotia leg iron .... Key you sent got sidetracked while in my possession."[3]

Roterberg mistakenly thought the "scarce" leg irons were of little concern to Houdini and suggested, "We can safely omit if you wish."[4] But Houdini knew others, including his magic dealer, W.D. LeRoy, also owned sets of the challenging Nova Scotia leg irons. And Houdini was always mindful of rival escape artists, with insider's knowledge, who could show up at a performance ready to embarrass him with manacles he was unprepared for. He wrote Roterberg a swift reply, asking that the Nova Scotia irons remain a part of his inventory of sixty-one restraints that comprised his 1908 Defiance Handcuff Act. "Regarding Nova Scotia Leg Iron, as LeRoy has that iron I believe you ought to add it. You have all the blanks, and it only means little expense. Let me know if you have really lost it and I'll cut you another."[5]

The Monday opening at the Academy of Music now had serious financial consequences for Professor Dooley. After the cancellation of the Fredericton and Moncton shows, he was bankrolling two full weeks of salaries, hotel rooms, and meals for his idle assistants. Throw in train tickets, printing, and other incidental expenses and this Halifax downtime was a financial disaster for Dooley, a humble church organist and choirmaster who had never made more than fifty dollars a month in salary. And now he had coughed up even more cash for large advertisements that started appearing in all of the Halifax newspapers to promote Monday's Marco opener.

Professor Dooley felt he had good reason to be optimistic about Halifax's voracious appetite for entertainment. On Thursday, extra streetcars were pressed into service to bring citizens to an evening concert at the Public Gardens, and the beautiful Victorian gardens were jam-packed for the concert.

On the weekend before opening night, Professor Dooley finally convinced the Halifax newspapers to publish small reports about his upcoming stand at the academy. Another press release announced a matinee for Wednesday, but it was never mentioned again. The Marco Magic Company now had one last weekend to promote their Monday night opening at the Academy of Music.

Houdini's visit to the Halifax police station had generated some free publicity for the company and provided Houdini with two new clippings for his press book. He wasn't finished with his promotional work quite yet.

But Harry Houdini should have left well enough alone — his next Halifax publicity stunt would find him flirting with disaster.

>─┤◆>─○─<◆├─<

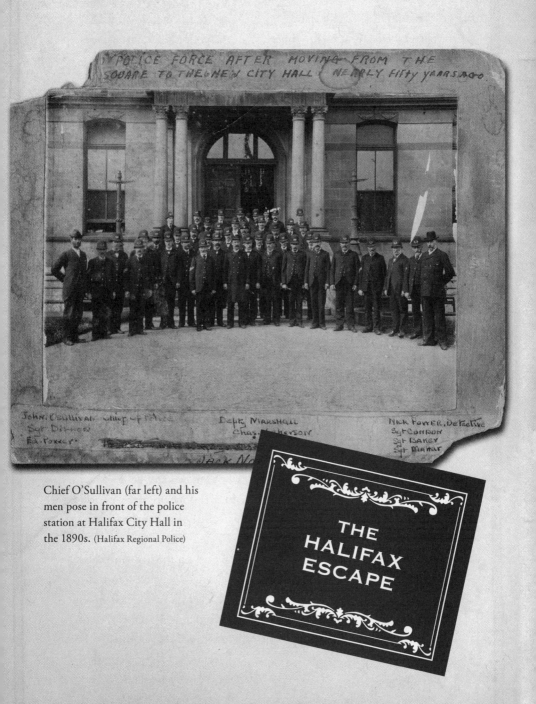

POLICE FORCE AFTER MOVING FROM THE SQUARE TO THE NEW CITY HALL NEARLY FIFTY YEARS AGO

John O'Sullivan, Chief of Police
Sgt Dickson
Ed. Foxxey

Depty Marshall
Chas. Paterson

Jack No...

Nick Power, Detective
Sgt Condon
Sgt Baker
Sgt Mahar

Chief O'Sullivan (far left) and his men pose in front of the police station at Halifax City Hall in the 1890s. (Halifax Regional Police)

THE HALIFAX ESCAPE

HARRY HOUDINI'S jail escape was recalled in a detail-rich November 4, 1936, article in the *Halifax Mail*. "One of the sensational feats of the great Houdini while in Halifax was to escape from the police lock-up in City Hall. His clothes were placed in one cell and, dressed in a bathing suit, he was locked in another. Shortly after being locked up, police received a phone call from the Queen Hotel asking that Houdini's clothes be returned. He had escaped."

Houdini wrote up his own fanciful account of the jailbreak in 1896. Somehow he managed to get a newspaper to publish the tale, claiming it was a bona fide report from the comically misspelled "Halifax Cronical." Aside from providing Houdini with another clipping for his press book, the story, entitled "A Slippery Prisoner," added some fun embellishments to the Halifax escape:

> A strange young man was arrested this morning by officers Pring and Killen, at the instigation of Mngr. Clark of the Academy of Music, who claimed the stranger was a dangerous criminal.

After being brought to the police headquarters, Chief O'Sullivan securely handcuffed and shackled his limbs together and, producing a pair of recently purchased double lock handcuffs, joined the leg shackles and handcuffs together. It certainly appeared as if the prisoner was secured. Nevertheless, five minutes after, the chief, wishing to question the unknown man, sent for him when the startling feat became known that the prisoner had escaped handcuffs, shackles and all. As the only exit from the cell led through the chief's office it certainly was a Mystery how the prisoner had escaped. Chief O'Sullivan was in a quandary when a messenger boy entered and delivered a neatly done up parcel addressed to chief of police. On being opened the parcel was found to contain the handcuffs and shackles which were linked together like a huge chain and also contained a card with the inscription, "Compliments of mysterious Harry Houdini,

good for one box at Academy of Music—come and see a good magician."

Some have suggested Houdini engineered a jailbreak a year earlier near Providence, Rhode Island, after the Welsh Brothers acts were thrown in jail for performing on a Sunday. The claim originates with a story told by Bessie Houdini: "In the lock-up the Fat Woman wept bitterly. Her cell was too small, and she was wholly uncomfortable and miserable. So after the sheriff had gone off and everything was quiet, Houdini deftly picked the locks of the jail and the whole company stole quietly back to the big tent."[6]

But Bessie's story has one big problem—in 1895 the Welsh Brothers only played one town outside of the state of Pennsylvania—Union City, New Jersey. The Houdinis rejoined the Welsh Brothers in 1898, when the circus played outside its home state, so it's possible the circus jailbreak happened then.

It would appear that in Halifax, Nova Scotia, Harry Houdini, the handcuff king, was able to add another proud title to his escape artist's calling card—jailbreaker.

After escaping from the police lockup in his bathing suit, Houdini made his way through the busy streets of Halifax to the Queen Hotel. (Nova Scotia Archives)

CHAPTER TWENTY-TWO

COUNTDOWN TO
CURTAIN TIME

Halifax, Nova Scotia
Friday, June 26, to Sunday, June 28, 1896

"It isn't any fun taking your life in your hands."
—Harry Houdini, *Pittsburgh Leader*, March 1, 1908

ON FRIDAY, THE DUST SWIRLING around the Houdinis' hotel was almost enough to blind someone out walking the streets. With the recent hot spell, downtown merchants were losing their battle against the airborne road filth that kept churning into their shops and restaurants. Frustrated businessmen banded together, demanding that Hollis, Granville, and Barrington streets should each have their own street-watering carts, especially with summer tourists now flooding the city.

Elsewhere were sure signs that summer had arrived in Halifax. Friday's *Acadian Recorder* reported that Thursday evening's concert at the Public Gardens drew one thousand people to the bandstand, praised for its "magnificent electrical illuminations." Also in the papers, Harry Houdini got plenty of press for his handcuff work at city hall, but "Mademoiselle Marco's" mind-reading demonstration

---

Houdini eventually replaced his boyhood pet chicken, Banjoe, with a more fearsome fowl named Abraham Lincoln. Although Houdini billed the bird as "the only tame eagle in the world," the fine-feathered fellow was really a red-tailed hawk. (Harry Ransom Center, The University of Texas at Austin)

received only one sentence in one paper. Bessie's demonstration might have been successful, but Halifax had seen much, much better.

During his 1887 stand in Halifax, the Swedish magician, Balabrega, conducted a severe test of his mind-reading abilities in a very public way. Witnessed by a large gathering at the Halifax Hotel, he challenged two prominent citizens of Halifax to select an object and hide it anywhere within a one mile radius of the hotel, predicting he could locate the object solely by reading the men's thoughts.

Alderman Alex Stephen and Captain Trott chose a small brass pin about two inches long and headed out to find a hiding spot. Once the pin was hidden, Trott and Stephen returned to the Halifax Hotel with a sizeable crowd of spectators in tow. After telling the men to concentrate on the hiding spot, Balabrega left the Halifax Hotel blindfolded, holding Alderman Stephen's hand. By now, the mob following the action was fairly wild and growing in numbers by the second. Like a bloodhound on a scent, Balabrega found the pin tucked in a curtain at the rear of a tailor's shop. But more importantly, Balabrega had successfully promoted his show to an admiring crowd and a bevy of reporters.

HOUDINI HORSES AROUND

Like Balabrega, Houdini had already observed how outdoor events — concerts at the Public Gardens, Walter L. Main's circus parade, and the fugitive Townsend's dash for freedom — all caught the fancy of this harbour town. And Houdini wasn't going to be left out. His outdoor promotional plan was a simple one; he would be tied to a horse and escape in plain view of an audience. The curious scheme was intriguing, attracting a few newspapermen to a field outside of downtown Halifax to see what the young showman was up to.

Houdini's stunt likely happened at the Halifax Common where horses were plentiful at the adjacent riding clubs. At the appointed time, a stableman brought Houdini a horse. Somehow, wires had gotten crossed. Houdini had asked for a docile older animal. Instead, he was offered a frisky young steed who wasn't too pleased about being part of this strange ritual. Here again, Houdini found himself faced with an unexpected turn of events. Just like the Maniac Cuff in Saint John or police chief O'Sullivan's British naval irons, Houdini couldn't back down in front of reporters now that the moment had arrived.

A crowd gathers at the Halifax Common to watch a circus set up. The ladder for the high diving act can be seen at centre. (Nova Scotia Archives)

While the disgruntled animal was held at bay, Houdini mounted the horse and draped himself over its back like a human saddle. The unhappy steed took an instant disliking to Harry Houdini, flaring his nostrils and peeling back his ears. Then the horse got downright ornery, stomping, while several men tied Houdini's hands and feet together underneath his belly. Once the men finished their rope work, it was Houdini's turn to impress the crowd with some fine escapology.

But the angry horse had another plan.

The renegade animal turned and took off running at full speed, giving his unwanted passenger the ride of a lifetime. Houdini had to hold on as if his very life depended on it—because it did! A galloping horse could easily spin Houdini around until the magician was under its belly. If he was foolish enough to start untying the ropes while the horse was on the run, the risks multiplied. If only partly freed, Houdini could be flung off the horse and dragged or even trampled to death.

There was only one choice—Houdini had to let the horse run itself out. Finally, the horse tired and stopped. Houdini made sure he untied himself from the contrary animal forthwith before it caught a second wind. But nobody was there to see him escape. By now, his audience had lost sight of the equestrian escape artist and had wandered back to their downtown offices.

The uncooperative horse taught Houdini a significant lesson: never, ever attempt a publicity stunt without thoroughly checking all the details in advance. Not surprisingly, Houdini never referred to the embarrassing Halifax horse episode for the rest of his life. The story only came to light thanks to Bessie Houdini, who contributed her "recollections and documents" to a biography written two years after Houdini's death.

NORTH END COMPETITION

Professor Dooley was making his own share of blunders. His latest misstep came when he began promoting the following week's shows at St. Peter's Hall in Dartmouth. Dooley started by having the *Acadian Recorder* publish a note in the paper's Dartmouth section: "Marco performs at Dartmouth next week." This note, along with the Marco posters he pasted onto fences and dead walls across the harbour in Dartmouth, only served to slow ticket sales at the Academy of Music. Now there was no need for Dartmouthians to cross the harbour to see Marco; he would be playing in their own backyard next week.

Back on the Halifax side, the Academy of Music manager, Harshaw Clarke, didn't do Professor Dooley any favours when he bumped the Marco Magic Company from June 22 to June 29. Now, the amateur magician had to go head-to-head with a mid-week holiday, Dominion Day, and worse, the Nautical Fair set to open in the south end of Halifax.

ONE HOT WEEKEND TO OPENING NIGHT

Saturday, June 27, was a sweltering day. Large crowds seeking relief from the brutal heat crowded the beaches along the Northwest Arm, others cooled off in the waters of the Bedford Basin. Saturday evening found a large crowd attending a concert at the Public Gardens, while just six blocks away, the London Belles closed their week-long stand at the Academy of Music.

Directly across from the stifling Saint Mary's Basilica, Professor Dooley's stage assistants, Budd Trout, Jack Kenny, J. M. "the Irishman" Whitehead, Chas Bryant, and Burton Kilby were outfitting the stage for Monday's big opener. With the London Belles gone, the Marco Magic Company now had the full run of the Academy of Music. Good thing. It had been weeks since the troupe had performed and a rehearsal was badly needed. Not to mention the lighting and dozens of props that had to be installed and tested.

Tomorrow, Halifax would be buzzing with talk about a famous magician who would be performing at the Academy of Music.

But it wasn't Marco or Houdini.

THE
NAUTICAL
FAIR

Prices—25 and 35 cts.

Je18

Nautical Fair

— IN AID OF THE —
HALIFAX SAILORS' HOME,
UNDER DISTINGUISHED PATRONAGE,
— At the —
Halifax Exhibition Building
June 29th & 30th, July 1st, 2nd, 3rd & 4th
— GRAND OPENING —
Monday Evening, 29th June

At 8 o'clock. Continuing every afternoon and evening during the week. Grand Marches of over 100 Young Ladies each afternoon at 4.30 o'clock, and each evening at 8 o'clock. Booths representing Old Warships, Nautical Scene, etc. Fancy Stalls, Refreshments. Five O'clock Tea, etc., etc. Grecian Art Tableau by 25 young ladies in costume. Under direction of Miss Holmstrom. Grand Military Tournament and Mimic Battle, and many other interesting events, day by day, including a Bicycle Tournament.

BANDS every afternoon and evening. Season tickets, 50 cents; daily admission, 10 cents.

Arrangements will be made for excursion rates on railways.

GOD SAVE THE QUEEN

Je18 a&c 2t cw

(above) The Nautical Fair was held at the Halifax Exhibition Building where a mock-up of Halifax harbour, complete with vessels, was built.

(right) Thanks to extensive newspaper advertisements, the Nautical Fair attracted thousands of visitors during the Marco Magic Company's stand in Halifax.

(Nova Scotia Archives)

IF ANYTHING conspired to doom the Marco Magic Company in Halifax, it was the week-long Nautical Fair. The extravagant event was opening Monday, June 29, the same night as Marco, serving up a crushing dose of night-for-night competition for Houdini and his co-stars.

The fair took over the cavernous Halifax Exhibition building, creating a spectacular mock-up of Halifax Harbour. Replicas of ships complete with masts and rigging had been built to house booths selling ice cream and candy. One group built a stunning reproduction of a man-of-war as well as a British houseboat. The army and navy had also joined in the effort with a display featuring real cannons. And a copy of the *MicMac*, the Dartmouth ferry, was central to all the other displays. The brilliant transformation of the rink won praise from the *Halifax Herald* in a report that read, "One can hardly realize that it is terra firma under one's feet."[1]

Marching bands were scheduled for every evening as well as performances by almost every musical ensemble in the city. One of the most anticipated events was the military tournament that promised to include a storming of entrenchments and a battle with Arabs. The Gypsy Cave offered fortune telling, palmistry, black art, and a live Zulu.

Fair organizers, bracing for huge crowds, had arranged for extra streetcars to deal with the crush expected at the Tower Road rink. The organizers were right. The fair packed the enormous building to the rafters for the entire week.

Tickets for attending the Nautical Fair for a full week were only 50 cents. Tickets to see Houdini and Marco were 25 to 75 cents for each performance.
(Nova Scotia Archives)

CHAPTER TWENTY-THREE

ENTERTAINMENT
FOR THE FEW

Halifax, Nova Scotia
Monday, June 29, 1896

*"Occasionally the young man who defies jails and jailers
refers to his diminutive assistant as 'my sister,' but there is a gentleness
and affection between the performer and his assistant which is altogether
too warm for brotherly and sisterly attachment."*
—*Pittsburgh Post*, October 21, 1906

WITH MERE HOURS UNTIL CURTAIN TIME, a press release from Academy of Music manager, Harshaw Clarke, sent chills through the Marco Magic Company. The world's greatest magician, Herrmann the Great, was coming to Halifax in four weeks' time.

Alexander Herrmann and his wife Adelaide were two of the world's biggest stars. The fact they were coming to Halifax was a point of great pride for Haligonians. But this was a devastating blow for Dooley—the entire Marco production, except for Houdini's escape act, was little more than an amateur knock-off of Herrmann's celebrated show. Dooley must have wondered what Clarke was thinking. Why would he make the Herrmann announcement just as the Marco

☛ The regal interior of the Academy of Music.
(Nova Scotia Archives)

219

Magic Company was kicking off a one-week stand? It must have been an oversight on behalf of the academy's manager; surely he wouldn't have deliberately tried to undermine a troupe appearing at his own theatre.

Upstaged or not, with two weeks of promotions behind them, the Marco show had to go on. In light of Herrmann's impending visit, Professor Dooley's tireless efforts to distance his Marco persona from the magician named Markos now seemed vain and pointless. Nevertheless, the *Echo* tried to help Dooley's campaign when they ran a note in Monday's afternoon edition: "Marco, the prestidigitator and illusionist, opens at the academy this evening. Halifax people who saw Marco's show in St. John [*sic*] say it is a good one. A similarity in names leads some people to believe Marco was here before; but he wasn't—it was Markos."

The Academy of Music was readied for opening night as it had been untold times in its nineteen-year history. The box office opened, houselights were switched on, and ushers took their stations. Sidewalk signs announcing the appearance of the Marco Magic Company were placed on both sides of the Academy's front entrance doors, strategically placed to entice pedestrians strolling down Pleasant Street (now Barrington Street) and Spring Garden Road.

On June 29, 1896, the citizens of Halifax learned that magicians Adelaide and Alexander Herrmann would be appearing at the Academy of Music. Adelaide, seen here with her pet duck, kept many animals, including a monkey. When her pets died, she had custom coffins crafted, and buried the pets with a formal funeral in a private cemetery at the couple's Long Island estate.
(Harry Ransom Center, The University of Texas at Austin)

Halifax playing card issued by the Intercolonial Railway.
(New Brunswick Railway Museum)

Clarke had taken care of printing the programmes. The four pages were mostly filled with advertisements for restaurants and shops, but two columns were dedicated to Marco, Monarch of Mystery. Dooley changed his billing from the one he used in Saint John, giving Houdini his own act entitled, "Twenty Minutes with Mysterious Harry Houdini." The twenty-minute turn was familiar territory for Houdini, who was used to slotting his act in between a dozen others at vaudeville theatres. Despite his many troubles, Professor Dooley showed he was a good sport about the whole Marco/Markos affair. In the programme, he renamed Bessie Houdini's mind-reading act, "Mlle Marco in Karmos," the word "Karmos" being a rearrangement of the letters in "Markos."

As showtime grew near, only a handful of seats were occupied in the spacious theatre, with at least three reporters sitting among the tiny audience. Outside, streetcars overstuffed with citizens were passing by the academy on their way to the Nautical Fair, where well over one thousand people were already lined up for the grand opening featuring a speech from the lieutenant-governor.

Inside the academy, even the ushers knew they were witnessing a dud. The few theatre patrons shifted uneasily in their crimson-covered seats and gazed at the wonderful Italian garden scene painted on the academy's drop curtain, a curtain that has survived, and in 2012 still does service at a rural community theatre in Upper Musquodoboit, Nova Scotia.

This photo taken from the Academy of Music stage offers a view of the balcony and gallery above. The image also offers a glimpse of what Houdini saw in Halifax—empty seats. (Nova Scotia Archives)

Professor Dooley rang up the purple-toned curtain at eight o'clock and greeted his embarrassingly thin audience from the same stage once graced by Oscar Wilde and Balabrega. Putting on a brave face, he began a half-hour set of sleight-of-hand magic. Once Dooley finished warming up the audience with his traditional routine, he put aside his silks and coins and introduced his "daughter," Mademoiselle Marco.

Bessie took a seat at the centre of the stage where she was put into a "mesmeric trance" by Marco and, for good measure, blindfolded. Houdini prowled the aisles of the near-empty academy asking the audience to dig trinkets out of their purses and pockets, so Bessie could identify them using her powers of second sight.

The show continued with *Trilby*, the same levitation illusion Dooley performed with Bessie in Yarmouth and Saint John, although, for his sophisticated big city audience in Halifax, he renamed the performance the Mystery of L'Hassa. Next up for Dooley was the Cremation of Floribel—the same act the company flubbed in Saint John. Once again, Bessie stood atop the little wooden table awaiting her demise, and after a lengthy dramatic prattle from the professor she was instantly burned to ashes. Then Dooley introduced the Voodoo Temple of Brahma, explaining the audience would witness "the astral projection of a human body through space." In this act, Burton Kilby as Buttons disappeared from a cage near the footlights, instantly reappearing at the rear of the stage.

As usual, Professor Dooley explained he was on his retirement tour and introduced his successors, his daughter "Mlle Marco" and her husband, the "Mysterious Harry Houdini." Harry, in turn, introduced the couple's trunk mystery, Metamorphosis, although Dooley listed it on the Halifax programme using Alexander Herrmann's title, the Asiatic Trunk Mystery. The *Acadian Recorder* June 30 review indicates the Houdinis performed their signature act with some help from the Halifax audience: "Houdini, with a coat on, his hands tied and placed in a sack, was put in a trunk, which was securely tied with ropes by a committee from the audience; in a few seconds Houdini was out of the trunk, without his coat and his hands untied, while when the trunk was opened Mlle Marco was found to have taken his place in the bag, wearing the coat and with her hands tied." The review closed with a compliment to Harry and Bessie: "The trunk mystery has been done here before, but never so clever as by Harry Houdini and Mlle Marco."

By the close of the opening show, it was obvious to all that Professor Dooley couldn't draw flies—even in his own hometown. As the audience headed for home, Harry Houdini lurked near the Academy of Music exits and eavesdropped, later recalling, "As they left we could hear remarks all over to the effect that 'This is not the same Marco we had here last time.'"[1] When Houdini wrote this some years later, he neglected to mention which "Marco" the audience liked better.

If the Marco Magic Company stand in Halifax could be salvaged, it would be up to Harry Houdini. And tomorrow night, he would give it his best shot, with a little help from a friendly cook.

CHAPTER TWENTY-FOUR

TRY, TRY AGAIN

Halifax, Nova Scotia
Tuesday, June 30, 1896

"There are tricks in all trades but mine."
—Harry Houdini speaking to an audience at the sheriff's office
in Waukegan, Illinois, March 16, 1897, *Daily Register*, March 16, 1897

TUESDAY MORNING, HALIGONIANS were taking cover from a violent
windstorm that was hammering Halifax Harbour and tearing buildings apart on
McNabs Island. While the wind howled and rolling thunder shook the city, Harry
Houdini scoured the papers for any mention of his opening night performance.
He clipped one *Halifax Herald* article entitled "Marco's Fine Entertainment" and
pasted it in his press book.

> "Marco" failed to draw a large audience at the academy last night, but
> he attracted a highly pleased gathering. His many wonderful tricks
> well-earned for him the title of "monarch of mystery." The performance
> is divided into four acts, each of which was interesting and
> bewildering. He is ably assisted by Mlle. Marco and Harry Houdini.

The Marco Company performed at the Academy of Music, a 1,250-seat
theatre that first opened its doors in 1877. (Nova Scotia Archives)

225

"The congress of nations," "Mlle Marco in Karmos," "Metamorphosis," "The "Voodoo temple of Brahma," "The Hindoo Brahmin in the mysteries of Mahomet," "The cremation of Floribel"—all these made an entertainment of interesting character. Marco will hold the boards again tonight and for the remainder of the week.

ESCAPE FROM DORCHESTER

On Tuesday, Professor Dooley was counting on a brand new attraction, starring Harry Houdini, to draw paying customers to the Academy of Music. Houdini's new act was billed Escape from Dorchester in honour of the Maritimes' most notorious prison, Dorchester Penitentiary. Dooley neatly swiped the name from another prison-inspired act performed by Alexander Herrmann entitled Escape from Sing Sing.

Dooley can't be blamed for his thievery. His crosstown competition was intensifying and he needed a drawing card in the worst way. The Nautical Fair was offering a special Tuesday discount for members of all Halifax organizations and clubs. Groups like the Royal Nova Scotia Yacht Squadron and the Wanderers Athletic Club now had another reason to skip the Marco show in favour of the fair, where organizers put together a stellar lineup for Tuesday evening. As a bonus, a shooting gallery was set up for marksmen willing to test their aim for a shot at some big prizes.

The fair's club promotion worked. For the second straight night, the Halifax Exhibition building was packed to the rafters. Unfortunately for Professor Dooley, Tuesday evening at the Academy of Music found an even smaller audience than Monday's meagre gathering. The small assembly heard Dooley reiterate his retirement speech—but with a rambling twist. "Ladies and Gentlemen: Being now on my farewell tour, I have retired from all hazardous work and will introduce my daughter and her husband, Houdini, who is my successor, and who will do my famous handcuff act."[1] Dooley was really stretching the truth with this declaration; Bessie and Harry, along with the rest of the company chuckled, knowing full well that Dooley didn't know a handcuff from a leg iron.

For Tuesday's Escape from Dorchester challenge, Houdini recruited some prominent citizens of Halifax to join him on stage. Sergeant William Collins of the Halifax police department, who had just finished duty at seven o'clock that evening, agreed to help the young escape artist. So, too, did the chef of the Halifax Hotel, Louis Urnan. Chef Urnan and Houdini had something in common—both could speak German. The thirty-four-year-old cook immigrated to America in 1881 and had led a gypsy life ever since. Probably landing in Halifax as a galley cook on board a steamship, Urnan would spend little time in Nova Scotia, eventually returning to Brooklyn, where he worked as a chef at a department store.

Houdini took centre stage and explained his Escape from Dorchester challenge to more than a thousand empty seats and a handful of spectators. Sergeant Collins and Chef Urnan's footsteps echoed through the near-empty theatre as they climbed up into the footlights and spent several minutes trussing Houdini into a ridiculous predicament with rope. For good measure, Collins handcuffed Houdini and chained him into an even more difficult dilemma that inspired the *Chronicle* to report

Professor Dooley was a member of the dubious Egleston English Opera Company in 1883. Their dreadful Halifax performance of the opera *Iolanthe* caused one critic to suggest, "The company did injustice to author, composer and audience."

(Nova Scotia Archives)

Academy of Music.

ONE WEEK ONLY.

Commencing Monday Jan. 29th. Matinees Wed. & Sat.

THE EVENT OF THE SEASON.

Engagement Extraordinary of the

EGLESTON

English Opera Company

Monday and Tuesday Evenings. January 29th and 30th. and Wednesday Matinee.

Gilbert and Sullivan's latest production

IOLANTHE

— OR, THE —

PEER AND THE PERI.

(Costumes specially prepared at a cost of $4,000.) Notwithstanding the great expense, there will be no advance in prices. Reserved Seats 75 cents. General Admission 50 cents. Gallery, 25 cents. Matinee Prices. Adults 50c. Children 25c. Sale of seats commencing at Academy Box Office on Friday, Jan. 26th at 9 a. m.

the next day, "After they had finished it looked indeed impossible." But it wasn't impossible for Houdini. He retired behind a curtain and reappeared one minute and four seconds later with the ropes untied and the handcuffs unlocked.

As the disappointed troupe closed their performance at ten o'clock, crammed streetcars were returning from the wildly popular Nautical Fair. A brand new crisis was brewing for Professor Dooley, thanks to a reporter who recognized him from thirteen years earlier. This writer already knew the professor was a born-and-raised Haligonian, and he had somehow discovered that Dooley had played the Academy of Music years ago. Naturally, the reporter planned on reminding his readers about Dooley's past performance at the academy. It was a performance Professor Dooley would rather forget.

During the season of 1883, Dooley took a break from his organist position with the church and joined the Egleston English Opera Company. The company was touring the east coast and offered the aspiring musician a chance to return to his hometown of Halifax. Unfortunately, Dooley discovered too late that he had joined a poorly rehearsed and ill-managed troupe.

In return for their pitiable performances, the Egleston English Opera Company received some of the worst theatrical reviews in the history of Halifax. One Halifax reviewer, who described Dooley's company as "an exceedingly second class troupe," didn't mince words in summing up the dreadful effort offered by Dooley and his co-stars, writing, "The disappointment was pretty severe."[2] The same reviewer, perhaps regretting his caustic comments, returned the following night to give the company a second listen. Afterwards he wrote, "The orchestra shone out in continuous discord, exceedingly painful to listen to, and there was no sensible improvements in the vocal part."[3]

After tasting the sour sting of life on the road with the maligned opera company, Dooley had beaten a hasty retreat back to his old job with the Catholic church. On this evening in Halifax, thirteen years removed from the Egleston English Opera Company, the Catholic church job was starting to look good once again. As Professor Dooley tried to sleep Tuesday night, he couldn't help but fret over Wednesday's upcoming problem — Dominion Day. And his worries were completely justified.

⋗ ⋅ ⧁ ⋅ ○ ⋅ ⧀ ⋅ ⋖

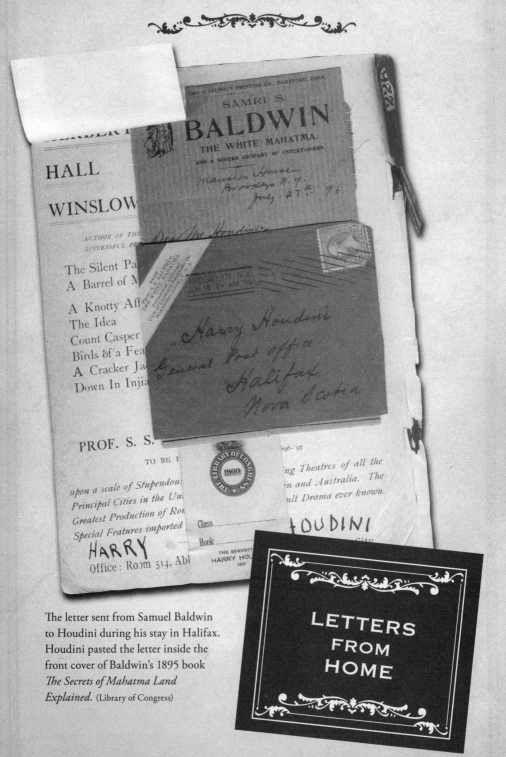

The letter sent from Samuel Baldwin to Houdini during his stay in Halifax. Houdini pasted the letter inside the front cover of Baldwin's 1895 book *The Secrets of Mahatma Land Explained.* (Library of Congress)

LETTERS FROM HOME

IT'S BEEN ESTIMATED Houdini wrote over 150,000 letters in his lifetime. In one letter dated June 19, 1919, he wrote, "Pardon brevity, am writing all day and have over 56 letters to get away." By 1896 Houdini was corresponding relentlessly with other magicians and his magic suppliers August Roterberg and W.D. LeRoy.

Like all performers, Houdini counted on having his mail forwarded to him while he was on tour. Whenever possible, he posted his upcoming dates in the *New York Clipper*. That way, mail could be sent to him in care of a theatre or post office along his route.

To let his friends and business contacts know he was touring Canada this summer, he paid for two small banner ads in the June 20, 1896, *New York Clipper*. One stated, "Harry and Bessie Houdini, the real and only recognized introducers of Metamorphosis, are touring the principal cities in Canada. Regards to friends." Another note in the weekly *Clipper* gave more details. "Harry and Bessie Houdini announce a successful

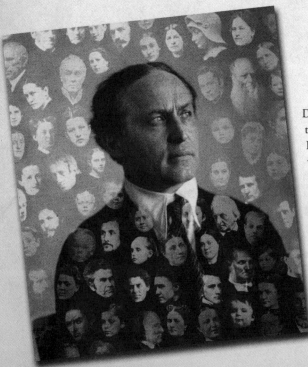

During his 1920s campaign to discredit fake mediums, Houdini experimented with "spirit photography" producing images like this one. (fantasmamagic.com, Roger Dreyer Collection)

Canadian tour. They will be at the Academy of Music, Halifax, N.S. the week of June 21." Of course, this note was inaccurate since the Marco Magic Company was bumped from their original slot.

Houdini was in for a pleasant surprise when he checked in at the Halifax post office on Bedford Row. The clerk handed him a small blue envelope addressed to Harry Houdini, General Post Office, Halifax, Nova Scotia. When Houdini looked closely at the envelope, his heart skipped a beat. A diagonal yellow stripe on the top left corner of the envelope was labelled, "From Prof. SS Baldwin, The White Mahatma."

After returning home from Saint John, serious medical problems had landed Baldwin in a Brooklyn hospital where he underwent surgery. Now he was recovering and found time to write the talented young man, Harry Houdini, he had met in Canada.

Dear Mr. Houdini,

Illness has prevented my replying sooner. Hope you've made a barrel full but I fancy a small keg will hold all any magician can make at low Tonies [slang] in Canada. Your work however is so cleverly done that you perhaps may succeed where others would fail.

I was much pleased with St. John [*sic*].

Come over and see me and bring the fairy queen when you get back to N.Y.

Regards to your pretty wife.

Yours Truly,
S.S. Baldwin

Houdini would never part with the letter or the small blue envelope. He pasted both onto the inside front cover of Professor Baldwin's book, *The Secrets of Mahatma Land Explained*.

The struggling young magician, so anonymous on this day in Halifax, would one day be the biggest act in the world. And he would one day write Samuel Baldwin, humbly telling him, "It will please you to know that I am considered as the biggest drawing card in Great Britain today. Am breaking all records." That letter is dated February 23, 1920, twenty-four years after Baldwin first predicted Houdini's success.

THE TRIBUNE

Is published at Springhill, N.S.

SATURDAY, JULY 25, 1869

A Slippery Prisoner

OPERA HOUSE
MONCTON

Monday and Tuesday
AUG. 17th and 18th.

SPECIAL ENGAGEMENT OF
"MYSTERIOUS"

Harry Houdini
The Wonderful Magician.

... ASSISTED BY ...

BEATRICE HOUDINI
World's Greatest Mind Reader
and Clairvoyant.

MIRTH AND MYSTERY

THE EVENING MAIL

WEDNESDAY, JULY 1, 1896.

HALIFAX, N. S. W

ACADEMY OF MUSIC.

Mysterious Harry Houdini, of the Marco company, who tested the handcuffs of Chief O'Sullivan last Friday and succeeded in releasing himself from all that were put on, made the same test at the Academy of Music last night. When the announcement was made from the stage that Houdini could get out of any handcuffs that might be brought, Sergeant Collins came forward with handcuffs and with the assistance of Mr. Urnan, chef of the Halifax hotel, chained him in such a   that he seemed impossible of release.

It was an easy task for Hou d. , as he released himself in one minute and four seconds. To-night Houdini will be put to a hard test and he promises to release himself in less than two minutes. This performance in Marco's bill is called "Escape from Dorchester."

The Daily Times

ESTABLISHED 1877

MONCTON, TUESDAY, AUG.

MONCTON, N. B.

Prices 15, 25,

COMING!
Gunn's Opera House.

JULY 15th & 16th

SPECIAL ENGAGEMENT

Mysterious Harry Houdini and
Madamsell Beatrice Hou

Local Items Etc.

The hand is slicker than the eye go and see Houdini at Pioneer Hall Sat. 25th.

Halifax, Nova Scotia
Wednesday, July 1, 1896

"Many amateurs with money commence their career at the top of the ladder,
lose their money and slide ungracefully to the bottom."
—Harry Lindley, actor/manager, from his book *Merely Players*

WHEN PROFESSOR DOOLEY CRACKED OPEN the Wednesday morning edition of the *Echo*, he found a brief note about his Halifax roots: "Marco, who is now performing at the academy, is said to have been born in Halifax, but left here some years ago." So now, along with all his other troubles, the "Monarch of Mystery" had been exposed as nothing more than a plain old Haligonian. But, mercifully, there was no mention of his previous visit to Halifax with the laughable Egleston English Opera Company.

The Escape from Dorchester act was mentioned in two of the Halifax papers, giving the eagle-eyed Houdini two new articles for his press book. The review in the morning edition of the *Chronicle* tried, half-heartedly, to drum up some interest in Houdini's act by reporting, "To-night [*sic*] Sergeant Collins and a number of

Houdini saved this 1896 Halifax clipping for the rest of his life.
(Sidney H. Radner Collection, History Museum at the Castle, Appleton, Wisconsin)

233

gentlemen who talked of the escape will bring handcuffs and shackles that they think will hold him."

Overall, the skimpy reviews of the Tuesday Marco show were lost amid the flood of ink praising the Nautical Fair. The *Chronicle* review of Tuesday night's fair offers a glimpse of the activity at the Exhibition building while Houdini was playing to empty seats at the academy. "The nautical fair was the centre of attention last evening. The attendance was very large, uncomfortably so, in fact. The marches were done with great precision and loudly applauded."

As if the fair wasn't enough opposition for the Marco Magic Company, today was Dominion Day—a major national holiday that commemorated the day Canada became a country in 1867. For many, Dominion Day was an excuse to take in some of the countryside and scenic coastline. The Intercolonial Railway was offering excursion trains to Windsor, Pictou, and Truro, while the SS *Lunenburg* set sail from Halifax, crowded with day trippers bound for Chester on the South Shore. For those who stayed in the city, there was plenty of fun to be had on a sunny holiday in Halifax. The thousands who turned out for the afternoon horse races at the riding grounds kept overflowing the fields, forcing race officials to delay the runs while the troublesome melee was brought under control.

Up on Tower Road, the Nautical Fair flirted with its own crowd control disaster scenario after admitting a frighteningly large daytime audience that overloaded the bleachers to watch the special Dominion Day lineup. Following a military tournament with a full battle re-enactment, many wandered over to the Gypsy Cave to see a startling new attraction—X-ray.

Dooley had planned a Wednesday matinee performance, but there is no record that the Marco Magic Company followed through. It is possible Houdini cashed in on the Dominion Day festivities by reviving a Punch and Judy wooden puppet show from his Welsh Brothers Circus days. In a 1925 letter to Harvard drama professor, George Pierce Baker, Houdini wrote of the incident without naming the exact location. "Remember once in Canada, they were giving a great big children's festival and I was asked to entertain one thousand kiddies and despite the fact that I only had twenty-four hours' notice, I cut a miscellaneous set of figures overnight and the paint was hardly dry. The only colors I had were red, white and black, but doubt if at any time in my life was I such a tremendous hit as I was to those children who had never before seen a Punch and Judy show."

Professor Dooley now knew he was fighting a losing battle. From the very start—when he was bumped by Rose Sydell and the London Belles—everything that could go wrong had gone wrong in Halifax. The beleaguered organist had stumbled into a perfect storm of opposition with the federal election, the lovely weather, the Nautical Fair, the imminent arrival of Herrmann the Great, and now, Dominion Day. Not to mention the confusion between Marco and the popular Markos and the *Echo* exposing "the Monarch of Mystery" as nothing more than a regular Haligonian.

On this day in Halifax, the supposed impostor Markos hardly mattered anymore. Bigger trouble, it seems, was in the offing.

TRADING PLACES

Likely because of Dooley's unpaid hotel bills, and circling Marco Magic Company creditors, Bessie and Harry Houdini quietly checked out of the Carleton House Hotel and signed into the Halifax Hotel. Although he had brazenly signed the Carleton House registry as "Harry Houdini and wife" two weeks before, he chose a clandestine sign-in for the Halifax Hotel. Combining his stage initials with his real surname, "the mysterious Harry Houdini" modestly signed, "H.H. Weiss and wife."

This was Professor Dooley's third week of carrying his company in Halifax. And so far, all he had to show for his ongoing investment was two embarrassingly small houses at the Academy of Music. All the while, of course, Dooley had to pay his assistants' salaries. The stagehands and his young magician Burton Kilby would have been earning from five to ten dollars a week, but it is unlikely the Houdinis were making less than the twenty-five dollars per week they earned with the Welsh Brothers Circus. Dooley certainly had reason to shed some assistants, and it appears Chas Bryant and J.M. "the Irishman" Whitehead had already been sent home, while Kenney, Kilby, and McKierney remained in Canada.

In Halifax, it would be easy for Dooley to end up deep in the red with merchants willing to extend credit for printing, lodging, meals, supplies, and cartage. There were few secrets amongst the businessmen in this relatively small harbour city. Whether theatre companies were successful or not, the Carleton House Hotel and other businesses would expect Harshaw Clarke to cover the unpaid bills of his performers.

And now Clarke was face to face with another failure on the stage of his theatre—the Marco Magic Company.

By showtime Wednesday evening, Dooley knew better than to ask for a count of advance ticket sales. Who in their right mind would plan on sitting in a dim theatre to watch a fledgling magic company on a beautiful summer evening like this one? Not to mention how the city was alive with Dominion Day celebrations at virtually every park, beach, and backyard. And for the third straight evening, the Halifax Exhibition building was full to bursting with spectators cheering on the Nautical Fair.

Clarke had been the lessee of the Academy of Music long enough to smell an imminent disaster. He knew there would be no last-minute rush of patrons filling his theatre to see this third-rate Marco. All tonight could promise was yet another failure. Clarke could only dream that Edward James Dooley and the Marco Magic Company could somehow fill his theatre like Willis Skinner and the Markos Modern Miracles Company had done last fall. But this Marco was no Markos, and the local papers had repeatedly warned Haligonians that this wasn't the same magician who lit up the academy audience nine months earlier. Now, Clarke could only dream about Willis Skinner's Markos stand, recalling fond memories of putting his beloved Standing Room Only sign on the Halifax sidewalk.

When the house lights dimmed, the city outside the academy doors was alive with music and unrestrained summer merriment. But inside, the academy was nearly empty, with bill collectors and ushers outnumbering the paying audience. Professor Dooley swallowed his pride and started performing. Bessie and Harry could only stand in the wings and watch the train wreck as Dooley went through the motions knowing that the demise of the Marco Magic Company was nigh at hand. Still, Dooley's assistants would offer a smattering of applause as he ran through his opening act.

Clarke had seen enough of Dooley's farcical attempt. The sullen businessman was already looking at carrying a dark theatre for the next four weeks. The acts booked to follow Marco's stand, White Crook and Jed Prouty, hadn't contacted him in some time and he assumed the productions had folded. His next attraction was Herrmann the Great, but not until July 27.

With the lean Marco receipts behind him—and no gates ahead of him for almost a month—Clarke had to recover his impending losses from the Marco

Magic Company. Going by the book, the manager summoned the sheriff to the academy.

While revellers could be heard celebrating Canada's twenty-ninth birthday outside, the sheriff stepped on stage, informing the crestfallen Professor Dooley the show was over. Furthermore, he was claiming the company's assets on behalf of creditors. The undignified finale was recalled in a November 4, 1936, *Halifax Mail* article published more than forty years later. "The troupe was having a few bad breaks, and one night, the sheriff leaped across the footlights and seized all the company's apparatus for debt."

On Dominion Day 1896, in Halifax, Nova Scotia, Professor Dooley's beloved Marco Magic Company had given its last-ever performance. The next day, the failed impresario and his assistants would have to make arrangements to return to America. The next sailing to Boston wasn't until Saturday, July 4, meaning Dooley still had to bankroll two more days in Halifax.

But Bessie and Harry Houdini weren't ready to admit defeat and slump home to America. It was agreed the Houdinis would stay in Canada to honour the Monday and Tuesday dates Dooley had booked at St. Peter's Hall in Dartmouth. Finally, after six years of going unnoticed in dime museums and circus tents, the name Harry Houdini would be top of the bill.

LOSING LOOT IN HALIFAX

Academy of Music manager Harshaw Clarke dropped the curtain on the Marco Magic Company on July 1, 1896. (Nova Scotia Archives)

THE MARCO MAGIC COMPANY wasn't the first troupe to lose a bundle in Halifax. Harry Lindley, an actor/manager who had been touring the Maritimes since 1870, once landed in a Halifax jail after he was unable to pay his creditors. His New York actors were left stranded while he lounged in prison unable to make bail. He finally won his freedom by surrendering his theatrical property along with most of his expensive clothing.

For Harshaw Clarke, Professor Dooley and Houdini were just the latest in a string of deadbeat performers playing his Halifax theatre. Clarke didn't like losing money on any show, although as owner of a beautiful home on South Park Street and proprietor of the Steam Lithographic Company he could easily survive a few poor stands.

Some weeks earlier, Clarke endured a disastrous stand by a variety company from New York. The production had opened to overflowing houses before the popular lead comedian of the show, Douglas Flint, failed to appear one evening. The police found Flint in hospital recuperating from a drinking binge. A stand-in actor tried to replace the lead man but couldn't fill the bill. With business ruined, Clarke closed the scheduled three-week stand leaving thirty-five actors scrambling to get home to New York.

Clarke faithfully published reports about troublemaking performers in the influential *New York Dramatic Mirror*. Clarke let loose with a damning report on Flint's drinking binge, but mercifully he didn't comment on the failure of the Marco Magic Company or its Halifax-born proprietor, Edward James Dooley.

Douglas Flint. (University of Washington Libraries, Special Collections, S-F-332)

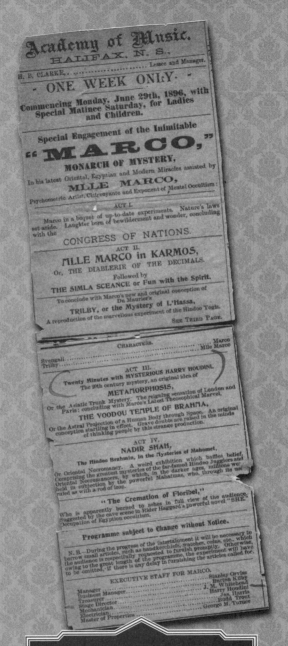

CHAPTER TWENTY-SIX

MARCO LOSES HIS MAGIC

Halifax, Nova Scotia
Saturday, July 4, 1896

"I guess we all occasionally
think of that unfortunate Marco tour."
—Edward James Dooley in a letter to Houdini, August 30, 1900

ON THURSDAY, AS THE REMNANTS of the Marco Magic Company took stock of their sorry situation, the Marco advertisements kept running in the Halifax newspapers. The only mention of the company's collapse was a gentle one-sentence report in the *Halifax Herald* that read, "Marco, who has given such excellent entertainments in magic, etc., at the academy of music this week, put on his closing performance last night." Thankfully, none of the papers reported on the sheriff's role in bringing down the curtain on poor Marco.

Luckily, Harry managed to save his all-important Metamorphosis trunk from the sheriff's clutches. He also rescued a few other Marco props, including the mechanism for the *Trilby* levitation. But the sheriff still had quite a collection with the Marco Magic Company's gear; an earlier article in the *Acadian Recorder*,

☞ Bessie Houdini's sister Marie Hinson gave this Halifax programme to a magic collector decades ago. It has since been purchased by Roger Dreyer for his Fantasma Magic Houdini Museum.

(fantasmamagic.com, Roger Dreyer Collection)

Edward James Dooley, the
Nova Scotia-born organist
turned magician, made a
pilgrimage to Rome in the
early 1890s. (from microfilm:
Connecticut State Library)

describing Dooley's stage outfit suggested, "He carries more paraphernalia than almost any magician we have ever had."[1] Exactly what happened to Dooley's seized property remains a mystery. In 1908 Houdini wrote; "He disbanded the company and left all his paraphernalia in Halifax, where it is perhaps still stored."[2]

John Kenney was the only assistant from the Marco entourage invited to stay on with the Houdinis. The thirty-three-year-old would serve as carpenter, stage crew, assistant, and actor. There simply wasn't a budget to allow for anyone else to have a spot on the payroll.

Friday's *Chronicle* finally noted the real reason for the collapse of the Marco show. Under the sadly appropriate heading, "Can you hear them drop?" was a single sentence, "Marco couldn't conjure with the Halifax public." Houdini carefully clipped the sentence, keeping it as an ironic souvenir for his press book.

Houdini clipped several Halifax articles for his press book. ☞
Showing great attention to detail, he carefully included
the newspaper name and date with each clipping.
(Sidney H. Radner Collection, History Museum at the Castle, Appleton, Wisconsin)

T. JOHN DAILY SUN

is published by

SUN PRINTING COMPANY, (Ltd)

ST. JOHN, N. B., JUNE 9, 1896.

...RCO AT THE OPERA HOUSE.

...good audience gathered at the ...house last night, the attraction ...Marco, "the monarch of mys... assisted by Mlle. Marco, a ...y young lady, and Mons. Houdini, ...cialist of no mean order. Bow-...orchestra made its first appear-...ce and acquitted itself very credi-...y, the opening selection being loud-...pplauded.

...rco gave a long and varied pro-...me, in which it introduced some ...ries new to St. John. The trunk ...ery was splendidly executed and ...the hit of the evening. The rap-...with which Houdini and Mlle. ...o changed places was simply as-...ing; Trilby, whom Marco made ...in the air in the full sight of ...audience, was a sensational feat-...of the programme, but the crema-...of Floribel and the growth of ...mango tree did not come up to ...xpectation of the audience. Taken ...whole the performance was inter-...t, if not brilliant, but much al-...nce must be made for a first night ...strange stage. A much better ex-...on may be looked for this even-...when several changes will be in-...ed. The box office will be open ...ay for the sale of tickets.

...e Gazette.

T. JOHN, ... TUESDAY, JUNE 2, 1896.

Opera House Last Evening.

...large ...ience attended the Opera ...se last evening to witness Marco the ...narch of mystery assisted by Mlle. ...rco and Signor Houdini make their ...t bow to a St. John audience. Marco ...not the 'Markos' who appeared here ...t September, he is a very superior ...gician in every way. More clever in ...ts of magic and the originator of many ...cks of legerdemain performed by him-...f and others. Marco is assisted by a ...mpany of performers any one of which ...an artist himself.

In the first part of the programme ...arco introduced new slight of hand ...cks which were the best ever attempt-...here. His cabinet manifestations ...re good, while the trunk mystery beat ...very attempt ever made by other magi-...ans in the past. While Mlle Marco and ...gno Houdinioa were the principals in ...s act and they exchanged places by ...ignor Houdinio getting out of the trunk ...nd the lady taking his place in less ...han six seconds.

...Nadir Shah or the black art mysteries ...was a clever performance. The per-...ormance was a long and interesting one ...nd was highly appreciated. Tonight ...here should be a good crowd present as ...he show is well worth the admission ...asked. A new orchestra made its first ...appearance at the Opera house last even-...ng and performed very creditably:

THE DAILY SUN.

ST. JOHN, N. B., JUNE 10, 1896.

IMPOSSIBLE TO HOLD HOUDINI.

Marco made a number of changes in his programme last night and will each evening introduce new features to his very entertaining performance. A spe-cial feature was made last night of Larry Houdini's mysterious way of releasing himself from handcuffs, schakles, ropes, etc. He proved that it was apparently impossible to bind him with irons or anything else. An-nouncements have been made that last night he would test anything in St. John that could bind him and requests were made for any person that had dif-ferent handcuffs or schackles to bring them to the theatre. Officer Baxter, Arthur McGinley, John McCafferty and others brought chains, thinking he could not release himself from them, but they only proved playthings to this mysterious magician. They handcuff-ed him with his hands behind, at the same time shackled his feet, put it would only take a few seconds for him to release himself. It is certainly a marvellous performance, and many people last night avowed that he must certainly be in league with the spirits. Marco should attract large audiences the remainder of the week. The per-formances will amuse and mystify all who attend.

St. John, N. B.

The Daily Telegraph

ST. JOHN, N. B., JUNE 12, 1896.

THE DAILY TELEGRAPH is ... d at 23 and 25 Canterbury street, ev... rning

At the Opera House.

There was a fair attendance at the Opera House last evening, when Marco, the magician, with his troupe mystified those present by his slight of hand work and illusions. Mysterious Harry Houdini, who performs the wonderful act with the trunk, invited a number of gen-tlemen from the audience—among whom were some well-known citizens—to tie him up in the trunk.

The gentlemen tied Houdini's arms behind his back; the latter was then put in a bag, and the top of the bag securely tied and sealed. He was then locked inside a large trunk, which was bound with ropes and placed inside a cabinet. Mlle. Marco also went inside the cabi-net, and in less than three seconds from the time the curtains were drawn a complete change had been made, the young lady being inside the trunk se-curely bound, and Houdini set free. The trick is a good one, and is one of the finest ever shown in St. John.

HALIFAX, N.S. ...

THE EVENING MAIL

THURSDAY JUNE 25 1896.

HE'S A WONDER.

Houdini the famous handcuff-breaker, with Marco, the wonder worker, mysti-fied the chief of police and officers at the police station this morning. He removed with ease every pair of handcuffs placed on his wrists by the chief and other officers. Houdini took off all kin... of cuffs, from the old ones used in days long gone by, to the very latest. Houdini's most remark-able feat was the way in which he re-moved three pairs of cuffs placed on his wrists by the chief of police. These cuffs were shackled to three other pairs. It took Houdini just two minutes to do the trick, much to the surprise of all present. Houdini experienced the hardest task with a pair of naval cuffs which took him four minutes to displace. He also gave an interesting exhibition in mind reading.

HALIFAX, N. S.,

The Acadian Record

(Established 1813.)

THURSDAY, JUNE 25, 1896.

A wonderful performer.

Harry Houdini, one of the members of the Marco Company, which appear at the Academy Monday, gave a most interesting exhibition at the Chief of Police's office this morning to members of the press and others. The Chief put on him the most severe pair of handcuffs in his possession, and Houdini released himself in 32 seconds. The Chief then put on three pairs of hand-cuffs, including two of the old style used here, which Houdini had never seen be-fore, and then placed another pair of cuffs around the others. Houdini said he was never so badly shackled before, but re-leased himself in 3 minutes 4 seconds. He was then shown how they were unlocked, and when put on him again released him-self in 20 seconds. One of the party thought of a card, and a messenger was sent to the Carleton House to Mlle. Marco, with the question "What card was thought of?" and she sent word back correctly that it was a queen. While waiting for the answer, He did some marvellous tricks with cards, excelling any eye seen here, fairly mystifying all present. He also did some clever feats in mind reading, and stamped himself a remarkable per-former.

THE EVENING MAIL

TUESDAY, JUNE 30, 1896.

MAGIC AND MYSTERY.

"Marco" failed to draw a large audience at the Academy of Music lase night, but he attracted a highly pleased gathering. His many wonderful tricks well earned for him the title of "monarch of mystery." The performance is divided into four parts, each of which was interesting and bewil-dering. He is ably assisted by Mlle. Marco and Harry Houdini. "The congress of nations," "Mlle. Marco in Karmos," "Trilby, or the mystery of L'Harza," "Metamerphosis," the "Voodon temple of Brahma," "The Hindoo Brahmin in the mysteries of Mahomet," "The cremation of Floribel"—all these made an enter-tainment of an interesting character. Marco will hold the boards again to-night and for the remainder of the week.

HALIFAX, N.

The Morning Chronicle

WEDNESDAY, JULY 1, 1896.

"The Escape From Dorchester."

Mysterious Harry Houdini, of the Marco company, who has relieved him-self from all handcuffs or irons of any kind that might have been brought to him since his arrival in the city, was put to even a more difficult task at the academy of music last night than Chief O'Sullivan put him to at police head-quarters last Friday. It was announced that he would get out of any handcuffs, shackles, ropes, etc , that would be brought to the academy last night, and when they were called for Sergeant Col-lins and Mr. Urnan, chief of the Halifax hotel, came on the stage to try and put him in a position that he could not re-lease himself from. After they had finished it looked indeed impossible, but it proved an easy task, taking one minute and five seconds to free himself. To-night Sergeant Collins and a number of gentlemen who talked of the escape will bring handcuffs and shackles that they think will hold him. Marco calls this performance the "Escape from Dor-chester," and it is surely a very mystify-ing and wonderful study.

In Saturday's *Chronicle*, a note confirmed what so many in Halifax's tight-knit Irish community already knew: "Marco and his assistants leave for Boston this evening. As already stated by the *Chronicle*, Marco is a Haligonian. Anybody who knew Michael [*sic*] Dooley, who used to live on Tower Road years ago and went to St. Mary's School, will notice a resemblance between him and the 'monarch of mystery.' Marco was here with the Eggleston [*sic*] Opera Company some years ago." The article made it official; Professor Dooley was now limping home minus his carefully crafted mystery man status.

On Saturday evening, Harry and Bessie Houdini waved goodbye to Professor Dooley, Burton Kilby, and Jack McKierney. The steamship docket listed Professor Dooley as holding forty dollars in cash but mentioned no assets for Kilby or McKierney. In 1908 Houdini recalled that Professor Dooley was able to meet his obligations to his employees, but he couldn't say the same for his partner Jack McKierney. "[Dooley] paid all his debts, even to the last penny, although Jack McKieran [*sic*], his partner in this provincial tour, to this day has failed to pay his share of the unpaid salaries of that tour."[3]

Once the SS *Olivette* pulled away from the Halifax pier, the Houdinis could look across at the east side of the harbour where the town of Dartmouth would welcome them to St. Peter's Hall on Monday evening. Following their frustrating experience in Halifax, they had to hope the apples were riper on the Dartmouth side of the harbour.

>–⋅‹›⋅O⋅‹›⋅i–‹

PART FIVE

HOUDINI THE HEADLINER

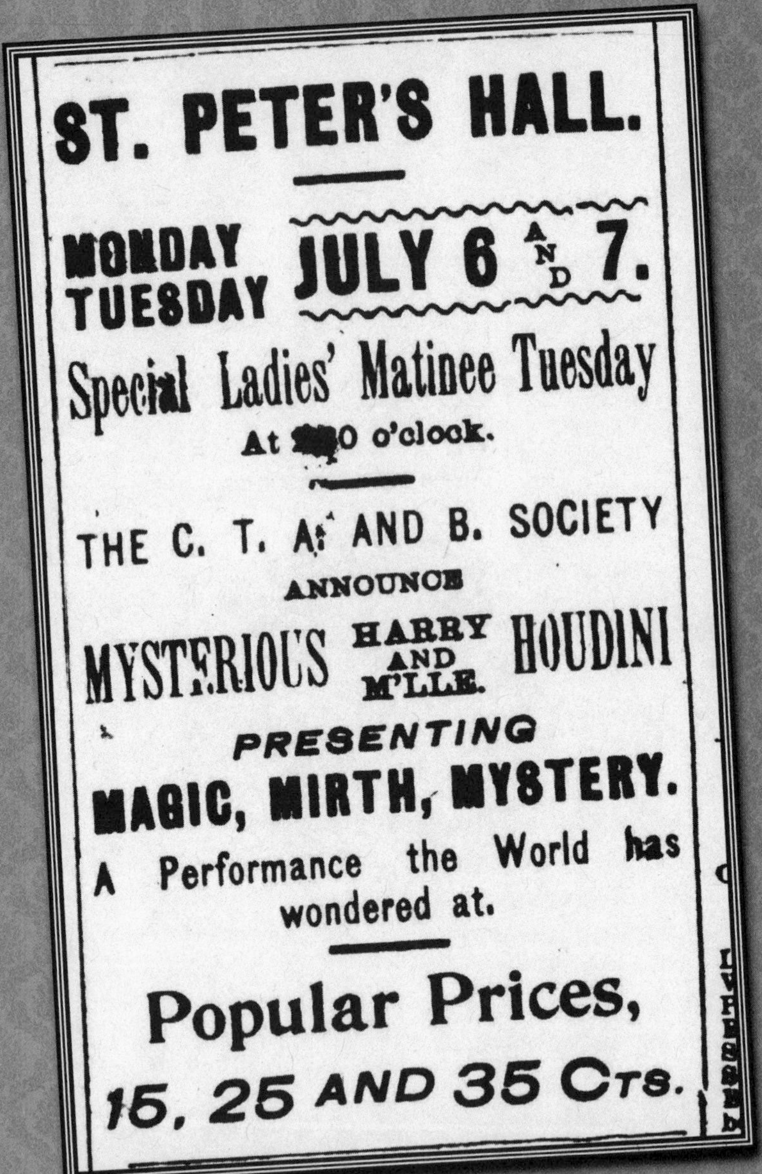

ST. PETER'S HALL.

MONDAY TUESDAY JULY 6 AND 7.

Special Ladies' Matinee Tuesday

At [illegible]0 o'clock.

THE C. T. A. AND B. SOCIETY

ANNOUNCE

MYSTERIOUS HARRY AND M'LLE. HOUDINI

PRESENTING

MAGIC, MIRTH, MYSTERY.

A Performance the World has wondered at.

Popular Prices,

15, 25 AND 35 CTS.

CHAPTER TWENTY-SEVEN

REDEMPTION

Dartmouth, Nova Scotia
Monday, July 6, to Wednesday, July 8, 1896

"I believe in myself."
—Harry Houdini speaking to a reporter days before his famous escape
from the custom-built Mirror handcuffs, *Daily Express*, London,
Monday, March 14, 1904

THE RUMBLING ENGINES COUPLED WITH the acrid smell of the coal-fired boilers aboard the *MicMac* brought back bad memories to Houdini. Thankfully, the Dartmouth ferry wouldn't torture the unseaworthy magician with a long voyage like his crossing on the SS *Yarmouth*. The large paddlewheel vessel shuttled passengers and horse carts across the mile-wide Halifax Harbour in less than half an hour.

As they disembarked in downtown Dartmouth at the foot of Portland Street, the Houdinis had to brush past the group of chronic loafers who made it their business to hang around the gates of the Dartmouth ferry station from dawn to dark. Aside from the practiced profanity of the sidewalk mob, the Dartmouth air was filled with a pungent mix of dried fish, sugar refinery caramel, and industrial smoke tinged with the pleasant odours emanating from the nearby soap and spice factory.

This Dartmouth advertisement for Harry and Beatrice Houdini's shows at St. Peter's Hall in *Atlantic Weekly* was their very first print advertisement outside of America. (Alderney Gate Public Library)

Harry Houdini's very first international performance as a headliner
was given at St. Peter's Hall on Ochterloney Street in Dartmouth.
The Hall is the first building at right. (Dartmouth Heritage Museum)

On Sunday, July 5, a brutal rainstorm pounded through the day. The rain
tapered before nightfall allowing Harry Houdini the opportunity to explore the
community of six thousand he would be performing for on Monday evening.
Dartmouth was an industrious community, home to foundries, a tannery, a rope
factory, sawmills, forty-five stores, and several hotels. The pearl of Dartmouth
industry was the downtown Starr Manufacturing plant. Starr, a medal winner at
the 1893 Chicago Columbian Exposition, was known the world over for producing
ice skates.

CATHOLIC BENEVOLENCE

One block from the harbour, at 40 Ochterloney Street, stood Houdini's upcoming
venue, St. Peter's Hall. The church hall still had a good coat of varnish on its
hardwood floors from its opening less than two years earlier. Built on the site of an
early schoolhouse, the hall was located a quarter mile from Saint Peter's Church, a
Maple Street parish anchoring a growing working-class neighbourhood with row
upon row of Maritime box-style homes.

Harry and Bessie took the Monday and Tuesday, July 6 and 7, bookings that

The town of Dartmouth circa 1896 with the ferry *MicMac* approaching from Halifax. This photo was taken by Dartmouth's Street Superintendent Watson Bishop who appeared on stage with Houdini at St. Peter's Hall. (Nova Scotia Archives)

Professor Dooley had arranged weeks earlier for his show. The Houdinis' Dartmouth stand was sponsored by the St. Peter's Catholic Total Abstinence and Benevolent Society with the blessing of their president, Alex Hutchinson.

The society was open to Catholic men between the ages of eighteen and sixty who pledged to abstain from all intoxicating drinks. All Catholic men, that is, except for Dartmouth's large contingent of brewery workers, who were forbidden to join because they were "employed in the manufacture or sale of intoxicating liquors." The society's amusement committee ran a small billiard hall and occasionally hired entertainers to work benefit shows.

On July 4, the abstinence society placed a small advertisement in the *Dartmouth Atlantic Weekly* for the Houdinis that St. Peter's Hall would be treated to "Magic, Mirth and Mystery." The Houdinis, on their first-ever trip outside of the United States, boldly added the line, "A performance the world has wondered at." Ticket prices for the Dartmouth shows were set cheaper than the Marco tickets at fifteen, twenty-five, and thirty-five cents.

Without the support of Dooley's capable assistants, the Houdinis found themselves short-handed. Their only stagehand, Kenney, already had his hands full as carpenter, prop master, and ticket taker. Harry Houdini needed some extra hands to operate the curtains and assist with his illusions. Rather than look for experienced stagehands from Halifax, Houdini hired some local Dartmouth boys, including Tim "Dee" Martin who lived with his family above a downtown store. Tim's brother John would one day become Dartmouth's most illustrious historian, writing about Houdini in his comprehensive 1957 book *The Story of Dartmouth* where he recounted his brother's experience with the magician.

By showtime on Monday night, Bessie and Harry had reason to celebrate. St. Peter's Hall was packed to capacity with Dartmouthians. Stepping onto the Dartmouth stage marked a monumental event in their lives — their very first performance as headliners outside the United States of America.

Houdini had no problem recruiting two of the town's most prominent officials for the Metamorphosis act. Thirty-year-old Daniel Brennan, who lived three blocks away from the hall at 53 Pine Street, served on Dartmouth's three-man police force and also acted as the town's health inspector and dog catcher. Brennan's days were typically spent patrolling the downtown, breaking up drunken quarrels, and reminding boys and men to cover up when bathing at Dartmouth Cove so as not to offend the ladies.

Houdini also recruited Street Superintendent Watson Bishop, who was responsible for overseeing Dartmouth's sewers and wells along with the town's wooden sidewalks and streets.

At St. Peter's Hall, the Dartmouth audience watched attentively while Houdini summoned Brennan and Bishop onstage to tie his hands and feet for the Metamorphosis illusion. The men then helped him into the large sack which they also tied off at the top. The crowded theatre tittered with excitement as the men locked the large Metamorphosis trunk lid on Houdini and wrapped it with rope. The Houdinis didn't use their usual curtained tent-styled enclosure at St. Peter's Hall. Instead, a local boy closed the right stage curtain to hide the trunk.

Seconds later, Tim Martin, who was manning the left stage curtain, glanced over at the trunk and couldn't believe his eyes. There was Harry Houdini, completely free and walking towards him! Bessie stood behind the right curtain and

Houdini's Dartmouth shows were sponsored by the St. Peter's Catholic Total Abstinence and Benevolent Society. While in Dartmouth, Houdini may have visited and possibly performed at the Mount Hope Insane Asylum. The 1896 hospital records are incomplete but the superintendent's correspondence does mention holding concerts and recitals for patients. (Archdiocese of Halifax)

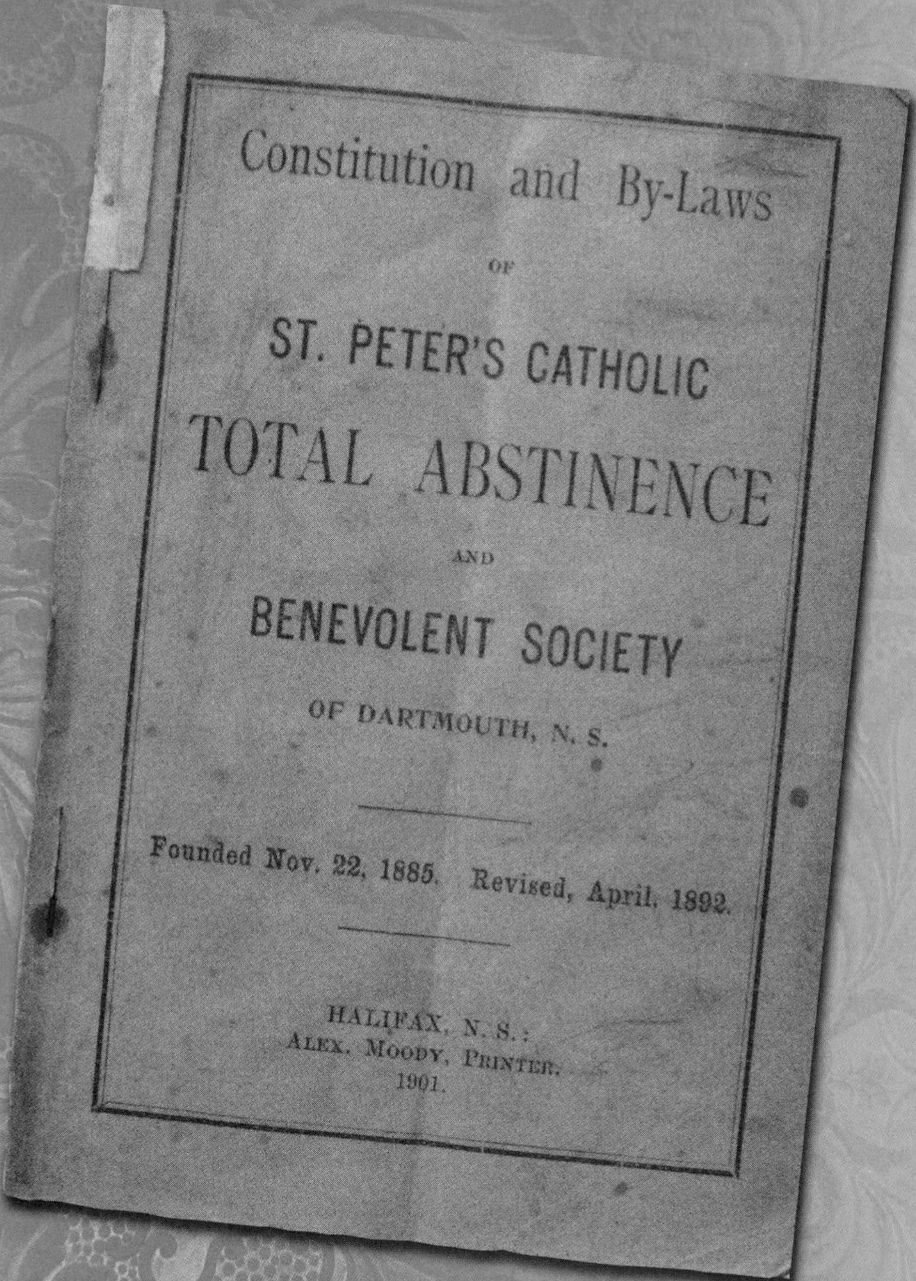

Constitution and By-Laws

OF

ST. PETER'S CATHOLIC

TOTAL ABSTINENCE

AND

BENEVOLENT SOCIETY

OF DARTMOUTH, N. S.

Founded Nov. 22, 1885. Revised, April, 1892.

HALIFAX, N. S.:
ALEX. MOODY, PRINTER.
1901.

told the audience she would clap three times and instantly change places with Houdini in the trunk.

The young Martin boy watched with his mouth open as Houdini clapped three times in place of Bessie. In his state of bewilderment, Tim didn't notice Bessie had disappeared into the trunk. At the third clap, the curtain was flung open revealing Houdini standing where Bessie had been just seconds before. The illusion was so startling that the Houdinis had grown accustomed to the typical audience reaction—silence. After a few seconds to recover from the unexpected shock of seeing Harry and not Bessie, the Dartmouth crowd let loose with a wild round of applause. Houdini and the stage boys quickly untied the trunk to reveal Bessie inside the sack with her hands tied behind her back. The crowd applauded again after Bessie was untied and took a centre stage bow with her husband.

For the first time in over a month, the Houdinis had played to a full house. Even the *Acadian Recorder,* on the Halifax side, reported on the successful stand, but with a curious reference to Professor Dooley's now-defunct show. "The performances of Marco at St. Peter's Hall attracted good houses Monday and Tuesday."

On Tuesday, the heavy rain returned and fell without respite all day long. Nonetheless, the Houdinis held a special ladies matinee at 2:30. St. Peter's Hall was packed again for their evening show. The Tuesday evening show was supposed to be the Houdinis' third and final Dartmouth appearance. But the Catholic Benevolent Society had other plans for the couple as noted in Dartmouth's paper, the *Atlantic Weekly.* "The Houdinis presented their wonderful performance in St. Peter's Hall on Monday and Tuesday evenings as advertised and also held their Tuesday afternoon matinee. The entertainment proved so popular that it was necessary for the managers to repeat Wednesday, on which day they gave a matinee admitting all for ten cents."

Unfortunately, the Houdinis couldn't extend their success in Dartmouth beyond their fourth show on Wednesday afternoon. St. Peter's Hall had to ready itself for one of the biggest events of the year—a three-day strawberry social and fair that was to be a fundraiser for a new Saint Peter's Church. The fair promised good eats along with the sale of "useful and fancy articles." It also offered musical entertainment with the Harpers and a Dartmouth favourite—the obligatory pie-eating contest, a tradition that was repeated many times at the Dartmouth hall that stood until 1983, when it was demolished to make way for a gravel parking lot.

Policeman Daniel Brennan
handcuffed Houdini on stage at
St. Peter's Hall on July 6, 1896.
Brennan, who was born on
Sable Island, gave up policing to
operate a grocery business before
opening an REO car dealership.
(Noella Brennan Fisher Collection)

The ladies organizing the fancy fair and strawberry festival at St. Peter's Hall sent a note about their fundraiser to the *Echo* newspaper. They also included a note about the Houdinis. "The mysterious Harry Houdini, a skilled magician, introducing the latest Oriental and modern miracles, assisted by Mlle. Bessie Houdini, the wonderful clairvoyant medium, who will answer all questions given her in sealed envelopes, is performing through the province."[1]

The ladies of Saint Peter's Church were correct—the Houdinis were indeed continuing their tour through Nova Scotia. If they had planned on returning to America after their Dartmouth stand, their marvellous success at St. Peter's Hall had changed their minds.

On this beautiful summer day, with their confidence riding high and their purse full, the young couple boarded a train bound for a Nova Scotia railway town—a town where Harry Houdini would accept a challenge...and wish he hadn't.

>-!-<>-•-○-•-<>-!-<

DEAR
HEARTS IN
DARTMOUTH

THE HOUDINIS were given a special welcome when they first landed in Dartmouth. The same 1936 article that described the sheriff's actions at the academy on Dominion Day, also recalled a heartening episode. Referring to the Houdinis, the article states, "Dartmouth citizens came to the aid of the unfortunate couple. A benefit performance was arranged across the harbor, and stage hands dug deep to provide enough money for the passage to the states of Mr. and Mrs. Houdini."[2]

The short write-up also names two individuals who came to the Houdinis' aid. "Mr. Fraser and A. Brunt, of Halifax, are perhaps the only two Haligonians living who contributed to the purse collected to help the magician get back to New York."[3]

Perhaps out of pride, Houdini never mentioned accepting charity following the collapse of the Marco show. He offered few details when he wrote about the incident. "Our show closed in Halifax, Nova Scotia, and I thereon determined to proceed by myself, and give the whole show."[4]

Houdini apparently never forgot the kindness of Allen Fraser, a Halifax printer who later became a photographer. Houdini dined with Fraser in Boston following his 1910 world tour where the escape artist became the first man to fly a plane in Australia. There is no record of Houdini ever reconnecting with the donor Alfred Brunt, a Halifax fireman.

Dartmouth's kind charity was just the start. Before they moved on, the Houdinis would have even more fond memories of the friendly town to carry close to their hearts.

Harry Houdini made several acquaintances in Halifax and Dartmouth including Allen Fraser. Fraser is remembered for images he took of the aftermath of the 1917 Halifax Explosion. (Nova Scotia Archives)

CHAPTER TWENTY-EIGHT

TIED UP IN TRURO

Truro, Nova Scotia
Wednesday, July 15, and Thursday, July 16, 1896

"String me up just as high as you can. If I drop I want to be sure
it's going to be the finish. I'd rather have a lily in my hand
than go through life crippled and a burden to others."
—Harry Houdini before being hoisted upside down
from an office tower in San Antonio, Texas, 1916

AFTER ALMOST A FULL MONTH within a stone's throw of Halifax Harbour, Harry, Bessie, and Kenney finally left Nova Scotia's capital and arrived in Truro, where they were booked to play two nights. With a week between their Dartmouth and Truro stands, it's possible the Houdinis tried to pick up at least one date along the way.

As they disembarked in Truro, the Houdinis knew they had arrived in a busy and prosperous town. Truro, which was noisy and dusty thanks to the ongoing trenching for new water lines and the installation of more street lighting, was the fourth largest town in Nova Scotia with a population topping five thousand. The

Houdini wrote a book in which he warned aspiring escape artists that, "The first thing for the performer to ascertain is, if any member of the committee has followed the sea, or for any other reason is familiar with knots. If such a one is found he should be used for tests where difficult knots and secure binding does not interfere with the effect." (Library of Congress)

local economy was thriving thanks to factories and mills like the one owned by Charles Stanfield that made underwear featuring the innovative drop seat.

Over twenty trains made scheduled arrivals and departures from Truro every day, including two daily express trains to Boston. Across from the rail station, the Esplanade was flanked by several large hotels offering high-end accommodations and fine dining. Much like the Carleton Hotel in Halifax or the Hotel Dufferin in Saint John, the Learmont was the hotel of choice for entertainers playing Truro.

Harry Houdini and Kenney only had to transport their props and trunks across the street from the train station. The seven-hundred-seat Gunn's Opera House was located on the top floor of Daniel Gunn's building at the Esplanade end of Inglis Street. The two-year-old theatre featured seating laid out in a semi-circular fashion on a sloped floor. Houdini had his choice of four dressing rooms and five complete sets of scenery.

Theatre companies visiting Truro promoted their shows by displaying their photographs in the windows of the Prince Street pharmacy, a jeweller, and G.B. Faulkner's music store on Inglis Street. The Houdinis would have to be careful about what posters they put up in the store windows. Bessie Houdini often appeared in tights with a short tutu-styled skirt. It was a standard stage outfit for a showgirl of the day, but it wasn't acceptable in this town. Truro's council had recently passed a bylaw stating, "No person shall post up or exhibit any indecent or immoral placards, writings or pictures, or shall put up or exhibit any pictures of the human form in a nude or seminude state or in what is known as 'tights,' or shall perform any indecent, immoral or lewd play or other representation within the town."[1]

Houdini had two policemen to work with in Truro, James McKenzie and William Green. During Houdini's visit, the two lawmen were keeping a watchful eye out for low-life. Reports of American pickpockets appeared in Truro and across Nova Scotia. Many of the professional thieves had come to the Maritimes with Walter Main's circus and were sticking around for the upcoming Halifax Carnival. Houdini had no luck involving the busy policemen in his pre-show publicity. Or if he did, the local paper didn't see fit to report on the interaction. But a small note in Saturday's paper offered some information about the unknown Houdinis: "The mysterious Harry Houdini, a skilled magician, introducing the latest Oriental and Modern Miracles, assisted by Mlle. Bessie Houdini, the wonderful Clairvoyant Medium, who will answer all questions given her in sealed envelopes, will appear in the Opera Hall here on the 15 and 16 of July. These performers are said to be

The interior of Gunn's Opera House. (Colchester Historeum)

among the best magicians who have ever visited our Province. Those interested in this kind of entertainment will be well pleased with these people."[2] The wording of the small promotional blurb was almost identical to the note published following the Dartmouth stand, suggesting Harry felt he should capitalize on Bessie's mind-reading act.

On Wednesday, under the headline, "A Wonderful Event," another note about the Houdinis appeared in the *Truro Daily News*. "That a human being is able to read another's mind is demonstrated by Mlle. Houdini, who appears at Gunn's Opera House tonight. Houdini is also a Wonderful Worker, and the Halifax and Saint John Newspapers speak in highest praise of the show."

SHOWTIME IN TRURO

Houdini opened Wednesday's show with traditional sleight-of-hand magic, stretching the opening set by throwing in some extra card tricks. While some of the grander illusions like the Cremation of Floribel were now gone, courtesy of Harshaw Clarke and the Halifax sheriff, Houdini still had the apparatus required to perform the *Trilby* levitation. A full theatrical production of the *Trilby* novel had played Gunn's months earlier. But this was the first time Truro had seen the *Trilby*-inspired levitation illusion.

After Bessie was released from her hypnotic *Trilby* trance, it was time for Houdini's escape act. Luckily for Houdini, he already had a policeman in the house. When he opened his theatre two years earlier, Daniel Gunn made a promise to the citizens of Truro: "Take warning: In operating my new Opera House I am

CONSTABLE WILLIAM GREEN
1884 TRURO POLICE DEPT. 1903

Policeman Green handcuffed
Houdini on stage at Gunn's
Opera House on July 15, 1896.
Green's whistle is still on display
at the Truro Police Station.

(Truro Police Service)

determined that good order shall be maintained and that it shall be kept clean and decent. To this end I will have a policeman present at every performance."[3]

On the Houdinis' opening night, sixty-year-old Constable William Green was on duty at the theatre. Before joining the Truro police department ten years earlier, Green worked on a large stock farm at Oakfield. For Green, moonlighting at Gunn's augmented his policeman's salary of $8.25 a week.

When summoned by Houdini, the constable made his way onto the stage and shook hands with the escape artist. After Green handcuffed Houdini, the magician retired to a small curtained enclosure. Within seconds he returned with Green's unlocked handcuffs.

The performance continued with Professor Dooley's Cabinet of Phantoms. Spirit manifestations had been summoned in Truro before, by performers including Willis Skinner. Anna Eva Fay also performed the spirit cabinet at Gunn's on a stopover show between her Halifax and Moncton appearances the previous summer.

After the spirits were sent packing, a blindfolded Bessie performed her mind-reading and clairvoyant act at centre stage. The Houdinis closed with their signature illusion, Metamorphosis. As with all the Houdinis' shows in the Maritimes so far, Metamorphosis was the most well-received performance of the evening. A brief review in Thursday's *Truro Daily News* mentioned the Gunn's audience was "delighted" by the show. Houdini clipped the sentence and pasted it in his press book right below one of his small advertisements from the Truro paper.

For their second night in the opera house, the couple performed the same show with one exception; Houdini would not repeat the handcuff escape. Instead, he would accept a challenge to be rope-tied by a member of the audience.

In his 1915 book, *Magical Rope Ties and Escapes*, Houdini suggests that rope escapes were often more impressive than opening handcuffs: "Rope ties have one distinct advantage over all other forms of escape, namely, no possible suspicion is attached to the ropes themselves. In many cases where locks, chains, handcuffs, trunks, pillories and the like are used, the apparatus is more or less under suspicion." Houdini also recalled that the mid-1890s was a period of evolution in his rope escape act that saw him do his rope escapes in full view of the audience. Escapes from handcuff and leg irons were still tackled in a curtained cabinet, but Houdini believed "In straight escapes [i.e. rope escapes] the cabinet hopelessly weakens the effect."[4]

Houdini wrote that his goal with rope escape challenges was to "prove that I can free myself in less time than is required to secure me."[5] To keep him honest, a member of the audience or a stage assistant would be provided with a stopwatch. Houdini's rope-tying challengers were generally upstanding citizens like local politicians or town officials. Try as they might, the committee members rarely had much experience with ropes. Even sailors, who were masters of knots and ropes, lacked experience tying a live person.

On this evening in Truro, an unknown man in the audience accepted Houdini's challenge. Almost immediately, Houdini realized this stranger was no slouch with ropes or knots. This man had come to the theatre with serious intent—and his own rope! According to the stopwatch, he spent a full eight minutes roping Houdini's hands and feet. And then Houdini went to work.

Typically, Houdini would first free himself from whatever binding method was used to restrain his arms. More often than not, challengers tried to thwart him by trussing his wrists to his ankles behind his back. Once his arms were free, he would manoeuvre his hands to the front of his body. This would allow him to gnash at the wrist knots with his teeth. Once his hands were free, Houdini could make quick work of untying the ropes at his ankles and elsewhere. But on this night in Truro, something went wrong.

Houdini struggled to escape from the expertly tied rope for a full nine and a half minutes. Houdini had finally failed a rope challenge—and by a full minute and a half. Unfortunately for Houdini, a Truro reporter witnessed the failed challenge and included it in his review of the show. Needless to say, Harry Houdini didn't paste this article into his press book.

Twenty years later, Houdini warned young escape artists to be prepared for the worst if they chose to perform in full view of an audience. "Your show will require a great deal of strenuous and intelligent rehearsing, for you will eventually encounter a committee who will bind you so tightly that you will have to struggle for your life—that is to say, for your freedom."[6]

This incident contributed to a policy that Houdini would keep the rest of his career: never let the audience supply their own rope. Silver Lake sash cord was Houdini's preference. He would never use brand new rope but worked the rope until it reached a certain degree of softness that made untying knots much easier.

Later in his career, Houdini more or less admitted he had occasionally failed rope escapes in the past: "I have rarely missed finishing within the specified time." After one show in New York where he was accused of failing a rope escape on purpose to elicit extra publicity, Houdini fired back: "I hereby put it on record that I never have played with an audience, but always freed myself from ropes, fetters, or other restraints as quickly as I possibly could."[7]

ONWARD TO CUMBERLAND COUNTY

On Friday, as the Houdinis prepared to depart Truro, Sir Charles Tupper arrived in the town accompanied by his wife and son. The defeated prime minister was on his way to his summer home overlooking the Northwest Arm on Quinpool Road in Halifax. It is unlikely Houdini interacted with Tupper in Truro, but almost a century later, the two men would be linked by a chilling coincidence (see Epilogue 3).

The Friday edition of the *Truro Daily News* reported on the Houdinis' next show. "This Company plays Saturday at Springhill, where we bespeak for them a good audience, as their entertainment is worthy of patronage." Perhaps this was the plan, but it wasn't going to come to fruition for at least another week.

One thing that's certain is Houdini was ultimately heading to a coal mining town located high atop the beautiful Cumberland hills. Harry and Bessie Houdini were about to discover that fortune telling wasn't always a phony stage act. Sometimes it had life and death consequences.

Springhill had fifty-six widows and one hundred and sixty-five fatherless children to prove it.

Adelaide Herrmann almost stole the Halifax shows from her famous husband. In his report to the *New York Dramatic Mirror*, Halifax manager Harshaw Clarke wrote, "He [Alexander] made an immense success, and Madame Herrmann made a furor." (Harvard Theatre Collection, Houghton Library, Harvard University)

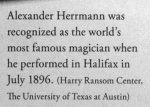

HERMANN "THE GREAT"

Anné Dupont   574 FIFTH AVENUE NEW YORK

THE COMPETITION

Alexander Herrmann was recognized as the world's most famous magician when he performed in Halifax in July 1896. (Harry Ransom Center, The University of Texas at Austin)

(top) Magician William Robinson was Herrmann's
assistant for many years, including the 1896 Halifax
appearance. This letter from Houdini's personal collection
appears to be the first exchange between the two magicians.

(above right) William Robinson in the guise of Chinese conjuror Chung Ling Soo.
Offstage Robinson spoke in made-up gibberish that passed for Chinese
fooling reporters who interviewed him through an "interpreter."

(Harry Ransom Center, The University of Texas at Austin)

AT NINE O'CLOCK Sunday evening, the SS *Olivette* bumped up against the jetty at the Plant Wharf in Halifax Harbour. The Boston steamship always drew a cluster of Haligonians, but on this night the cluster turned into a crowd.

The onlookers took over the Plant Wharf and spilled over to the adjacent piers. As the crowd surged forward, a small boy got pushed off the dock and splashed into the harbour. The *Olivette*'s crew wrung cheers from the crowd when they turned on their searchlight and swept it across the dark harbour as the boy was plucked from the chilly waters.

After several failed attempts to control the crowd with rope barricades, the passengers finally disembarked. One of the passengers was Alexander Herrmann, the world's greatest magician and his wife and co-star, Adelaide. The fifty-two-year-old "Herrmann the Great" was arriving on the eve of the week-long Halifax Carnival, and the city, much like the wharves, was overflowing with visitors. Herrmann was ready to cash in on the popular carnival with a week-long stand at the Academy of Music.

Herrmann's manager, Edward Thurmer, had already been in the city for a full week with an advance team of carpenters and electricians, preparing the Academy of Music for an elaborate show. Thurmer had handled the Herrmann promotions well; the *Echo* noted that photographs of Adelaide Herrmann "are to be seen almost everywhere in Halifax."

Among Herrmann's entourage was a magician named William Ellsworth Robinson. Houdini would introduce himself to Robinson in an 1897 letter, initiating a correspondence that saw the two become close friends, confidants, and eventually, rivals. Much of Herrmann's success was thanks to Robinson's mechanical ingenuity and creative illusions. In 1900, after assuming the persona of a silent Chinese conjurer named Chung Ling Soo, Robinson took command of British stages for the next eighteen years until his career, and life, came to a horrific end in front of a packed London theatre. On that night in 1918, Chung Ling Soo died in a pool of blood when his bullet-catching trick went terribly wrong.

Coincidentally, Houdini's father was related by marriage to Alexander

Hermann's late brother, Compars, also a magician. Houdini once wrote about the connection between the two men in a letter to a fellow magician. "My dear old Dad and Compars Herrmann were great companions, and for business reasons have never given out the facts, because they might think that at one time I was seeking publicity."[8] Honourably, the publicity master, Houdini, never would use his late father's Herrmann connection to promote his own career.

The carnival drew thousands of tourists to Halifax. Every hotel room in the city was booked, forcing the carnival committee to offer accommodations in private houses. Thanks to the influx of visitors, the advance tickets for Herrmann's seven shows at the Academy of Music were selling out quickly—and they were among the most expensive in the history of the theatre with the best seats costing a full dollar. The academy's manager, Harshaw Clarke, took the unusual step of restricting advance ticket sales to a maximum of four tickets per person.

Herrmann opened on Monday evening to a sold-out house.

The applause lasted minutes as Haligonians welcomed the satanic-looking performer, who entered wearing a classic tuxedo with white gloves, sporting his trademark pointed goatee and freshly waxed moustache. Once the crowd settled down, Herrmann offered a warning to his audience, "The closer you watch me, the less you will see."[9]

Herrmann began his show with some traditional sleight-of-hand work. William E. Robinson once described Herrmann's astonishing sleight-of-hand work in *Scientific American*. "His hands were trained to a marvelous state of responsiveness. His misdirection was simply beyond description. If his eyes looked in a certain direction, yours were bound to follow them, as if compelled to do so by some mysterious power."

After Herrmann finished his opening solo set—which included rabbits, canaries, watches, cards, and pistols—Adelaide joined him on stage for their *Trilby* illusion, the original production that Professor Dooley and many others had copied. Rumours circulating in Halifax pegged the cost of Adelaide's *Trilby* dress and diamond necklace at over

seven hundred dollars, enough money to purchase a house in the city.

Next, Herrmann's company performed a trunk trick very similar to the Houdinis' Metamorphosis. After a wildly applauded set of dances performed by Adelaide, came the magnificent Artist's Dream illusion, which began with Herrmann painting a picture of his lover. As he contemplates the painting he falls asleep. Suddenly, the subject of the painting comes to life and steps out of the picture frame and wakes the artist.

By the time the Herrmanns closed the evening, the audience had been entertained for three hours. The Herrmanns were forced to make several curtain calls and finally conceded to an encore performance to send their Halifax admirers home happy. The triumphant scene repeated itself for the entire week until they closed with a final performance on Saturday, attended by a large military contingent led by the admiral and the Governor General.

The Herrmanns would never return to Canada. After performing in Rochester, New York, five months later, Alexander Herrmann died on his private railcar, en route to a show in Pennsylvania, on December 17, 1896.

In spite of decades spent filling theatres and living at a magnificent nineteen-acre estate on Long Island Sound, Alexander Herrmann died poor. His widow Adelaide was forced to auction off most of the treasures the couple had purchased while touring the world. Amongst the thousands of exotic auction items, including a tooth from Napoleon's horse and an ivory skull, was listing number 1213, a souvenir silver spoon from Halifax, Nova Scotia.

During his triumphant stand in Halifax, Herrmann's legacy as the world's greatest magician was already in jeopardy. His successor would so ruthlessly overshadow the nineteenth-century conjurer, that Herrmann the Great would be all but obliterated from record.

In July 1896 that successor was seventy miles north of Halifax, struggling to fill small halls in Cumberland County, Nova Scotia. Yet this young man would one day be hailed the world over as the greatest magician in history— Harry Houdini.

Springhill, Nova Scotia
Saturday, July 25, and Monday, July 27, 1896

"There's a lot in that; You [*sic*] can tell a bank clerk from a bricklayer."
—Harry Houdini replying to a question about the science of palm reading
from the Advertising Club of Boston, September 21, 1926,
Boston Globe, September 22, 1926

THE HOUDINIS CHANGED TRAINS in Springhill Junction, rolling the last five miles into Springhill on board a clattering coal company train. Built atop one of the highest hills in Cumberland County, the town of five thousand offered a splendid view of the gentle rolling Cumberland hills, receding to the horizon in every direction, with nary a hint of the blue sea that otherwise defines Nova Scotia.

Houdini had competition in Springhill. Harry Lindley's large repertory company, fresh from two shows in nearby Acadia Mines (now known as Londonderry), was in town for the week. The British-born Lindley, no stranger to Springhillers, had been playing the North American circuit for more than forty years. Both an actor and a singer, Lindley could tell Houdini some hard luck stories about the entertainment business. Aside from his debtor's stay in a Halifax jail years

Trained bears entertaining the locals on Main Street
in Springhill, circa 1896. (Springhill Heritage Group)

earlier, Lindley had been treated to a stint in a Saint John lock-up after another Maritime show collapsed and creditors had him arrested.

Lindley brought his Big Show Company to Springhill for a reason. By 1896 the coal mining settlement had earned a reputation as an entertainment-loving town. Earlier in the year, the Wallace Hopper Company sold out five nights in a row at Fraser's Hall. So far this summer, the Webling Sisters, Rose Sydell's London Belles, and Professor Wormwood's Monkey Theatre all opened to big houses here. The profitable shows inspired Mr. Fraser to buy a downtown lot and begin planning for a new one-thousand-seat theatre to replace his existing Main Street venue.

Houdini was shut out of Fraser's Hall because of Harry Lindley's company. Instead, Houdini booked the coal miners' union hall. Pioneer Hall, newly re-shingled after a fire burned out most of Main Street in August 1895, was rarely used by travelling shows, but Harry Houdini somehow managed to book two nights: Saturday, July 25, and the following Monday.

Springhill offered Houdini only one policeman to help promote the Pioneer Hall shows. The uniformed Samuel Richmond could easily be found on his regular patrol, keeping loafers moving along before they made a mess of the town's sidewalks with their tobacco juice. But the newspaper made no mention of the policeman trying his handcuffs on Houdini. The other Harry, Harry Lindley, upstaged Houdini in the promotions game when his entire company played a friendly baseball match against some of the locals. Lindley made even more friends in the community when he hired the Springhill Band to accompany his troupe.

On Thursday, July 23, the *Springhill Advertiser* republished one of the Halifax articles about Houdini's Escape from Dorchester act. Houdini added a line that proves he was hedging on Bessie's mind-reading act to be popular with the townsfolk. "But the manner in which Mlle Houdini answers all sorts of questions while in a trance, actually reading the very mind, is simply marvelous and is worth going a journey of 100 miles to see."

Before anyone even had a chance to cough up the fifteen to thirty-five cents to see his show, Houdini extracted a few bucks from some unsuspecting "Hillers" in a poker game. As a public service announcement, the *Springhill Advertiser* ran a friendly warning about the slick showman in town fleecing the miners at poker. "Don't play poker with mysterious Harry Houdini. He is a slippery cuss with the cards. He beats playing cards and card shakers always keep shy of him as he generally does them good and plenty are going to learn to play poker at Pioneer

In Springhill, Bessie Houdini was called a "clever little woman."
Here in a photo snapped by Harry Houdini, Bessie (right) is cleverly
imitating a rather stern-looking lady. (Library of Congress)

Hall." Wisely, Houdini chose not to keep the warning note for his press book. But he did paste in the advertisement from the paper along with several tiny notices that stated "The hand is slicker than the eye go and see Houdini Pioneer Hall Sat. 25," and "Houdini is going to visit our town don't fail to see him."

Like card-playing coal miners everywhere, the Springhill men were a superstitious lot — especially where women were concerned. For instance, it was considered bad luck to see a woman on the way to work in the morning. The miners must have been intrigued by a note printed in the Springhill paper that read, "Bessie Houdini is certainly a clever little woman and is quite famous as a mind reader."

Bessie Houdini was indeed a clever little woman. Harry liked this description of his wife so much that he clipped the sentence and carefully pasted it in his press book. The couple had a fine mind-reading act in store for Springhillers. Houdini would work the crowd, asking audience members to show him a coin from their pocket, and then instruct them to hold it tightly in their hand while concentrating on the coin's date. A blindfolded Bessie seated at centre stage would read their mind to "see" the date for herself, always managing to call out the correct date.

SECOND-SIGHT

The Houdinis polished the coin-reading act during their stint with the Welsh Brothers Circus. The secret was a code used to feed Bessie the numbers making up the date on the coin. Bessie had to pay careful attention to Houdini's prattle to pick up on this pre-arranged code:

Pray = 1   Please = 6

Answer = 2   Speak = 7

Say = 3   Quickly = 8

Now = 4   Look = 9

Tell = 5   Be quick = 10

To feed Bess the numbers for a coin with an 1896 date, Houdini would simply blurt out nonsense containing the code for the four digits: "I **pray** you will **quickly look** at this coin... **please** tell us the date Mademoiselle Houdini."

The coin reading was only a warm-up for the second sight act where Bessie played the role of a fortune teller. Behind the scenes, Houdini called this act, "Looking into the future as well as the past."

Houdini would seek out the town's local gossiper and stock up on details of any local mysteries, disappearances, and murders. In Springhill, a good selection of talkative locals could always be found hanging around the Royal Hotel, where a sample room allowed local farmers and crafters to sell their goods. But on any evening, Houdini could strike gossip gold at Fraser's Hall. A crowd of storytellers could always be found at the entrance to the Main Street theatre, located directly across from the post office. Known in Springhill as "doorstep philosophers," these chatty loiterers had actually worn out Mr. Fraser's clapboard from leaning against the exterior wall while spending hours embroiled in conversation.

A smart operator like Houdini would have no problem getting some racy Springhill rumours to throw into Bessie's second-sight act. Likewise, he could gently steer the conversation toward mysterious events or unsolved crimes that took place in the town. In 2012 the town of Springhill maintains a Liar's Bench to commemorate the centuries-old tradition of storytelling on the streets of Springhill.

The second-sight act took a great deal of preparation and communication between Harry and Bessie. But the normally cooperative Bessie recalled a funny story about turning rogue on her husband while performing the act in the Maritimes:

Grand, Brilliant, Bewildering and Startling Spiritualistic Seance, given by

..Prof. Harry Houdini..

The Great Mystifier,

ASSISTED BY

Mlle. Beatrice Houdini

The Celebrated Psycrometic Clairvoyant

Spiritual forms materialized, tables and musical instruments float in midair when conditions are favorable; messages received from dead and departed friends.

The Houdinis used this image to promote their second-sight act in the mid-1890s. (Public domain)

I recall one evening, in a town over the Canadian border, Houdini had put me in a trance, and I was reading sealed messages from persons at the séance and answering them, according to our system. One of the questions read: "Where is my brother John? I have not heard from him in nineteen years (signed) Mary Murphy."

For such questions the answer was invariably simple and evasive like, "You will shortly hear from him, as he is on his way to you." But I had a lively recollection of a Mrs. John Murphy who kept an ice-cream parlor near the Weiss home in New York. Houdini was a great pal of hers and often spoke to her. So to Houdini's astonishment my reply broke all the rules of the game: "You will find your brother," I said "at East Seventy-Second Street, New York."

This seemed a harmless answer to me, for by the time Mary Murphy wrote and got a reply, we would be safe in another town.

But Mary Murphy fooled us. She wired. John Murphy of East Seventy-Second Street, New York, was indeed Mary Murphy's long lost brother, and if some bold realist had subsequently tried to explain to the good people of that Canadian town that Houdini and I really had no inside knowledge of the spirit world, no second sight, no occult knowledge whatever, he would have courted tar and feathers.[1]

Given Houdini's local research and his gifted stage ability as a showman, coupled with Bessie's improvised answers, audiences everywhere bought the second-sight routine hook, line, and sinker. Houdini recalled one such victorious second-sight act: "I had gone around to the cemeteries and read all of the inscriptions on the tombstones, looked over a few birth and death records and acquired a lot of information from the gossips. But the crowd was so anxious my information began to run out. Then I was amazed to find that no matter what was said it applied to somebody in the audience."[2] But as Bessie recounted, the couple dropped the money-making act along with private séances not long after this Maritime tour. "The work brought in a surer income than the concert halls, and the surroundings were cleaner, but very soon Houdini found that he could not go on with it. He was too straightforward for that. The people were so pitiable, so trustful. Our messages probably gave them comfort, but it was false comfort at best."[3]

HARRY AND HARRY PART WAYS

While the Springhill newspaper published a long, detailed review of Harry Lindley's performance, precious few details about the Houdinis' shows were reported. The lone review of the shows at Pioneer Hall read, "The concerts given by the mysterious Harry Houdini in Pioneer Hall on Saturday and Monday evening were the best of its kind ever given in Springhill."[4] The only other reference to Houdini's visit to Springhill was a single sentence reading, "Two show companies were in town on Saturday and Monday nights."[5]

Harry Lindley was spending a few more days in Springhill before heading north to play Dorchester, New Brunswick. The *Advertiser* reported, "Mr. Lindley made many friends during his short stay with us." Unfortunately, Mr. Lindley didn't make any money during his stay, losing over $100 in the coal town. Nonetheless, he offered his final performance free of charge as a benefit to raise money for the Springhill musicians who had accompanied his troupe. The local musicians returned Lindley's classy gesture with one of their own—as an act of respect for the old showman, the band refused to accept the cash raised by the benefit.

Tuesday was the only day off before the Houdinis' next show. As his southbound train left Springhill Junction, Houdini had to focus on promoting his upcoming shows in a town that had given birth to one of the world's greatest mysteries, thanks to writer Sir Arthur Conan Doyle.

> ⊶ I ◀◈▸ ○ ◀◈▸ I ⊷

IN SPRINGHILL, Nova Scotia, the locals would be able to teach any magician a heartbreaking lesson about clairvoyance. No magician—not even Harry Houdini—could ever top an ominous prophecy made by a real-life fortune teller who, to this day, remains a local legend.

Ellen Creighton was born at sea as her family emigrated from Scotland in 1833. She grew up in Miramichi, New Brunswick, marrying an Acadian named Edward Coo before moving to Stellarton, Nova Scotia, where she gave birth to six children.

In 1880 Ellen, a revered tea-leaf reader, forewarned an explosion would devastate a local coal mine on November 12, 1880. Some women hid their husband's boots and clothes,

Town of Springhill, N. S.

The town of Springhill with collieries visible in the background. Old Mother Coo (1833-1912) predicted the 1891 Springhill mine explosion that killed one hundred twenty-five men and boys.
(Mary Willa Littler Collection)

OLD
MOTHER
COO

while others broke down crying, begging their men to take the day off. At 6:30 a.m., high levels of methane gas in the Foord Pit exploded, killing forty-four men working the south side of the pit.

When her husband died in 1888, Ellen Coo moved to Boston. In 1891, by then known as Old Mother Coo, she sent word that a mine explosion would occur in Springhill, Nova Scotia, before Easter. In response to Coo's prophecy, provincial inspectors, union representatives, and company officials toured the thirteen-hundred-foot-deep mine, declaring it to be perfectly safe with adequate ventilation and no large amounts of volatile gas.

But the inspectors were dead wrong.

Five weeks before Easter, on February 21, 1891, an explosion tore through the east slope of the Springhill coal mine. One hundred-and-twenty-five men and boys were

Caskets containing victims of the 1891 explosion are hauled by horse sleighs to the Springhill cemetery. Horses and coal miners forged strong bonds while working underground together. When brought to the surface, horses had to be blindfolded until their eyes could adjust to the sun. (Nova Scotia Archives)

killed. Once again, Ellen Coo had made a tragically correct prediction. No surprise to the surviving miners who worked day and night, chipping away at the frozen ground to dig graves for their fallen brothers.

Houdini couldn't have missed hearing the story or seeing the explosion monument at the highest point of Main Street. The white marble statue, since moved to a central location, listed the names of the victims, many of whom still had widows and children living in the town. In his later years, Houdini conducted experiments intended to help miners who become trapped underground. Dr. McConnell at the United States Bureau of Mines complimented Houdini's research. "He was sincere and honest in every detail. He knew exactly what he was doing and he's studied every phase of the work."[6]

In his book *A Magician Among the Spirits*, Harry Houdini offers a heartfelt apology for his days spent cashing in on grieving audience members, like those in Springhill,

with a fake second-sight act. "I did not see or understand the seriousness of trifling with such sacred sentimentality. After delving deep I realized the seriousness of it all. I was brought to a realization of the seriousness of trifling with the hallowed reverence which the average human being bestows on the departed, and when I personally became afflicted with similar grief I was chagrined that I should ever have been guilty of such frivolity and for the first time realized that it bordered on crime."

Houdini would live the rest of his life knowing what the Springhillers knew: Old Mother Coo *had* predicted two coal mine disasters. Houdini couldn't possibly know if real spiritualists walked this earth, but he would spend the rest of his life looking for them. Unlike the ridiculous Boston medium and fraudster Margery Crandon, whom Houdini exposed in 1924, Mother Coo lived quietly at her East Boston home until she died on November 1, 1912.

CHAPTER THIRTY

WHERE MYSTERY
SETS SAIL

Parrsboro, Nova Scotia
Wednesday, July 29, and Thursday, July 30, 1896

"Houdini is far and away the most curious and intriguing character
whom I have ever encountered."
—Sir Arthur Conan Doyle in *AC Doyle: The New Revelation*

AFTER A TWENTY-SEVEN-MILE passage through the rolling Cumberland countryside, Harry and Bessie Houdini disembarked in Parrsboro, a town of two thousand on the Minas Basin. Little is known about Houdini's visit to the town, except that he posted the dates—albeit a week late—in the August 1 edition of the *New York Clipper*. Since Parrsboro records and newspapers from the time are incomplete and offer no mention of Houdini, this is the only evidence we have that the couple visited the town.

By Wednesday, the Halifax papers had reached Parrsboro, allowing Houdini to read the rave reviews of Herrmann's performances. The *Acadian Recorder* didn't hold back its praise: "Halifax has been visited by many magicians, but all pale into complete insignificance after seeing Herrmann, as one realizes that all others are almost mere imitators of a finished artist."

Magicians and fast friends Harry Kellar and Harry Houdini.
(Library of Congress)

Never one to lack confidence, Houdini wrote to Alexander Herrmann during his summer tour, hoping to land assistant roles for himself and Bessie. He also applied to Herrmann's principal rival, Harry Kellar, who wrote back declining Houdini's offer. But Herrmann never responded; or possibly Herrmann's reply, intended to reach Houdini per his published *New York Clipper* itinerary, simply languished unopened in a Maritime village's post office.

Fresh from Springhill, where Mother Coo loomed large, Houdini could learn of another compelling mystery, this one with Parrsboro roots. Of the many wooden ships launched from the Parrsboro shore, none was more famous than *Amazon*, built at nearby Spencers Island in 1861. In 1872 the world was fascinated when the ship, renamed *Mary Celeste*, was found drifting near the Azores in perfect running order but minus her crew. Interest in the mystery intensified when Sir Arthur Conan Doyle, who would one day become Houdini's friend and adversary, wrote a fictionalized account of the incident in his 1884 book, *The Captain of the Polestar*.

A very rare image of Parrsboro
taken in the 1890s.
(C. Byers Collection)

Amazon entering Marseille,
France, on her first voyage in
1861. This water colour was
painted by Honore Pellegreni.
(C. Byers Collection)

Simon Gibbons (1852-1896) was the world's first Eskimo priest. Born in Labrador, Gibbons spent most of his career in Cape Breton and Parrsboro often traveling by foot or snowshoes. Gibbons once astonished onlookers by submerging his hand in boiling water to pull out a potato. (C. Byers Collection)

Aside from shipbuilding and serving as a coal and lumber port, Parrsboro was a popular summer resort. Hence Parrsboro offered a bonus to Houdini: he could count on the presence of hundreds of summer tourists who might take in his show.

Even without the tourist trade, Parrsboro was large enough to support a theatre, but it didn't have a proper venue. Plans were afoot to convert an old Methodist meeting house on Spring Street to a theatre complete with a sloped floor and balcony. But in July 1896, Houdini had to choose from two halls: Smith's Hall on Main Street or St. George's Hall on Church Street.

The Anglican St. George's Hall, still standing in 2012, had been built sixteen years prior to Houdini's arrival and offered him a cozy venue with a stage and a balcony. St. George's Simon Gibbons, the world's first "Eskimo priest," was a remarkable fundraiser who built many churches in Nova Scotia. He happily rented out his church hall for political rallies and anyone else willing to pony up some cash.

After the Wednesday and Thursday shows in Parrsboro, the Houdinis and their assistant Kenney headed for another Cumberland County town that was home to a mystery easily rivalling the *Mary Celeste* or Old Mother Coo—a terrifying spirit phenomenon that was once widely reported from Nova Scotia all the way to New York City.

>─┤‹›─〇─‹›┤─‹

Amherst, Nova Scotia
Monday, August 3, 1896

A maiden followed by a man's afraid;
A ghost is worse if fresh from hell he's strayed.
— Walter Hubbell, *The Haunted House: A True Ghost Story;*
The Great Amherst Mystery (1879)

ON FRIDAY, JULY 31, Bessie and Harry Houdini arrived in Amherst, a town renowned for its stately Victorian mansions. Founded near Chignecto Bay, an inlet of the Bay of Fundy, Amherst was the birthplace of ousted prime minister, Sir Charles Tupper. Many of the thirty-five hundred citizens worked at local manufacturers, including a large shoe factory.

It would appear that Amherst was a last-minute booking. Houdini didn't submit the date to the *New York Clipper* even though his bookings before and after Amherst were published. However, there is evidence he did some advance promotional work — the *Amherst Daily News* had earlier published a brief note about the upcoming appearance of the mysterious Harry "Handini." Before he could book a venue, in accordance with Amherst bylaws, Houdini had to apply to the town clerk's office for an entertainment licence that cost two dollars.

Amherst's Victoria Street in 1895. Houdini would have certainly strolled along these wooden sidewalks during his stay in town. (Cumberland County Museum and Archives)

BEWARE THE STRANGER

Houdini entrusted his ticket sales to Harry Hillcoat who was no stranger to the theatre himself, having been a lifelong musician and former orchestra leader. But now he operated an Amherst store that stocked musical instruments along with furniture, sewing machines, and bicycles.

Turns out, it was a bad time for a stranger like Houdini to arrive in Amherst. The local newspaper printed a front-page warning about some unwelcome outsiders visiting the Chignecto region. "The country is now full of suspicious characters and our people should be on their guard. The toughs and criminals of the American cities have come to Nova Scotia to spend their summer and they no doubt will not be averse to combining business and pleasure if an opportunity presents itself."[1]

The newspaper was correct; several of the American crooks had been caught red-handed by nearby railway workers and small-town policemen. But no arrests were made. The brazen bandits escaped after threatening authorities with knives and revolvers. And now, the *Daily News* reported, the pickpockets and come-from-away thieves were close at hand. "A detachment of the gang has been doing Amherst the past few days."

Houdini must have been pegged as a suspicious character the moment he began strolling down the wide wooden sidewalks of Victoria Street. But the locals didn't have to worry about Houdini causing trouble—he was on his way to the town

Policeman Soy attempted to handcuff Houdini at the Amherst town clerk's office.
(From the collection of the late Leonard Harkness, courtesy of Doris Harkness)

Former band leader and store owner Harry Hillcoat sold tickets to Houdini's Amherst show. (Cumberland County Museum and Archives)

clerk's office, which also served as the police department. Houdini arrived with a new acquaintance—a reporter from the *Daily News*, happy to have a break from his office on a Friday afternoon. After the usual introductions and pleasantries were exchanged, Houdini challenged the town's two-man police force, Chief Dennis Madden and policeman Richard Soy, to test him with their finest handcuffs.

Soy was the first to snap his cuffs on Houdini. The thirty-five-year-old policeman had only recently rejoined the force. A year earlier, Soy's pregnant wife died in a horrific accident after she dropped an oil lamp that ignited her dress and quickly burned her alive. Soy had resigned from the force for a few months to console his two small children.

Houdini had little trouble with Soy's handcuffs, freeing himself within a minute and a half. Then Chief Madden tried, and failed, to restrain the confident showman. In a futile final attempt, the two policemen put both pairs of cuffs on Houdini, but, of course, he once again escaped easily.

Meanwhile, Chas Casey, the *Scott Act* inspector charged with enforcing liquor regulations, wandered into the clerk's office and was invited to try his hardware on Houdini. Casey's handcuffs had served as bracelets for plenty of Cumberland County black market rum dealers, but as was reported in the *Daily News*, the cuffs were no match for Houdini. "Scott Act Inspector Casey then had a try but met with no better success." The spelling-challenged paper also reported that mysterious

Harry "Houdine" produced a deck of cards and performed a few tricks for the lawmen.

On Friday evening, Houdini watched as much of the population of Amherst boarded the trains for weekend excursions to the Halifax Carnival. Now he had the hopeless task of promoting his Monday night magic show to an empty town. Houdini could take some comfort knowing the magician Markos, a.k.a. Willis Skinner, had sold out the Amherst theatre less than a year earlier. But Skinner was one of the very few performers who ever managed to fill the troubled Amherst Academy of Music.

A CURSED THEATRE

The six-hundred-seat Amherst theatre, the Academy of Music, was just over a year old and had been created by retrofitting a forty-year-old church. A Saint John architect had overseen the installation of a full forty-six-foot by twenty-six-foot stage and eight dressing rooms, along with a formal entrance on Victoria Street and a box office for ticket sales.

As handsome as the theatre was, Amherst had to live with an unfortunate reality — theatrical folk of the day widely believed that churches converted to theatres were bad luck. And indeed, the Amherst Academy of Music had been unkind to some performers of late. The previous summer, John L. Sullivan's touring show almost disbanded in Amherst when the former world champion boxer fired most of his entourage. The unsavoury company had run afoul of the law for a wide range of offences from intoxication to wife-beating.

So far this summer, Rose Sydell's London Belles had cancelled their scheduled June 13 show at the Amherst Academy of Music after their manager, John Sydell, received word of poor advance ticket sales at Harry Hillcoat's music store. Rufus Somerby, who knew the Maritime circuit better than anyone, visited many communities with much smaller populations than Amherst with his monkey theatre, but he chose to skip the town altogether in 1896. And in a matter of weeks, the cast of *On Southern Soil* would prove that the Amherst Academy of Music *was* cursed — or at least hazardous. In a scene featuring a shotgun, an actor aimed squarely at another actor's chest and fired. The wadding from the blank shot had enough force to knock the actor down, halting the show as the severely bruised man was helped to the wings.

While visiting Amherst, Houdini dropped by the Rhodes, Curry & Company and performed some close up magic for the workers. (Cumberland County Museum and Archives)

But not all companies had bad luck in Amherst. Fewer than two weeks before Houdini arrived, a Boston company of fifteen black performers filled the Academy of Music to capacity. After delighting their Amherst audience with two hours of dancing and singing peppered with plenty of jokes, the Sunny South Company agreed to a special request to hold over their minstrel show to the following night.

Sunday evening, an unusually long train arrived in Amherst. The train was so crowded with passengers returning from the Halifax Carnival that it had extra sleeper cars and was being drawn by two engines. As waves of Amherst citizens disembarked, Bessie and Harry Houdini had to wonder if the townsfolk had exhausted their entertainment budgets at the monstrous carnival.

The cursed Amherst theatre, which, fittingly, met its demise in a 1908 fire, appeared poised to claim its latest victim — Harry Houdini.

SHOW DAY

On Monday morning, Houdini hiked along Victoria Street past the red "shoddy stone" buildings that dominated downtown, across the railway tracks, continuing for a few blocks past Station Street. From here, he turned left and walked to the very end of Lusby Street. After passing through the ornate iron gates of Rhodes, Curry & Company, Houdini surveyed the thirty-five-acre grounds of the town's largest employer. Here, the enormous workings of the fabrication company were in full production mode. The high-pitched screams from the shop's saws, in chorus with the monotonous whine from planers, provided a background racket to the non-stop yard activity. Hundreds of labourers and tradesmen were busily loading carts and managing an inventory of millions of board feet of lumber destined for construction projects across the Maritimes. This was also a hectic summer for the men of the Rhodes, Curry & Company manufacturing shops and foundries who were building streetcars for the new street railways in Halifax and Moncton.

In spite of the busy shops, Houdini, no stranger to factory work himself, easily found an audience at Rhodes, Curry & Company for a little up-close street magic and wowed them with some slick card work. Houdini's visit won him another note in the afternoon paper. And true to form, the *Amherst Daily News* managed to find yet another way to misspell his name.

> "Mysterious" Harry Hondini called on some of his friends in Rhodes, Curry & Co's and was introduced to give an exhibition of his slight [*sic*] of hand work, as they had heard of his wonderful ability. He cheerfully responded and although they had expected a good deal of him, they never dreamed that such a clever thing could be done at so close a range. If his entertainment is in keeping with his slight [*sic*] of hand work, it certainly must be well worth witnessing at the Academy of Music tonight.[2]

Elsewhere in the paper was a brief note that finally spelled Houdini's name properly. "The Monarch of Mystery mysterious Harry Houdini gives an entertainment tonight in the Academy of Music."

On Monday evening, Bessie, Harry, and Kenney did their best to bring in an audience, likely even working Victoria Street in the grand tradition of sideshow hucksters, trying to cajole pedestrians in to the Academy of Music.

Any last-minute publicity didn't work.

On Tuesday morning, the Amherst *Daily News* printed a brief but telling two-sentence review of the Houdinis' show. "The performances of Harry Houdini at The Academy of Music last night were one of the very best exhibitions of magic ever given in this town. The attendance was very small."

Houdini didn't keep this clipping for his press book.

With the embarrassing Amherst show behind them, Harry and Bessie Houdini boarded the train and set out for a village that boasted some of the greatest natural phenomena on the entire planet.

>-!-◊->-⊙--<-◊-!-<

HOUDINI'S DOG-EARED COPY of *The Great Amherst Mystery* is now stashed in a vault at the Library of Congress in Washington, DC. Throughout the eighty pages he drew dozens of check marks, underlined passages, and scribbled notes. Houdini's booklet is deeply creased, suggesting he folded it in half, jammed it in his pocket, and spent his time in Amherst investigating a haunted house.

For a year spanning 1878-1879, Esther and Jennie Cox suffered an unwanted visitor in the form of a nasty poltergeist. After introducing himself to the Amherst sisters by knocking on floorboards under their bed, the ghost tipped over a box in the girls' room and hurled a pillow at the man of the house. The harmless antics soon turned dangerous with wall-shaking reverberations, stabbings, and unexplained fires. The spooky phenomenon even struck the kitchen when a bucket of cold water came to a rolling boil on a wooden table.

An Amherst doctor reported seeing the words "Esther Cox, you are mine to kill" appearing, freshly scratched, on the bedroom wall. Houdini was

THE GREAT AMHERST MYSTERY

Actor Walter Hubbell lived in the Amherst haunted house and published his book about the incidents he witnessed.

(Billy Rose Theatre Division, New York Public Library for the Performing Arts, Lenox and Tilden Foundations)

hinges, removed the axe handle from the position in which it had been placed, and, after throwing them some distance into the air, let both fall to the floor with a tremendous crash. Mr. White was speechless with astonishment, and immediately called in Mr. W. H. Rogers, Inspector of Fisheries for Nova Scotia. After bracing the door as before, the same wonderful manifestation was repeated, in the presence of Mr. Rogers. On another occasion, a clasp-knife belonging to little Fred, Mr. White's son, was taken from his hand by the ghost, who instantly stabbed Esther in the back with it, leaving the knife sticking in the wound, which bled profusely. Fred, after drawing the knife from the wound, wiped it, closed it and put it in his pocket. The ghost took it from his pocket, and in a second stuck it in the same wound. Fred again obtained possession of the knife, and this time hid it so that it could not be found, even by a ghost.

There is something still more remarkable, however, about the following manifestation: Some person tried the experiment of placing three or four large iron spikes on Esther's lap while she was seated in the Dining Saloon. To the astonishment of everybody, the spikes were not removed by the ghost, but instead, became too hot to be handled with comfort, and a second afterwards were thrown by the ghost to the far end of the saloon, a distance of twenty feet.

During her stay at the saloon the ghost commenced to move the furniture about in the broad daylight. On one occasion a large box, weighing fifty pounds, moved was a distance of fifteen feet without the slightest visible cause. The very loud knocking commenced again and was heard by crowds of people, the saloon being continually filled with visitors. Among other well known inhabitants of Amherst who saw the wonders at this period, I may mention William Hillson, Daniel Morrison, Robt. Hutchinson, who is John

A well-marked page from Houdini's copy of *The Great Amherst Mystery.* Notice the sword drawn in the margin. (Library of Congress)

intrigued by the account of this incident in his book. At the top of page thirty-three, above the story, he printed "mine to kill."

Houdini also underlined the names of dozens of Amherst citizens mentioned in the story, many of whom were still living in Amherst, perhaps hoping to interview them in person. Elsewhere, details were marked with exclamation marks; he drew a large one with a circle around it next to a description of lighted matches falling from the ceiling.

This gruesome description caught Houdini's full attention: "A clasp-knife belonging to little Fred, Mr. White's son, was taken from his hand by the ghost, who instantly stabbed Esther in the back with it, leaving the knife sticking in the wound which bled profusely."[3] Not only did Houdini underline most of the stabbing story, but in the margin alongside it, he also drew a knife.

The author of *The Great Amherst Mystery*, an American actor named Walter Hubbell, moved in with the family during the haunting. Somehow he convinced them to let him mount a lecture tour with eighteen-year-old Esther, the ghost's favourite prey. Following their appearance in Moncton, New Brunswick, the tour was roundly condemned by a church newspaper. At the next stop in Chatham, a violent mob formed outside the theatre and pelted Hubbell with rocks. Fearing for his life, he cancelled the rest of the tour and retreated to the safety of New York City.

Like Hubbell, Houdini must have been tempted to cash in on the great Amherst mystery. It had been done before by a magician. In September 1895 Willis Skinner sold out his Amherst Markos show after promising to reveal new details about the mystery.

It should have been easy for Houdini to exploit the great Amherst mystery. On July 23, fewer than two weeks before Houdini's visit, the thirty-six-year-old Esther Cox had returned to Amherst to marry her latest beau, Peter Shanahan. Amherst tongues were once again wagging about the mystery from seventeen years earlier.

Unfortunately, young Harry Houdini didn't yet know how to sell out a theatre in Amherst, Nova Scotia, by selling the supernatural, even when it was handed to him on a spooky platter. But one day, he would know how to fill theatres around the world by mocking the supernatural.

CHAPTER THIRTY-TWO

NATURAL PHENOMENA

Joggins Mines, Nova Scotia
Wednesday, August 5, and Thursday, August 6, 1896

"To succeed I must work, and work hard."
—Harry Houdini discussing his eight-hour-a-day practice regime,
Denver Times, October 2, 1899

HARRY AND BESSIE HOUDINI SCARCELY had time to get comfortable as their train sped alongside the Maccan River to the village of Maccan. In fifteen minutes, the first leg of their journey to Joggins Mines was behind them.

At Maccan, Kenney, Bessie, and Harry tossed their baggage onto a freight train owned by the Canada Coal and Railway Company. The lone passenger car, accompanied by six coal cars, was hauled by a smallish locomotive over a meandering route past collieries at Jubilee and Black Diamond. The Houdinis would find the coal train to be far from luxurious, or fast. Locals joked that a cow once raced the train—and won! Still, even with a flag stop in Hardscrabble Junction, the twelve-mile trip took less than forty minutes as the train crossed the River Hebert and chugged into the coastal village of Joggins Mines.

Harry and Beatrice Houdini spent numerous hours travelling from show to show aboard trains. (Harry Ransom Center, The University of Texas at Austin)

293

From the Main Street station platform, Bessie and Harry stepped out onto a windswept commercial street lined with stores and wooden sidewalks, but without a single electric street light. The Houdinis had arrived at an isolated coal mining town, seaside home to one thousand inhabitants and two of the Earth's greatest marvels.

Joggins Mines (now known as Joggins) stands where the Bay of Fundy narrows into Chignecto Bay. Here, the ocean level drops an astonishing—and world's record—forty-nine feet during low tide, allowing fishermen to erect tall weirs constructed from poles and netting. Twice a day, at low tide, the men would harvest the netted fish from the emptied ocean floor and haul their catch to buyers with horse-drawn wagons. Deep underground, below the sunburned weir fishermen, toiled the blackened miners, chasing a coal seam that extended ever outward under the Bay of Fundy.

Standing watch over the bay, the seventy-five-foot-high cliffs of Joggins Mines hold a treasure trove of the world's finest fossils. The huge petrified trees and fossilized reptiles, continually revealed thanks to erosion, enchanted scientists like Charles Darwin who discussed Joggins Mines in his groundbreaking book, *On the Origin of Species*. While outsiders were enthralled with the fossils, the locals were largely indifferent to the geological treasures, using them for doorstops.

Joggins Mines was booming in 1896, welcoming migrant workers from Newfoundland and Europe, including Houdini's native country of Hungary. It was claimed up to twelve languages were spoken in the town by 1896. Unbeknownst to the hard-working folks of Joggins Mines, their village was noted in two of the continent's leading entertainment journals of the day when Houdini listed his upcoming August 5 and 6 Joggins Mines appearances in both the *New York Clipper* and the *New York Dramatic Mirror*.

Listing his shows in the American papers helped Houdini's mail reach him while he was on tour—but it didn't help publicize his shows. And for the first time since leaving Boston, Houdini found himself without any policemen to help promote his handcuff escapes. Aside from an occasional visit from Scott Act inspector Casey to roust out bootleggers, Joggins Mines was remarkably free of crime and got by without a police force or lock-up.

The only venue available to Houdini in Joggins Mines was Melanson's Hall. Built above a Main Street general store owned by the Melanson brothers, the hall was normally set up with tables and chairs to host small functions for up to fifty people. But during the national election campaign, the *Amherst Daily News*

Bessie Houdini posing with a floral bouquet. This photograph was taken in the 1890s and used on the Houdinis' letterhead.
(Harvard Theatre Collection, Houghton Library, Harvard University)

reported a boisterous crowd of five hundred crammed into the tiny hall to hear a Liberal candidate speak.

So far this summer, Harry Lindley's Big Show Company had played Melanson's Hall, and so had Rufus Somerby with his Professor Wormwood's Monkey Theatre. In Joggins Mines, Somerby introduced a brand new cast member he acquired while touring Cape Breton Island—a friendly Newfoundland dog named Canso.

On Wednesday evening, taking the same stage pawed by Canso five weeks earlier, the Houdinis opened their two-night stand. The second show in Joggins Mines, on Thursday, marked the final time Harry Houdini would ever perform in Nova Scotia. Unfortunately, records of Harry and Bessie's visit to the town were lost in a 1928 fire that wiped out most of Main Street.

One mention of the Houdinis' stand in Joggins Mines is on record—sort of.

The Amherst newspaper, still seemingly hell-bent on getting Houdini's name wrong, outdid all their earlier blunders. This time, they managed to mix-up the magician Harry Houdini with the actor, Harry Lindley. A note about Houdini in the Joggins Mines section of the August 8, 1896, *Amherst Daily News* comically credited the wrong Harry: "Harry Lindley gave two of his mysterious entertainments here this week. He is a great wonder."

Bessie and Harry Houdini would visit many exotic and unusual places in their career—but few could pretend to rival the awe-inspiring high tides and fossil-rich cliffs of Joggins Mines.

>─┼◆>─Θ─<◆┼─<

IMPORTANT.

NOTICE.

I OFFER $100.00 to any human being living that can escape from all the cuffs I carry, and from which I release myself.

I escape from the celebrated Bean Giant Cuff with them locked behind my back, a feat no one else has ever accomplished. My hands can be fastened back or front. It makes no difference how many pair of cuffs are locked on me (**at the same time**), and I will allow the **keyholes to be stamped and sealed,** and as I bring out all the cuffs interlocked, it proves conclusively that **I do not slip my hands.**

I have escaped out of more handcuffs, manacles and leg shackles than any other human being living. As I carry a very rare, curious and costly collection of torture, antique and modern Handcuffs (of every style and make), I give a scientific and historic lecture on them; in fact, I have the ONLY complete act of this description in existence.

Harry Houdini

Of the Team ————

Harry and Bessie Houdini

>>>The Expert Handcuff Manipulator.<<<

NOTE.—There is a **$50.00 REWARD** offered to any one that can escape from the Bean Giant, but that offer is for the cuffs to be fastened behind the back.

Did you ever see any handcuff worker have his hands locked in back to escape from the Bean cuff?

CHAPTER THIRTY-THREE

BARNSTORMING

Sackville, New Brunswick
Saturday, August 8, to Monday, August 10, 1896

"As a rule, I have found that the greater brain a man has, and the better he is
educated, the easier it has been to mystify him."
— Harry Houdini in a letter to Sir Arthur Conan Doyle, April 20, 1920

DURING THEIR TRAIN JOURNEYS through the hills and valleys of Nova
Scotia, it's probable that the Houdinis performed — or at least attempted to
perform — in some of the smaller communities along the way. This was a common
hit-and-miss type tactic known in the trade as "barnstorming." Bessie Houdini
recalled arriving in several small Maritime towns and attempting to mount a show at
church halls without any advance publicity. While no specific towns are mentioned
by Bessie, there are some likely candidates.

One of the most sizeable country communities was Stewiacke, a settlement
between Dartmouth and Truro that supported a variety of stores, several hotels,
and at least one saloon. Stewiacke's Old Temperance Hall hosted mostly local
entertainers and dances but occasionally offered a performance by a visiting
company. Two men who travelled with a trained bear were regular visitors.

Houdini added a cash reward to his handcuff act. He also allowed
policemen to place postage stamps over handcuff keyholes which would
remain untouched while he escaped from the cuffs. (Library of Congress)

Another possible stopover for Houdini is Oxford, a town north of Truro.

Bessie and Harry quite likely performed at Acadia Mines, a booming town of three thousand, with an ironworks and rolling mill that was located between Truro and Springhill.

Although not a major player on the vaudeville circuit, Acadia Mines got its fair share of performers at St. Bridget's Hall thanks to being a stop on the Intercolonial Railway. Magicians, including Zera Semon, had played the community in the recent past. On Tuesday, July 21, 1896, the veteran actor Harry Lindley was opening the first of two nights at the hall with his Big Show Company. This left a coveted Saturday slot for the Houdinis after their Truro stand, with the potential for a matinee, followed by a Monday evening show.

Unfortunately, the Acadia Mines records were destroyed when much of the town burned to the ground in a devastating fire on May 31, 1920, so for now, it can't be proven that Houdini performed in the once-thriving mining town.

We do know that after their stand in Joggins Mines, Bessie and Harry Houdini climbed aboard an Intercolonial Railway car at Maccan, and settled in for their return trip to New Brunswick. Followed by scheduled stops in Nappan and Amherst, their train crossed the Isthmus of Chignecto on an elevated gravel railway bed, offering the Houdinis a grand view of the vast green Tantramar Marshes. Twenty minutes later, Bessie and Harry arrived at Sackville, New Brunswick, home of Mount Allison University.

Harry Houdini's visit to Sackville might be forever shrouded in mystery. Only two weeks earlier, the *Chignecto Post*—the only local paper—ceased operations because of financial troubles. Gone was the reporter who might have reviewed Houdini's Sackville shows. And gone was the reporter who might have described Houdini's visit to the Sackville police station.

But one vital record remains: Houdini submitted the Sackville dates to the weekly *New York Clipper*. The edition, with the Sackville listing, was published on August 8, 1896. The fact Sackville wasn't included with Houdini's Nova Scotia tour dates a week earlier, suggests the university town might have been a late—or come-by-chance—booking. It's interesting to note how the dates were listed as "Sackville 8-10," indicating a three-night stand, regardless of August 9 being a Sunday.

Sackville's only theatre was the Music Hall, at the corner of Bridge and Main streets. The sizeable Music Hall "block" was also home to a bank and five street-level stores, including a bookstore owned by William Goodwin, the lessee and manager

Harry and Bessie Houdini travelled the Maritimes onboard Intercolonial Railway trains. The railway issued playing cards bearing these images. (The New Brunswick Railway Museum)

of the top-floor theatre. The Music Hall, noted for superb acoustics, offered Houdini the real deal—a professional-sized stage at twenty-five feet by forty-five feet raised above hundreds of seats bolted to a sloped floor, giving all a good view of the stage.

Since opening for business in 1883, the Music Hall had welcomed a steady procession of American show companies. So far this summer, Professor Wormwood's Monkey Theatre, the Webling Sisters, and Rose Sydell and the London Belles had all played the facility. Looking ahead, the considerable cast and crew of *On Southern Soil* were booked to bring their lavish production to the Music Hall on August 17.

Assuming the Houdinis met with better success than magician Zera Semon, who closed his last Sackville appearance due to poor attendance, they would have performed on Saturday night and closed their Sackville stand on Monday evening. Over the weekend, a violent thunderstorm passed through the area. Lightning struck several houses, setting them ablaze, while strikes in nearby Memramcook shattered three power poles. Meanwhile, Maritime papers carried front-page stories about a deadly heat wave killing scores of Americans in the Houdinis' hometown, New York City, as well as Washington, DC, and Providence, Rhode Island.

The weekend storm, no doubt, dampened the spirits of Harry and Bessie Houdini. As a consolation, the best weather of the summer greeted the Houdinis as they boarded their train out of Sackville, bound for their next stand in a nearby shiretown.

HOUDINI WASN'T THE FIRST handcuff escape artist to play Sackville. That claim belongs to Professor Barrael, who first appeared at the Music Hall back in 1891, performing a special Saturday matinee across town at Beethoven Hall, a performance room at Mount Allison University's Conservatory of Music.

A review of Barrael's long-forgotten Sackville show offers us a rare glimpse of a pioneering escape artist who toured Canada years before Harry Houdini had slipped out of his first pair of handcuffs.

With hands tied behind his back and feet firmly lashed to the legs of the chair, by two well-known gentlemen from the audience, in about five seconds he appeared from his darkened cabinet with his coat off and with the knots as firmly tied as before. His tricks while handcuffed were equally good. With hands fastened behind by the manacles he did the same tricks. In response to a challenge Mr. David Lund stepped on the stage with Constable Bowes' handcuffs, tried and true. Prof. Barrael did the same tricks with these and ended by shaking them off his wrists and returning them to Mr. Lund open.[1]

Professor Barrael aside, Sackville was an unfriendly stopover for most magicians, hypnotists, and clairvoyants. The otherwise successful American production of *Trilby* was a notable failure in Sackville, as was Professor Dayton with his table-rapping spiritualism show. Even the popular magician Zera Semon, with his giveaway trinkets and door prizes, had struck out in Sackville.

ROLL OUT
THE
BARRAEL

☛ Professor Barrael promoted his 1891 Sackville stand by promising "Difficult feats performed with hands bound and handcuffed." (Image courtesy of Harriet Irving Library, UNB)

Music Hall, Sackville,
FRIDAY EVG., JULY 5

JOHN L. SULLIVAN'S
COMEDY Co.
— AND —
Athletic Exhibition,
A Company of 15 First - Class Artists

John L. Sullivan,
12 Years Champion of the World.
— AND —
Pabdy Ryan,
Champion for 11 Years.
— IN AN —
EXCITING GLOVE CONTEST
A Show Full of Specialties.
LADY DANCERS AND LADY SINGERS.
Buck and Wing dancers. And the famous
CALIFORNIA QUARTETTE.

A special train will run to the Cape Tormentine after the performance, one fare for the round trip.
PRICES 25, 35, & 50 cents which are for sale at Goodwin's Book Store. Seats can be secured in advance by letter telegraph or telephone.

Former world heavyweight boxing champion John L. Sullivan performed in Sackville in 1895.
(Image courtesy of Harriet Irving Library, UNB)

ZERA
SEMON
WITH A
New Company
IN
MUSIC HALL, SACKVILLE, N. B.
3 NIGHTS
Wednesday,
Thursday &
Friday,
Nov. 7th, 8th, & 9th.
HUNDREDS
f presents given away
EVERY NIGHT
ISSION 25c.   Reserved Seats 35c

Richmond, Virginia-based magician, Zera Semon, closed his 1894 Sackville stand early due to poor attendance.
(Image courtesy of Harriet Irving Library, UNB)

Prof. Barrael
WILL GIVE ONE OF HIS
Inimitable ENTERTAINMENTS
IN
Music Hall,
ON
Saturday Evening next,
AND A
MATINEE,
IN
Beethoven Hall,
same day at 3 o'clock.

New and Startling Manifestations !

Difficult feats Performed with hands
Bound and Handcuffed.

No objectionable features in the entire performance.

Popular Prices 15 and 25 cents

Says the St. John *Globe* of Dec. 8th :—
Prof. Barrael is without doubt one of the
cleverest performers seen in this city. His
exchanging of coats while in the spirit
cabinet was done in the twinkling of an
eye, the mystery being how he got his hands
which were securely tied, and in addition
handcuffed, free to take his coat off, and
even if he did how he put them back again.

To our dear
friend Dr Waitte,
merry Xmas & Happy New Year 1903
Harry & Bessie Houdini

Dorchester, New Brunswick
Tuesday, August 11, 1896

"I want this chair for sweet sentiments sake."
—Harry Houdini after an auction where he purchased an electric chair
used at Auburn Prison, *New York Telegraph*, August 2, 1910

ON A SWELTERING TUESDAY, Bessie and Harry Houdini hopped a train to the next stop on the Maritime theatre circuit. Their trip ended twenty-five minutes later at a small railway station below the hillside town of Dorchester.

Dorchester enjoyed one of the Maritimes' most charming settings, overlooking an expansive valley where the lazy Memramcook River cuts a serpentine path through lush green fields. The locals called this picturesque valley Shepody Bay, though it was really only the headwaters of the small ocean bay.

Harry Houdini might have appreciated the pastoral westward view, but his attention was most likely fixated to the east. Almost a mile above the train station, on the brow of a gentle hill, loomed a solitary stone building with castle-like turrets—the infamous Dorchester Penitentiary, forced home to almost two hundred men and seven women who fought the law, and lost.

Harry and Bessie Houdini, who sent inscribed cards and photos to friends at Christmas time, were probably not thinking of Yuletide greetings when they reached Dorchester. (Harvard Theatre Collection, Houghton Library, Harvard University)

During the ill-fated Marco stand in Halifax, Professor Dooley named Houdini's handcuff act Escape from Dorchester, adding a Maritime twist to Alexander Herrmann's famous act Escape from Sing Sing. Coincidentally, Alexander Herrmann visited Sing Sing prison on July 4, the very day Dooley sailed home from Halifax. The story of Herrmann's triumphant show, performed for fourteen hundred New York convicts, was printed in almost every newspaper in North America, including the Halifax *Echo*. And now, an inspired Harry Houdini had a chance to visit a prison himself.

Dorchester, the shiretown for Westmorland County, was home to the court governing the larger centres of Sackville and Moncton. Government amenities, combined with farming, textiles, and shipbuilding, fuelled a robust economy for the little town. Dorchester catered to a constant stream of visitors, offering them entertainment, accommodations, food, and more at "the corner," a commercial hub at the top of Main Street.

Despite laws to the contrary, the brand new Windsor Hotel dispensed liquor liberally—perhaps too liberally. One evening back in April, a group of hotel drunks put the boots to Dorchester's constable William Lawrence in a dispute over a bottle of gin. The day after the battered constable "kissed the dust," an army of lawmen and Scott Act inspectors descended on the town, determined to enforce Canadian liquor laws.

Until recently, Dorchester had two theatres. But following a performance by students from Mount Allison University, Robb's Hall burned to the ground. Since that fire, a hall owned by the Hickman family served as Dorchester's sole venue for entertainment.

Hickman's Hall stood on Main Street, a few doors down from the Windsor Hotel. The three-storey structure housed the Merchant Bank on the main floor, with offices for the Hickmans' lumber company on the second floor. The theatre occupied the entire third floor; Houdini and Kenney had their work cut out for them to carry the props, including the Metamorphosis trunk, up a steep narrow stairway.

The public entrance to the hall was on the right side of the building, where the door opened from a corner snubbed at a forty-five-degree angle to the sidewalk. On show nights, a closet was emptied and converted to a makeshift box office at the bottom of the stairs. Once upstairs, theatregoers found themselves in a small but respectable hall with ten-foot ceilings. Twelve large double-hung windows, set

The stable of the Dorchester Hotel was used for advertising shows at Hickman's Hall. Several posters from 1896 can be seen here including *Trilby* and the New York Comedy Company. Perhaps Houdini's poster is one of the torn or covered advertisements.

(Mount Allison University Archives, Westmorland Historical Society Collection)

high off the floor, let in plenty of natural light in the daytime and provided natural ventilation on hot stuffy evenings.

The stage itself was at the back of the building. Due to the ceiling height—low by theatrical standards—the stage platform was raised less than two feet above the hall's main floor. The thirteen-foot-deep stage ran the full width of the building, flanked by dressing rooms on both sides.

It had been a busy summer for Hickman's Hall. Harry Lindley's Big Show Company, the Sunny South Comedy Company, and Professor Wormwood's Monkey Theatre had all played the venue in July. Only days before Houdini arrived in Dorchester, the Phila May Company of New Hampshire also performed at Hickman's Hall.

Dorchester was a dream come true for a burgeoning escape artist like Harry Houdini. Not only was there a federal penitentiary in this town, there was also a courthouse and the Dorchester jail that hosted drunks and, sometimes, hangings. And, as an added bonus, the jail was directly across the street from Hickman's Hall.

But, just like nearby Sackville, there was one big glitch for Houdini's promotional plans — the recently defunct *Chignecto Post* had also served as the paper for Dorchester. Without newspaper ads or a friendly reporter to count on, Houdini had to rely entirely on posters and word of mouth to promote his show.

A poster from Houdini's Dorchester visit was displayed in the community for many years at a garage owned by the late Eugene Weldon. Regrettably, it sold at an estate auction in the 1980s and has yet to resurface.

MAGIC BY MOONLIGHT

Back in the village of Dorchester, cool evening air finally conquered the stifling afternoon heat. As the crickets began their evening symphony, Harry Houdini worked quietly, double-checking his props, concealed by the curtain at Hickman's Hall. The magician was joined by his petite assistant as the sun was setting behind the western hills. As the Houdinis opened at eight o'clock, a beautiful golden hue cloaked the valley below, just as the moon crept above the eastern hills in the New Brunswick sky.

Like so many performers before them, Harry and Bessie Houdini entertained the good people of Dorchester on the storied boards of Hickman's Hall, a building still standing in 2012.

Following Dorchester, Harry Houdini was heading an hour north, by train, to a city where a police chief was having a dreadful summer. And the last thing this lawman needed was yet another escape artist visiting his jailhouse.

HARRY HOUDINI READ lots of newspapers while he was in the Maritimes, sometimes saving clippings for his press book. He couldn't have missed the stories in the Halifax papers about Alexander Herrmann's spectacular performance at Sing Sing prison.

At the Fourth of July show, Lou Hannigan volunteered to hold Herrmann's pistol while the magician loaded gunpowder and pounded it home with a ram rod. The hushed crowd watched as Lou took over, driving four bullets deep into the barrel. Before prison guards realized

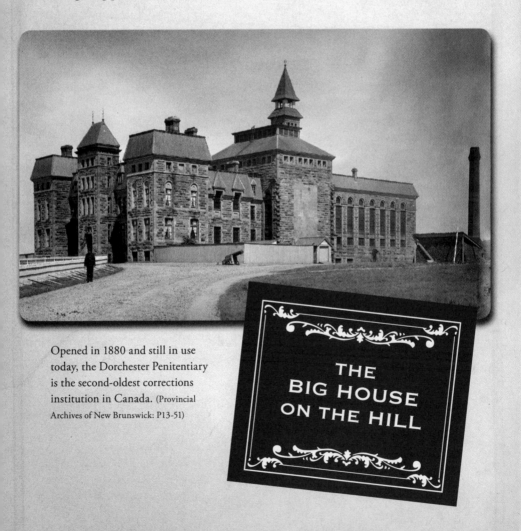

Opened in 1880 and still in use today, the Dorchester Penitentiary is the second-oldest corrections institution in Canada. (Provincial Archives of New Brunswick: P13-51)

THE
BIG HOUSE
ON THE HILL

what was happening, Herrmann had armed a convict.

From ten paces, the lawbreaker aimed the long-barrelled handgun at a ceramic plate held chest high by the magician. Herrmann drew a deep breath, paused, and shouted "Fire!" Before the gun smoke cleared, with the shot still echoing off the concrete walls, Herrmann held the four bullets at his fingertips. Fourteen hundred convicts leapt to their feet, cheering wildly for the world-famous magician who had defied death at the end of a pistol.

Just five weeks after reading about

163

DATE. 1896	SIGNATURE.	RESIDENCE.	Authority for Admission.
Aug	B. H. Leger	Sackville	pd Allen 50
	G. H. Hilson	Sackville	
	Kate O'Brien	Dorchester	pu
	Annie F. O'Neill	St. John N.B.	"
	Samuel E. Robb	Boston	Paid S. M.
	Percy Smith	Dorchester	
10	E. B. McKie	Ch. Town P.E.I.	Paid J. U.
	P. G. Armour	Ch. Town P.E.I.	J. R. F.
	Dale Armstrong	Boston	
	Harry Houdini	New York City	Gene D. M.
	Jas. Sheridan	Boston	
	Rev. E. Sirois, P.P.	Plympton N.S.	

Houdini's signature, extending into the margin of the Dorchester Penitentiary's Visitor register, was entered sometime between August 10 and 20, 1896.
(Mount Allison University Archives, Westmorland Historical Society Collection)

Herrmann's bullet catching at Sing Sing, nothing could stop Harry Houdini from making his way to the top of Prison Road where Dorchester Penitentiary stood on a hilltop plateau. The storybook structure, constructed from mammoth blocks of quarried-on-site stone, reigned over the idyllic New Brunswick countryside. At the crest of the road, Houdini could see why the prison was branded "The Big House on the Hill." From their tiny cells prisoners could see sweeping vistas of farmland with the Bay of Fundy shimmering in the distance.

Houdini approached the prison under the watchful eyes of sentries stationed in the observation towers rising above the prison's corners. The eighteen guards who manned the "towers and cages" had a vested interest in spotting escaping inmates—their families lived just below the prison in Guard Row, townhouses built especially for jail staff.

Harry Houdini signed the visitor's register, listing his residence as New York City. Two travellers from Boston named Dale Armstrong and Jas Sheridan signed in with him. The three signatures were bracketed and noted as "Free" men. The dating of the visit is unclear because ditto marks were used for all visitors between August 10 and 20. The leather-bound book has survived, stored in a vault at the Mount Allison University Archives.

Without a report from the *Chignecto Post*, which folded shortly before Houdini arrived, there is little we can know about the escape artist's visit to Dorchester Penitentiary. Warden John Forster's diary rarely offers more than daily accounts of weather and farm production on the six-hundred-acre grounds. But in one report, the warden explained how entertainment was provided on "a stage erected in the dining hall."

Perhaps Houdini did perform inside the New Brunswick prison after all. And perhaps when Houdini finally performed at Sing Sing prison on August 10, 1916, he had reason to recall his visit to the Big House on the Hill exactly twenty years earlier.

CHAPTER THIRTY-FIVE

CITY of JAILBREAKERS

Moncton, New Brunswick
Monday, August 17, and Tuesday, August 18, 1896

"For some time, past escapes from the lockup have been numerous
and it is evident that there is something decidedly wrong in connection
with the management."
—*Moncton Daily Transcript*, August 14, 1896

BACK IN JUNE, BESSIE AND HARRY HOUDINI were scheduled to play
Moncton with the Marco Magic Company. Now, two months after the Marco
dates were cancelled, they finally landed in the "Hub City."

So far this summer, the Houdinis had closely followed Rufus Somerby's tour
route—at least from Truro northward. And Somerby had brought Professor
Wormwood's Monkey Theatre to Shediac, a lively Acadian village eighteen miles
east of Moncton. Given there was almost a week between the Houdinis' appearances
in Dorchester and at the Moncton Opera House, it's possible they also performed
in this same coastal town, although no records of a Shediac show have been found.

The Houdinis arrived just as Moncton was overflowing with visitors. Less than
a week earlier, the Moncton Street Railway opened. Like a fairground attraction,

Marshal Charles Foster (fourth from right) poses with his men in front
of the Moncton police station in 1895. (Moncton Museum Collection)

311

the Rhodes Curry-built streetcars were amusing upwards of two thousand people a day with short jaunts the length of Main Street.

Houdini took the liberty of rewriting a review from Halifax and submitted it to the *Moncton Times*. The bogus review, supposedly from the *Acadian Recorder*, stated "A large audience greeted mysterious Harry Houdini at the Academy of Music last night." Missing from the fanciful rewrite was any mention of Marco, or the empty benches that really greeted Houdini during the disastrous Halifax stand.

Houdini would meet the new manager of the Moncton Opera House, thirty-eight-year-old Watson Lutz. Mr. Lutz, already an experienced businessman, proved to be a quick study of the entertainment business, subscribing to the *New York Dramatic Mirror* and contributing weekly reports about acts playing his theatre.

Some big names had graced the Opera House this summer. Ethel Tucker, Professor Wormwood's Monkey Theatre, and Rose Sydell's London Belles had all played multiple night stands. And featherweight boxer George "Little Chocolate" Dixon, from Africville, Nova Scotia, the first-ever black world champion, fought an exhibition match at the theatre on July 27.

With his show opening on Monday, Houdini was following hot on the heels of *On Southern Soil*, which played a one-night stand on Saturday. The Moncton papers trashed the American show company. "So low a standard has never before been used in this city by amateurs or professionals. It would pay the manager to give his company a lengthy leave of absence in order that they might learn something of the art."[1] Mr. Lutz agreed with the mean-spirited review; in his weekly report to the *New York Dramatic Mirror*, he wrote "Company one of the poorest seen in this section in years."

A TROUBLED MARSHAL

On Monday, August 17, Houdini paid a visit to the Moncton police station. Accompanied by two reporters, Houdini found the narrow three-storey stone building on Duke Street staffed by seven policemen under command of police marshal Charles Foster.

Moncton police operations had taken a bad turn lately, starting when Marshal Foster had to ask Chief Clarke to arrest a Moncton constable in Saint John. In recent months, over a dozen convicts had escaped from Foster's jailhouse. The local newspapers were cashing in on the escapes, using each getaway to fire barbs

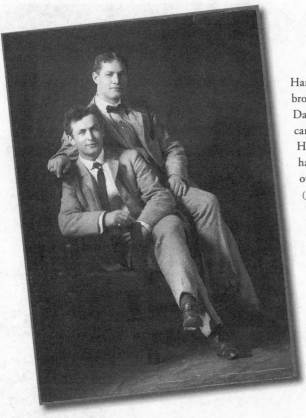

Harry Houdini (left) and his brother Theodore (Dash) Weiss. Dash also forged a successful career as an escape artist called Hardeen. Both brothers would have had little trouble breaking out of the 1896 Moncton lockup.

(John Cox Collection)

at the police department. Just three days before Houdini waltzed into the station, the *Daily Transcript* wrote, "By this time, the city council must be pretty nearly convinced that the police lock-up in its present condition will not hold prisoners who prefer the open air to confinement."

It wasn't just men who were escaping—at least five of Moncton's working girls had escaped through a window by removing an iron bar and climbing down a rope made from bed sheets. Two more ladies of the night managed to open their cell doors and escape through the basement.

It was bad enough that a newspaper editorial labelled his police station a "disgrace to the city."[2] Now, the beleaguered marshal had a professional escape artist visiting, with snickering reporters in tow! After patiently listening to Harry Houdini grandstanding about how he could escape from any restraint in the police arsenal, the marshal agreed to the challenge, handcuffing the magician in one of

The Moncton Opera House, located on the top floor of Moncton City Hall, opened its doors to the public in 1885. (Moncton Museum Collection)

the cells at the rear of the station. Before the marshal even returned to the reporters gathered in the front lobby, Houdini was free from the cell and brandishing the unlocked handcuffs.

A small report of Houdini's escape appeared in both Moncton papers. Unfortunately for Houdini, reading about escapes from Marshal Foster's police station was nothing new to the citizens of Moncton.

A NIGHT AT THE ODOUR HOUSE

The Opera House was an outstanding theatre, offering patrons luxurious iron seats decked out with bronze trim and scarlet upholstery. Twenty-seven feet above the seats, centred between rows of ornate iron columns, a grand chandelier hung from an arched ceiling. The stage itself was an enormous thirty-five feet by sixty feet, fitted with up-to-date workings from Boston. With trap doors and a trench for multicoloured footlights, the stage and large dressing rooms could easily accommodate the largest productions of the day.

The 750-seat Opera House wasn't the only enterprise located in city hall. The ground floor of the stately brick building hosted the farmers' market, where butchers and fishmongers sold their wares.

Like all acts playing this theatre in summer, Bessie and Harry Houdini would need to overcome the repulsive odour of rotten meat, hides, and fish. In spite of a new ventilation system featuring five separate ventilators and regular hosing of the market by the fire department, complaints still flew about the unbearable stench wafting up to the theatre. The smell ultimately forced the theatre to close in 1908, after twenty-three years of failed efforts to resolve the issue.

By showtime on Monday, the Houdinis' audience had already been treated to a warm-up act before they even took their seats in the Opera House. At nightfall, the electric lights above the Main Street entrance to city hall attracted swarms of moths and an army of beetles. Then the fun began! To cheers from the sidewalk, plump market rats would scurry along the ledge, snapping up the hapless insects.

Meanwhile, upstairs, the Houdinis prepared to ring up the curtain. Kenney would have to be extra careful with the *Trilby* machinations backstage. The August 8 edition of *Scientific American* was on the stands in Moncton. And it featured a detailed explanation of the levitation illusion complete with revealing drawings. The exposé of the popular act riled magician Alexander Herrmann, who wrote a widely published condemnation of the popular magazine. "Is it not the very mystery and miracle that gives the delight? And why all this [*sic*] cold blooded endeavors to rob a weary world of its relaxation and wonderment?" [3] asked Herrmann.

Sadly, the crowded city didn't translate to a large audience at the Opera House. Instead of a night at the theatre, many attended a fundraiser across town. The open-air social, complete with an orchestra illuminated by Chinese lanterns, drew a large crowd who indulged in ice cream and dancing, while Harry and Bessie played to mostly empty seats at the Opera House.

The review of Monday's show in the *Daily Times*, perhaps written by the same critic who ripped *On Southern Soil*, offers us a reasonable description of the Houdinis' Moncton performance.

> A performance which fully merits all that has been said about it, and is certainly ahead of anything in the same line ever seen in this city before, was the unanimous verdict of those who saw Harry Houdini, the magician, at the Opera House last night. The entertainment was perfectly free from anything objectionable, and was a wonderful exhibition of magic and mystery. Professor Houdini did all that any other slight [*sic*] of hand performer in the Moncton Opera House ever attempted, and a great deal more. His work with the cards is phenomenal. During the evening he gave an exhibition of getting out of handcuffs placed on his wrists by persons in the audience. *Trilby*, or the mystery of Mahomet, in which a human being actually floats in space without any visible means of support, was one of the startling features of last evening's performance. The trunk mystery, which has puzzled the minds of the most crafty, is another feature of Prof. Houdini's show, which is performed mysteriously and with lightning rapidity. Mlle Bessie Houdini, the clairvoyant medium, who answers all questions in sealed envelopes without touching them, is another mystery with which the audience are [*sic*] required to grapple. Her work is marvelous. This performance will be repeated at the opera house tonight, and those who enjoy this sort of entertainment may depend on seeing an exceptionally clever artist in Harry Houdini.

Both Moncton papers were kind to the Houdinis. The reviewer for the *Transcript* pleaded with his fellow citizens to support Houdini. "Give him a good house tonight. His show certainly merits it." Houdini kept both reviews along with a newspaper advertisement, pasting them in his press book.

Neither Moncton paper offered a review of the Tuesday night show. But one more review was yet to come. The dependable Opera House manager, Watson Lutz, mentioned Houdini in his weekly report, published in the August 29 edition of the *New York Dramatic Mirror*. "Harry Noudini [*sic*], magician. (August) 17, 18; good entertainment to light business."

FINALE

Summers are brief in the Maritimes. By now, the days were getting shorter and the nights were getting colder. Mornings began with a chill and the occasional whiff of smoke from a heating stove. Maritimers were throwing an extra blanket on their beds and shaking the moth balls out of their fall jackets.

Harry and Bessie Houdini had been in the Maritimes for almost twelve weeks. Their tour was, by far, the longest Maritime tour of the season. Now they were competing against a fresh batch of well-rested companies, arriving to open their Maritime fall tours. Magician Zera Semon was back working his favourite circuit, and so was a wild west show. Mrs. General Tom Thumb, widow of P.T. Barnum's famous "midget," Tom Thumb, had arrived for a New Brunswick tour and was opening at the Opera House in Saint John.

The companies that started playing the territory back in May, alongside the Marco Magic Company, had long since moved on. Rose Sydell's London Belles had enjoyed their summer break and completed weeks of rehearsals for a brand new season, already underway in Boston. Rufus Somerby and his Professor Wormwood's Monkey Theatre were now touring their way back to America through the Province of Quebec. And the Walter L. Main Circus had covered Quebec and Ontario and was now showing through New York State.

While the summer tours of 1896 were fading into memory, Bessie and Harry Houdini were still working the Maritime provinces after nearly three months on the road.

But enough was enough.

It was time to go home.

CHAPTER THIRTY-SIX

HOMEWARD BOUND

Yarmouth, Nova Scotia
Saturday, August 22, 1896

"I see that you have not yet acquired your sea legs.
It is a grand, good thing that Bessie is such a good sailor."
—Professor Edward James Dooley
writing to Harry Houdini, October 4, 1900

THE HOUDINIS' FLAT IN NEW YORK CITY was seven hundred miles from Moncton. But there wasn't enough money in the purse for the passage home, especially a full-day train ride. Instead, the Houdinis returned to where their Maritime tour began—Yarmouth, Nova Scotia.

Since 1896 the Houdinis' trail out of Moncton has gone cold. Passenger lists from local trains and the Bay of Fundy steamers are all but non-existent. The Houdinis might have travelled to Yarmouth entirely by rail. Or they might have returned to Saint John, hopping a side-wheel steamer across the bay to connect with the Dominion Railway at Annapolis or Digby. They also could have boarded the steamer *Alpha* from Saint John directly to Yarmouth.

Although an unlikely possibility for the Houdinis' route home, steamships bound for Halifax also sailed from the adjacent province of Prince Edward Island.

The seasick-prone Harry Houdini once wrote, "I am not even a fair weather sailor." (Corbis)

A group in Georgetown, Prince Edward Island, claim Houdini once performed at their theatre, a venue built in 1897. When queried, the directors were unable to offer any evidence to support the claim other than local oral history. The claim likely stems from Karland the Handcuff King's 1908 tour of Prince Edward Island. Houdini did not list any Prince Edward Island dates in the *New York Clipper* or the *New York Dramatic Mirror* and no mention of performances has been found in Prince Edward Island newspapers of the day. For now, it can't be proven or disproven that Houdini ever visited the island.

The best we can do is piece together their story from fragmented international steamship records and the recollections Bessie provided to a biographer in 1928.

Bessie remembered a last-ditch attempt to raise steamship fare just before leaving the Maritimes. Like a cleaned-out gambler throwing his watch on the table, Harry Houdini used the last of their cash to rent a church hall for one final show. The Houdinis pulled out all the stops, working the streets and hawking their show like circus pitchmen. And they were rewarded with a small audience. But at the end of the evening, their take barely covered the hotel and hall rental. The next night, the stranded troupe made do without a hotel, spending the evening bunked down in a hallway where Harry and Kenney used their coats to improvise a bed for Bessie.

Once back in Yarmouth, Harry came face to face with his worst nightmare — the SS *Yarmouth*! The very sight of the vessel gently bobbing at dockside, coupled with memories of his last crossing, was enough to make Houdini feel seasick.

If the couple were going to board the steamship, it would be up to the seaworthy Bessie to negotiate with the captain. The Houdinis and Kenney simply didn't have the five dollars apiece fare for the journey home. After listening to Bessie's woeful and practiced tale, complete with tears running down her cheeks, the captain agreed to let them board the ship at no cost. Bessie had brokered a deal — in return for a free ride, the Houdinis would perform for the passengers.

Back in May, the equipment that was going to launch the worldwide fame of "Marco, the Monarch of Mystery" weighed tons and filled dozens of trunks when it was unloaded in Yarmouth. Now, aside from a few props salvaged by Houdini, most of Dooley's gear stayed behind in Halifax. Since then, Harry had sold or bartered the remnants of Professor Dooley's props for hotel rooms, hall rentals, train fare, and food. Now, the Houdinis were leaving Canada with one item only — the Metamorphosis trunk they started out with.

Bessie Houdini on
board the *Malwa*.
(Patrick Culliton Collection)

The steamship cast off in early evening and nosed out of Yarmouth Harbour, passing by fishing boats returning to port. By the time the hull of the SS *Yarmouth* thumped into the choppy waters of the Gulf of Maine, Houdini was crippled with full-blown seasickness. A furious storm battered the northeast on Saturday evening, making the crossing much rougher than usual. The storm damaged docks and wrecked seven vessels at Nova Scotia alone.

Bessie—who gave her name and age for the steamship manifest as "Miss Rahner, 20"—set up a table with Harry's gear, while a crowd gathered in the ship's lounge. Pale as a sail, "Mysterious" Harry Houdini introduced himself to the suddenly skeptical passengers, then lurched toward the table to begin his show. As he got underway with his usual patter, his hands shook uncontrollably and his speech dropped to an incoherent mumble. Then he started to faint, catching himself before striking the floor. A stunned audience watched as Houdini struggled to right himself—and then his nose began to bleed.

The show was over.

Houdini stumbled back to the deck and resumed his retching overboard into the pitiless Atlantic Ocean.

The passengers began to laugh. And who could blame them? They gathered for a magic show, and then this ridiculous spectacle unfolded like a well-rehearsed vaudeville comedy. Bessie didn't know what to do. There were two hundred sixty-seven people on board and she had promised the captain they would be entertained.

Her exhaustion from the long summer tour, her hunger, and the sight of the laughing audience suddenly overwhelmed Bessie. Tears formed in her eyes and the passengers grew silent, firing sidelong glances at one another. Then a lady asked if Bessie could perform in place of her husband.

Bessie started working Harry's routine the best she could. But her husband was the magician. Bessie knew how the tricks were done, but she hadn't practised them herself. After botching two tricks, the audience rewarded her for her bravery. A man took off his hat and passed it around. When the hat was presented to Bessie, she counted more than twenty-five dollars.

Clutching her earnings, Bessie went looking for her husband. She found him on deck, still drained of his colour and sweating. While Harry suffered with each heave of the SS *Yarmouth*, Bessie excitedly explained how she came by her windfall. A thoroughly humiliated Harry Houdini was in no mood to listen to her cheerful story. He knew the passengers' charity was a direct result of his embarrassing performance.

Still, Bessie was hungry and asked, "May I spend for some eats?"

"No!" shouted Harry.

Bessie later recalled, "I think it was the only really bitter word he ever addressed to me in all our 33 years together."[1]

In spite of her husband's orders, Bessie couldn't resist the delightful aromas wafting from the ship's galley. "I reentered [*sic*] the lounge to gather up our apparatus, and the same kind woman who suggested that I give the show asked me if I would like something to eat. The look in my eyes answered her. She took me into the grand dining room and I gorged myself with food."[2]

Later on, the storm clouds cleared and a full moon lit up the sky, paving a glorious sparkling road across the Gulf of Maine. Just after midnight, passengers gathered on deck to witness an eclipse of the moon.

At midday on Sunday, the steamship entered Boston Harbour. After three months in Canada, and seventeen hours aboard the SS *Yarmouth*, the Houdinis finally landed back in America.

And here, as longshoremen tie off the SS *Yarmouth* at the Lewis Wharf in Boston, we'll ring down the curtain on the story of Bessie and Harry Houdini and their Maritime summer.

But thy eternal summer shall not fade.[3]

>∙⋯◆∙○∙◆⋯∙≺

EPILOGUE

THE REST OF THE STORY

Edward James Dooley

(Harry Ransom Center, The University of Texas at Austin)

ONE

PROFESSOR EDWARD JAMES DOOLEY
LIFE GOES ON FOR MARCO

"Drop me a line when you get a chance and don't forget
that I have a kind remembrance of you from the Marco days.
With best regards to yourself and Bessie."
—Letter to Houdini from Dooley, 1900

AFTER THE FAILURE OF HIS MARCO TOUR, Professor Dooley settled back
into a boarding house at 86 Ann Street, his Hartford home for the last twelve
years. He returned to playing organ at St. Patrick's Church and started teaching
music lessons at a Main Street studio. He also resumed his position as leader of the
Hartford Opera House orchestra.

Within a year, the Nova Scotia expat had recovered from his Marco losses.
With new savings in hand, he resigned from the church and jumped right back
into the fire as an impresario. This time, Dooley partnered with his Elks Lodge
brother, Colonel Edward Graves, a wealthy Hartford businessman who purchased
the performance rights to a stage show called *Bimbo of Bombay*.

Bimbo of Bombay was a freakish three-act play combining music, comedy, and
magic—at one point in the production, a group of five skeletons danced and sang
onstage. Dooley, using the alias Sydney Marlow, played the lead role of the *Bimbo
of Bombay*, described as "a Hindoo adept in the necromantic art."[1]

To fill two minor supporting roles, Professor Dooley recruited some old friends from the Marco Magic Company. Charles Bryant played the part of John, a butler, while Burton Kilby played a pageboy named, not surprisingly, Buttons. Dooley also landed Thomas Gossman, a brilliant stage carpenter and mechanic who spent years contriving illusions for the late magician, Alexander Herrmann. The lavish production ultimately failed. Dooley left Hartford, briefly working as an organist in Bridgeport, Connecticut, before settling in Albany, where he hung out his shingle as a teacher in "voice, culture and piano." He also revived his magic career, performing at local clubs.

In a letter dated September 5, 1903, Professor Dooley sent Houdini a rather glum update on his colleagues from the 1896 Maritime tour.

> I have done nothing in the magical line in years and have lost my interest in it. The Irishman is in New York selling tape in some dry goods house. He married a widow with a family of three so he is getting his share of trouble. Bert is still working magic as a side issue and is getting to be very clever at palming coins and cards. I have lost all track of Budd and don't know what has become of him. Have not seen nor heard of him in three years. Kenney has gone to the dogs completely from booze and his whereabouts are unknown, so you can see that the Marco Company has not panned out well, with the exception of yourself.

After a failed attempt to start a school of astrology in Manhattan, Dooley took a steady organist gig at a church in Oswego, New York. For a time, he mounted an original burlesque, *Cinderella Up-to-Date*, which turned a small profit for about a year, prompting him to write Houdini, "This is better than the Marco game for me." In 1904 Dooley moved in with his sister at her Hartford home and started teaching music at a Sumner Street studio and the St. Thomas Seminary. Dooley was hired as organist and choirmaster for St. Joseph's Cathedral.

In 1906 Dooley published a book, *The Maria Immaculata*, a collection of pieces played at Catholic services, including a few of his own songs complete with Latin lyrics. In spite of his work as a teacher, author, organist, and choirmaster, Dooley still found time to revisit his old magic career. This time it wasn't as a performer. Instead, he created two new magic plays. *The Pink Venus* and *Bimbo of Bombay*

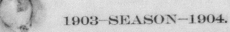

1903–SEASON–1904.

Pronounced by Press and Public in every City where it has been produced,

"THE MOST MAGNIFICENT SPECTACLE EVER PRODUCED HERE."

Cinderella ❧ ❧
❧ ❧ Up-to-Date.

A SPECTACULAR, OPERATIC, FAIRY EXTRAVAGANZA in 3 Acts,
BY EDWARD J. DOOLEY.

Produced with a WEALTH OF GORGEOUS SCENERY AND TRANSFORMATIONS, MAGNIFICENT
NEW COSTUMES, NEW AND POPULAR MUSIC, ETC.

Hartford, Conn. Sept. 5th. 1903.   190

My dear Harry.

I received your souvenir postal card from Moscow and am more than
pleased to hear from you and that you are doing so well and hope you will continue to
do as well that, when you return to America, you will be able to buy the big ocean
liner that will carry you over. I have read your letters to the "Dramatic Mirror"
and enjoyed them and laughed more than once at your witty jokes. You have made
wonderful progress in the English language and your letters are as good as any University man could write. It is just a year since I wrote you last from Oswego and
I stopped, not through forgetfulness, but from lack of knowledge where to reach you,
and, "being on the road" I could not always get the Mirror regularly to see where you
were. I am now home here in Hartford and this will be my permanent address from this
time on.

I wrote this burlesque opera and produced it in Oswego and it made such a
success there that I had many applications from other cities to produce it with their
home talent that I gave up my church position and went at it. It has paid as well
and proved a big success wherever produced. I would go to a city where it was called
for, organize a crowd of amateurs and rehearse them for four weeks and then leave with
from three to five hundred to the good as my share of the green. I invested heavily
in scenery and costumes, but got it all back. I make Hartford my headquarters and
have enough dates booked in this State to fill my time next winter. I have tried to
sell the piece to some New York managers, but they won't pay enough for it, so will
hold on to it till I get my price.

This is better than the Marco game for me and I hope to do well this season.
I think you told me once—or did I read it in some paper——that you were to be the
manager of Thurston and his new act. He introduced it at Keith's in N.Y. and
played there three weeks. I did not see the act, but he is booked here to open
Poli's new theatre the 14th' and I will see it then. Some foreign performer has
introduced a new Levitation act at Hammersteins in N.Y. and it has made a sensation
and is puzzling all the magicians. I did not see it but hope to when next I go to t
to the City. Outside of this Illusion, there is nothing new in the country and magic
is very tame. Kellar has just returned form Europe but I do not know if he found anything worth bringing back. Herrman is doing a living business in the South and West
and that is all. Magic seems to be dead here owing to the want of something new.

I have done nothing in the magical line in years and have lost my interest in it
It is the man who comes along with a new and puzzling Illusion that has the chance to
make some money in the Vaudevilles, but Europe has nearly all our best performers .
I never hear of anyone here trying your handcuff act, except the fellow in Worcester
who advertised himself as Houdini, but he quit as soon as the Mirror exposed him.

I had a lot of fun over that Russian comic paper you sent me. I could not find
anyone here who could read it and I am keeping it as a curiosity.

A letter to Houdini typed on Edward James Dooley's letterhead for his
original show *Cinderella Up-to-Date*. (Harry Ransom Center, The University of Texas at Austin)

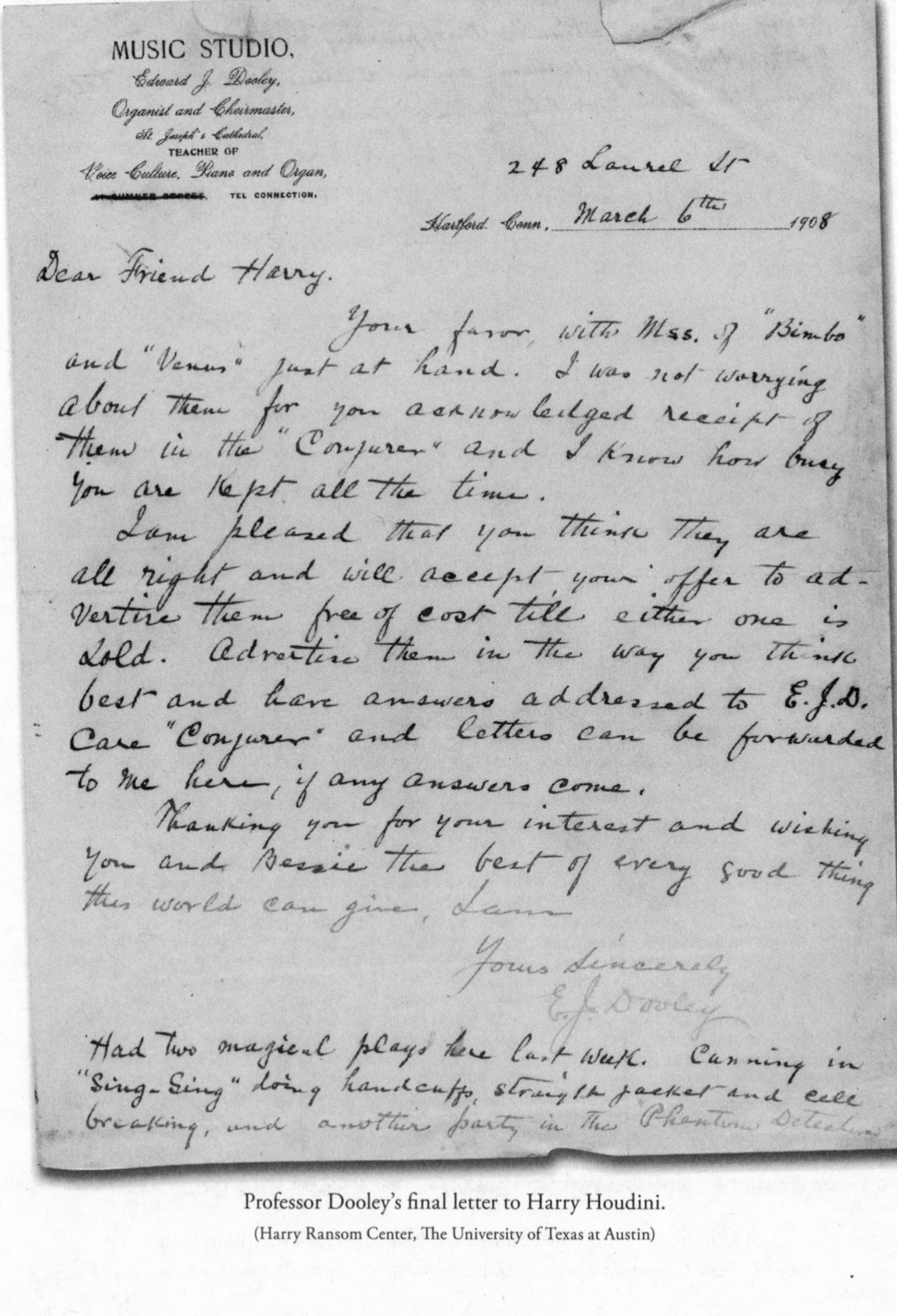

MUSIC STUDIO,

Edward J. Dooley,

Organist and Choirmaster,

St Joseph's Cathedral.

TEACHER OF

Voice Culture, Piano and Organ,

~~SUMMER COURSE~~ TEL CONNECTION.

248 Laurel St

Hartford Conn, March 6th 1908

Dear Friend Harry.

Your favor, with Mss. of "Bimbo" and "Venus" just at hand. I was not worrying about them for you acknowledged receipt of them in the "Conjurer" and I know how busy you are kept all the time.

I am pleased that you think they are all right and will accept your offer to advertise them free of cost till either one is Sold. Advertise them in the way you think best and have answers addressed to E. J. D. Care "Conjurer" and letters can be forwarded to me here, if any answers come.

Thanking you for your interest and wishing you and Bessie the best of every good thing this world can give, I am

Yours Sincerely

E. J. Dooley

Had two magical plays here last week. Cunning in "Sing-Sing" doing handcuffs, straight jacket and cell breaking, and another party in the Phantom Detective

Professor Dooley's final letter to Harry Houdini.

(Harry Ransom Center, The University of Texas at Austin)

In 1904, Professor Dooley moved in with his sister at her
248 Laurel Street home in Hartford. (Bruce MacNab photograph)

were one-act scripts inspired by Dooley's brief tenure as actor Sydney Marlow in the *Bimbo of Bombay*. Dooley copyrighted the two works in the United States, giving him a total of five copyrights on his original dramatic compositions. Conversely, Harry Houdini only copyrighted three of his stage acts in America during his lifetime: Buried Alive, Challenged, and Walking Through a Brick Wall.

At Christmas 1907 Dooley asked Houdini to advertise his new plays for sale in *Conjurers' Monthly*, a magazine Houdini had started for professional magicians. Houdini wrote back, offering to place the ads free of charge until the pieces sold. On March 6, 1908, Dooley wrote Houdini a brief letter, thanking him for the favour. The professor ended his note with, "Wishing you and Bessie the best of every good thing this world can give."

Professor Dooley spent his last years as organist and
choirmaster at Hartford's St. Joseph's Cathedral.
(Archdiocese of Hartford)

Professor Dooley is buried with his sister
at Mt. Calvary Cemetery, Boston. (Bruce MacNab photograph)

On Thursday, April 9, 1908, Professor Dooley wasn't feeling well and was admitted to St. Francis Hospital, right across the street from the seminary where he taught music. His flu-like symptoms, known then as the grippe, worsened through the weekend. His chronic kidney problems resurfaced along with complications from hepatitis. At 9:30 p.m., Monday, April 13, 1908, Professor Edward James Dooley breathed his last breath.

Houdini wrote a brief eulogy to Dooley in *Conjurers' Monthly*, closing with: "Poor Marco! A dear, good fellow, a failure as a magician, a huge success as a man. May his soul rest in peace!"[4]

Edward James Dooley died unmarried without any children or a will. His assets were insufficient to cover the $153.65 invoice of the undertaker. This Nova Scotian — the first man to genuinely recognize the budding talent of Harry Houdini — rests in a hillside Boston grave that doesn't even bear his name.

[N. Y. TELEGRAPH, FEB. 11, 1906.]

"You have made wonderful progress in the English language
and your letters are as good as any university man could write."
—Professor Dooley writing to Houdini September 5, 1903 (Library of Congress)

*

*   *

*

TWO

HARRY HOUDINI
OVERNIGHT FAME AFTER A DECADE OF WORK

"Time flies. It brings back to me memories of the dim past
when those who have gone before were still with us and
all you and I thought of was our small, honest expenses."
—Harry Houdini writing to Bessie Houdini, January 1, 1917

SAFELY BACK IN MANHATTAN, Harry Houdini submitted a note to the *New York Clipper*, which was published in the September 5, 1896, edition. "Harry and Bessie Houdini have just returned from a trip through the Canadian provinces and are now at their home."

Wasting no time, Houdini started writing American theatre managers, looking to score bookings for the fall season. While he was soliciting work, he was still paying off debts racked up six months earlier by Fred Harvey, manager of the American Gaiety Girls. Trying to generate some cash, he contacted several New York City reporters, offering to sell his handcuff secrets for twenty-five dollars. There were no takers.

By the end of September, Houdini's letter-writing campaign was paying off. The Imperial Music Hall in Buffalo, New York, replied, requesting a week's booking starting October 19. The theatre offered a respectable seventy-five dollars for the week—three times the couple's salary with the Welsh Brothers Show.

In late November 1896 Houdini would once again cross paths with Samuel Baldwin. Houdini wrote: "When he was in the height of his success, I was working in the Gregory Dime Museum, Milwaukee, Wisconsin. He was playing at the Davidson Theatre. He came into the Dime Museum and told the audience that Houdini was the cleverest mystifier he had ever seen and predicted a wonderful future. It is of rare occurrence that big men in the show business will put themselves on record in mediocre theatres, but such a sacrifice of dignity on the part of Baldwin only goes to show that his heart was in the right place."[5]

In the summer of 1897, after months of playing small Midwest theatres, Harry and Bessie seemed to catch a break. Houdini was planning on touring with Samuel Baldwin, his admirer whom he had met in Saint John, New Brunswick. Although still recovering from his illness, Baldwin negotiated a tour with Houdini, and even invited Harry and Bessie to visit him at his secret enclave at 317 West 32nd Street. In a handwritten letter sent on July 27, 1897, he wrote:

Dear Mr. Houdini,

Please to see you any morning at 11 or evening at 5.
Have been very ill—am not feeling well now.
Keep the address private as I don't want to be bothered by anyone but
real friends and as such regard you and your wife.

S.S. Baldwin

The tour seemed to be a done deal; Houdini wrote his Chicago magic dealer Gus Roterberg and told him he was signing on with Samuel Baldwin. Roterberg wrote back a congratulatory December 10, 1897, letter. "Am glad to hear that you are going out with Baldwin. That is your proper place." However, the tour never came off as planned, perhaps due to Baldwin's illness. Instead, the couple returned to the grinding tour regime of small-time theatres and dime museums.

For several months in 1898 the Houdinis went on the road with Dr. Hill's California Concert Company, little more than a trumped-up medicine show selling the usual collection of dubious health remedies. The show's cast included Joseph and Myra Keaton, who travelled with their infant son Joseph Junior. Baby Joseph was dropped one night and didn't seem at all fazed by the accident. In honour of the baby's toughness, Houdini started calling him "Buster," a name that would stick even after the child grew up and became a famous Hollywood actor.

After leaving the medicine show in 1898, bookings were few and far between. Houdini contemplated quitting show business altogether to "work by day at one of my trades being really proficient in several."[6] Houdini didn't completely quit show business, but he published a magic catalogue and tried to recruit students for a magic school. Plans for a school were soon abandoned. Reuniting with old friends, Harry and Bessie logged another summer season with the Welsh Brothers Circus.

In 1899 Houdini finally caught a break in St. Paul, Minnesota. A big-time vaudeville manager, Martin Beck, watched his show and liked what he saw. But the manager ordered Houdini to make drastic changes. Beck told Houdini to drop the traditional magic—such as cards and coins—and focus on his escapes. It was golden advice. Almost immediately Houdini's career started to take off.

In February 1900 Houdini returned to Canada, appearing at Shea's Theatre in Toronto. Houdini had reason to recall his first visit to Canada in 1896; in Toronto, he took over the venue from Professor Wormwood's Monkey Theatre, who held the boards at Shea's the previous week.

On May 30, 1900, Harry and Bessie Houdini sailed for England aboard the SS *Kensington*. For the first time since leaving Nova Scotia, Harry Houdini would once again battle seasickness on the Atlantic Ocean.

It was well worth it.

The British public went wild for Houdini, reading about his exploits and lining up for his shows. After he took England by storm, Houdini travelled to Germany where managers fought over his bookings.

After a decade of hard work and struggle, Harry Houdini had made it to the very top.

Word of Houdini's success spread quickly throughout the four corners of the world. Back in Halifax, Nova Scotia, a theatre reviewer wryly noted, "Harry Houdini, who appeared to empty seats in Halifax, is playing at a salary of $800 a week in England."[7] While Houdini was selling out Russian theatres in 1903, another Halifax theatre critic recalled how Houdini and his co-stars were treated in the fickle harbour city. "The company which Houdini was with in Halifax played to such small business that Manager Clarke received a portion of the proprietor's stage property to hold for an amount due him."[8]

And the rest is Houdini history.

On October 31, 2010, some of Houdini's fans left a pumpkin inscribed
"To Harry Houdini from Mario and Victoria" on the granite exedra.
(Bruce MacNab photograph)

*
*   *
*

THREE

END GAME
THE CONSEQUENCES OF COINCIDENCE

"Occasionally coincidences occur in the performance of magical feats that are so
startling as to cause even the artist surprise. And such might easily be mistaken for
actual manifestations of something occult by those who are believers in such things."
—Harry Houdini, from *Houdini on Magic*

HARRY HOUDINI OFTEN COMMENTED on the role of coincidence in life
and in magic, and he wrote about the subject regularly. Perhaps it was fated that
Houdini should die, so fittingly, on Halloween day. And there's another startling
oddity regarding Houdini's demise—one that connects his death to his Maritime
tour in 1896.

On October 20, 1926, eleven days before he died, Houdini was in full flight,
raging against spiritualists and false mediums at Montreal's McGill University
between shows at a downtown theatre. At the end of his lecture, he was swarmed by
students, including a young man who asked him to autograph a portrait he sketched
during the lecture. Houdini quite liked the drawing, and asked the student-artist,
Sam "Smiley" Smilovitz, to sketch him later in the week. Smiley happily accepted
Houdini's request.

On Friday, October 22, Smiley and his McGill friend, Jacques Price, arrived
at the Princess Theatre dressing room, finding Houdini immersed in a stack of

mail. The boys observed a petite lady, whom Harry introduced as his wife, Mrs. Houdini. Shortly after the boys settled in, Bessie exited the small room. The students discovered Houdini was hobbled by an ankle injury from a recent stage accident in Albany, New York. To keep weight off his leg, Houdini lay on a couch as he methodically opened and read his mail, occasionally chatting with the boys.

As Smiley sketched Houdini, a third McGill student, Joscelyn Gordon Whitehead, entered the cramped eight-foot by ten-foot dressing room. Smiley wasn't pleased when the older student began distracting his sketch subject by asking contentious questions. Whitehead mischievously asked the Jewish entertainer what he thought of the Bible, prompting an agitated Houdini to look up from his mail and snap, "I don't discuss these matters."[9]

The thirty-one-year-old Whitehead then steered Smiley and Price's line of questioning away from Houdini's intellectual pursuits to his athleticism. The two chatted about physical conditioning until Whitehead abruptly asked Houdini if rumours about his physical endurance were factual. More precisely, Whitehead asked the fifty-two-year-old performer if it was true that he really could withstand powerful punches to his stomach. Houdini, still reclining on the couch, muttered in the affirmative without even lifting his eyes off his mail.

Suddenly, without warning, Whitehead sprang at Houdini like a wildcat, punching him over and over in the stomach. Jacques Price jumped to his feet and yelled, "Hey there, you must be crazy! What are you doing?" Houdini held up his hand at Whitehead. "That will do. Stop there," he ordered.[10]

In spite of the bizarre punching, the boys hung out with Houdini for another hour or so until Bessie returned with Harry's lunch. Sensing it was time to leave, Smiley presented Houdini with his sketch. Houdini looked it over and commented, "You make me look a little tired in this picture. The truth is that I do not feel very well."[11] Smiley's sketch has never surfaced, causing some to wonder if Houdini might have destroyed the unflattering drawing.

Houdini finished his stand in Montreal, then boarded the train for Detroit, reportedly giving an interview at a brief stopover in London, Ontario. After struggling through a sold-out performance in Detroit, Houdini was rushed to hospital where his appendix was removed from the left side of his body, opposite of most. The organ had ruptured, wreaking havoc with Houdini's abdomen after peritonitis set in. Houdini seemed to recover somewhat, but then his condition worsened, prompting a second operation.

Harry Houdini performs a straitjacket escape from a construction crane.

(fantasmamagic.com, Roger Dreyer Collection)

Jacques Price, who witnessed the infamous dressing room punch, retired to Sir Charles Tupper's former cottage. (Nova Scotia Archives)

On October 31, 1926, Houdini looked up at his brother Theodore from his Detroit hospital bed and whispered, "I'm tired of fighting Dash. I guess this thing is going to get me."[12] He drifted off, mumbling a few words about the late agnostic lecturer Robert Ingersoll. Moments later, Harry Houdini passed away.

Possibly to ward off controversy, doctors claimed the punches delivered by J. Gordon Whitehead weren't the root cause of Houdini's death. But mystery still surrounds Whitehead's acquaintance with Houdini. The McGill student met at least twice with Houdini in Montreal, lending him an edition of *Scientific American*. Perhaps this Whitehead was somehow related to "Irishman" Whitehead from the Marco tour and gained access to Houdini by exploiting the connection.

The late Don Bell spent twenty years investigating Whitehead and the dressing room incident for his book, *The Man Who Killed Houdini*. J. Gordon Whitehead lived a reclusive life following the punching episode and died in 1954. Bell managed to locate J. Gordon Whitehead's brother, but the man wanted nothing to do with Bell or his investigation.

Mr. Bell had an easy time finding and interviewing the sketch artist, Samuel J. Smilovitz, who was alive and well in Montreal. But the other dressing room witness, Jacques Price, was a difficult quarry. Not knowing if Price was dead or alive, Bell searched for many years in a circuitous hunt that led him to Scotland before picking up a trail in Windsor, Nova Scotia, where Smiley's old friend had worked as a town engineer. And before long, the tenacious Don Bell discovered that Jacques Price was still alive.

When he finally caught up with the elderly Jacques Price in 1990, he found him living near the Northwest Arm in Halifax, Nova Scotia. Sixty-four years had passed since the dressing room incident, but Mr. Price was reluctant to speak about what he saw that fateful day.

Curiously, Jacques Price was living in the house once owned by Sir Charles Tupper, the former prime minister of Canada, the very man whose election campaign made it so tough for Houdini to promote the Marco Magic Company back in 1896. It was to this Quinpool Road house that Tupper was returning when he and Houdini were both in Truro, on Friday, July 17, 1896.

Even from beyond the grave, it would seem Harry Houdini was still racking up more of his beloved coincidences.

Harry Houdini

Shackled - Padlocked
Handcuffed And Chained.
Freed himself in
10 Minutes.

From the start of his escape artist's career in the Maritimes, challengers tried
to defeat Houdini by chaining his hands to his ankles behind his back.
(Harry Ransom Center, The University of Texas at Austin)

*
*　*
*

ACKNOWLEDGEMENTS

UNCOVERING HOUDINI'S 1896 MARITIME ADVENTURE was only possible because so many people loved this story and offered their help and enthusiasm. Many well-known Houdini collectors and magic scholars responded, including Kevin Connolly, Patrick Culliton, James Hamilton, Sidney Radner (1919-2011), Dorothy Dietrich, James Randi (following his 2011 Halifax lecture), Raymond and Ann Goulet, Joe Lauher, Tom Boldt, John Cox, Dr. Bruce Averbook, Richard Hatch, Kent Cummins, Ron Cartlidge, Roger Dreyer, and Jim Baldauf.

Archivists, librarians, historians, and others were invaluable to my research; I'll list as many as possible. In Appleton, Wisconsin: Matthew Carpenter and Terry Bergen at the History Museum at the Castle. In Austin, Texas: Helen Adair and Rick Watson at the Harry Ransom Center at the University of Texas. In Washington, DC: Eric Frazier, Clark Evans, Mark Dimunation, Sherlita Jones, Dr. Joan Higbee, Lisa Shiota, and Margaret Kieckhefer at the Library of Congress; Yvonne Carignan and Adam Lewis at the Historical Society of Washington, DC; and staff at the National Archives and Catholic University of America. In New York City: Dr. Alexis Lynne Pavenick and Bill Kalush at the Conjuring Arts Research Center; John Calhoun, Eadey, Karen, and Louise Lareau at the New York Public Library; Eva Halfon of the Jewish Museum; Ken Silverman; Marianne Giosa; Gunnar Berg at YIVO Institute for Jewish Research; and David Rosenberg at the Institute for Jewish Research.

In Hartford, Connecticut: Jeannie Sherman at the Connecticut State Archives; Cynthia Harbeson, Judith Johnson, and Sierra Dixon at the Connecticut Historical Society Museum and Library; Brenda Miller and Eileen Colletti at the Hartford History Center; Maria Medina at the Archdiocese of Hartford; Karen Lesiak at the Archbishop O'Brien Library; and Roberta Tuttle, the editor of the *Catholic Transcript*. A very special thank you to Chris, along with the other staff and residents, who allowed me to wander through Professor Dooley's old Hartford house, now an assisted living facility.

In Massachusetts: Micah Hoggatt and Emily Walhout at the Houghton Library; Henry Scannell, Diane Parks, Nancy Walsh, Sean Casey, Kim Reynolds, and Susan Glover at the Boston Public Library; Anna Cook and Elaine Grublin at the Massachusetts Historical Society; Marie Daley and Jade Luongo at the New England Historic Genealogical Society; Edward Butland at the Boston Catholic Cemetery Association; Eileen Marcelonis at the Salem Probate Court; Autumn and Regina at the Massachusetts State Archives; and Steven J. Babbitt and Margaret Dee at the Lynn Museum Library.

Elsewhere in America: Andy Moul, Ann Dodge, Gayle Lynch, and Rosemary Cullen at the John Hay Library in Providence, Rhode Island; Charlese L. Farmer, William Fee, and Susan Mazza at the Pennsylvania State Library; Marjorie Mckensie at the Harrisburg, Pennsylvania, Library; Jamie Kingman Rice at the Maine Historical Society; Anthony at the Maine State Archives; and Ernie Plummer at the Kennebec Historical Society.

In my old hometown of Dartmouth, Nova Scotia: Crystal Martin and her colleagues at the Dartmouth Heritage Museum; Susan McClure and Dave Cogswell at the Halifax Regional Municipality Archives; Harry Chapman, Mrs. Fisher, David and Marie Jones, and John Lushington; Noella Fisher; and Helen Thexton at the Alderney Gate Public Library. In Halifax, Nova Scotia: Philip Hartling, Garry Shutlak, Barry Smith, Lois Pyke, Chris Rogers, George, Anjolie, and Gail at the Nova Scotia Archives; Mike O'Sullivan, Marlene Miller, Chief Beazley, Ron Grantham (retired) of the Halifax Regional Police; Jean Howell at the Cambridge Military Museum; Provincial Privacy Officer Sue Jakeman; Sharon Riel at the Archdiocese of Halifax; and Harry Carrigan and Phil Newell at Halifax City Hall.

In Truro, Nova Scotia: staff sergeant Randy Mackenzie; and Colchester Museum and Archives director Nan Harvey. In Springhill, Nova Scotia: Don Tabor; Russell Fisher, and Ron Samura of the Springhill Heritage Group; Mary-

Willa Littler; Kevin Misken; and Jason Farnell. In Amherst, Nova Scotia: Shirley Nickerson, Kristen Holloway, and Peggy O'Brien at the Cumberland County Museum and Archives; John McKay; Marney Gilroy; Margo at the Cumberland County Genealogy Centre; Rebecca Purdy at Amherst City Hall; and Doris Harkness. In Parrsboro, Nova Scotia: Paul Morse, Edward Gilbert, Reverend Tory Byrne, Kevin Yorke, Marilyn Orr, Susan Clark, and especially Conrad Byers. In Joggins, Nova Scotia: John Reid and the late historian Gary Vickery. In Yarmouth, Nova Scotia: Jamie Serran and Gail O'Sullivan at the Yarmouth County Museum and Archives; Ross Paro; Daniel MacIsaac; and Kathy Mohle. In Prince Edward Island: Peter Llewellyn, Bernice DeLory, Nathan Mair, and Lisa MacKenzie; Gillian Booker at the Public Archives and Courtney Matthews at the University of Prince Edward Island library.

This book would not have been possible without Rob Gilmore at the Provincial Archives of New Brunswick who helped me understand the complex world of genealogy and showed me how to find clues hidden in census records, vital statistics, and probate papers. On my many trips stateside, Rob always answered my barrage of emails, offering steady guidance from his office in Fredericton. On many occasions, Rob back-tracked my research and found details I had overlooked. I'd also like to send a special thank you to all Rob Gilmore's Provincial Archives of New Brunswick colleagues, especially: Fred Farrell, Julia Thompson, and Heather Lyons. Also in Fredericton: Christine Jack, Yolande House, and Lyn Richardson at the Harriet Irving Library, The University of New Brunswick; Fredericton residents: Ernie Fitzsimmons, Colin Rayworth, Joy Jamer, Koral LaVorgna, and Tina Tu.

In Moncton, New Brunswick: Bridget Murphy and Brenda Orr at the Moncton Museum; Pierre Goguen at the Moncton Library; Kenneth Breau at the University of Moncton; and Ed Boews and Art Clowes at the New Brunswick Railway Museum. In Saint John, New Brunswick: Janet Bishop and Jennifer Longon at the New Brunswick Museum Archives; and David Goss, Harold Wright, Katherine Biggs-Craft, and Mary E. Smith. In Sackville, New Brunswick: Rhianna Edwards, Anita Canon, Dr. Carrie MacMillan, and David Mawhinney at Mount Allison University. In Dorchester, New Brunswick: 102-year-old Art McCready, Nora Williams, Ernie Partridge, Wayne Feindel, Dennis Reid, Libby Stultz, Betty Adams, Denyse "Dee" Milliken, and Marlene and Bobby Hickman.

This project would not have been possible without employment during the years of research. Art Cole and Glen Carvery gave me work in my trade. Kit Jillings hired me for a term at the Nova Scotia Community College. Grail Sangster, of the Guysborough Adult Learning Association hired me early in this project. Denise Manuel of the Nova Scotia Worker's Compensation Board helped me procure reading glasses. Thank you to Laurent Le Pierrès, Deborah Wiles, and especially Paul O'Connell for publishing my stories in the *Halifax Chronicle Herald*. Thanks to Mark Reid and Nelle Oosterom who published my Houdini story in *The Beaver*. And to Linda Forbes of the Heritage Trust of Nova Scotia for publishing my work in *The Griffin*. Thanks to Goose Lane Editions. Special thanks to Paula Sarson for her keen eye in copy-editing and to Jaye Haworth for her design work.

My parents Ron and Mary Macnab were unfailing in their love and support as were my siblings Paul, Catherine, and Susan. My sister-in-law Marianne Ward read many early versions of this book and helped me with her editing skills. Cynthia Brown offered her love and friendship throughout the entire project.

Thank you all for such an incredible journey.

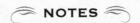

CHAPTER 1

1. "Houdini Unmasks Spiritualism," *The American Hebrew*, 115, no. 5 (June, 13, 1924): 173. Silverman notes YIVO.
2. Will Goldston, *The Magic Annual, 1909-1910* accessed in Ken Silverman's notes at YIVO Institute for Jewish Research.
3. "Houdini Unmasks Spiritualism," *The American Hebrew*, 115, no. 5 (June, 13, 1924): 173. Silverman notes YIVO.
4. Harry Houdini, introduction to *Unmasking of Robert-Houdin* (New York: Publishers Printing Company, 1908).
5. Houdini, *Unmasking of Robert-Houdin*.
6. Ibid.
7. Quote from Dorothy Young noted in *The Secret Life of Houdini Laid Bare: Sources, notes and additional material*, 33. Additional source (variant of same quote) Ken Silverman notes YIVO.
8. Harold Kellock and Beatrice Houdini, *Houdini: His Life Story* (New York: Blue Ribbon Books, 1928), 48. Excerpts from *Houdini: His Life Story by Harold Kellock from the Recollections and Documents of Beatrice Houdini*, copyright 1928 by Harold Kellock and Beatrice Houdini and renewed 1956 by Katherine Kellock and Melville Cane, reprinted by permission of Houghton Mifflin Harcourt Publishing Company. All rights reserved.
9. Kellock and Houdini, *Houdini: His Life Story*, 47-48.
10. Joe Hayman, "My Pal Dash," *Conjurors' Magazine: Hardeen Memorial Issue* 1, no. 6 (July 1945): 28.

CHAPTER 2

1. Houdini letter to Quincy Kilby, January 2, 1919, Boston Public Library, Rare Books and Manuscripts.
2. Houdini diary, Collection of Dr. Bruce Averbook. Sourced from William Kalush and Larry Sloman, *The Secret Life of Houdini Laid Bare: Sources, notes and additional material*, (Pasadena, CA: The Conjuring Arts Research Center & Mike Caveney's Magic Words, 2007), 35.
3. Kellock and Houdini, *Houdini: His Life Story*, 75.
4. Ibid., 76.
5. *New York Dramatic Mirror*. October 25, 1902.
6. Kellock and Houdini, *Houdini: His Life Story*, 79.
7. *Boston Daily Globe*, September 22, 1926, 5. Via ProQuest.
8. *York Dispatch* (York, PA), September 28, 1895, 3.
9. Houdini letter to H.J. Moulton, January 31, 1919. Robert Lund Collection, American Museum of Magic, Marshall, Michigan. Sourced through Silverman notes YIVO.

10. *York Daily* (York, PA), September 28, 1895, 1.
11. *Evening Call* (Woonsocket, RI), April 14, 1896. Clipping from Houdini's press book.
12. Ibid.
13. *Conjurers' Monthly Magazine*, II, no. 9 (May 15, 1908): 261.
14. *Hartford Courant* (Hartford, CT), February 18, 1896, 6.

CHAPTER 3

1. *Yarmouth Light* (Yarmouth, NS), May 28, 1896. 1.
2. Dooley letter to Houdini, Albany, New York, October 4, 1900, Harry Ransom Center.
3. *Dispatch* (Woodstock, NB), July 29, 1896, 8.

CHAPTER 4

1. *Yarmouth Telegram* (Yarmouth NS), June 5, 1896.

CHAPTER 5

1. *Yarmouth Times* (Yarmouth, NS), May 29, 1896, 2.
2. Kellock and Houdini, *Houdini: His Life Story*, 77-78. Permission granted for usage.

CHAPTER 6

1. *Yarmouth Light* (Yarmouth, NS), June 2, 1896, 2.
2. William Lindsay Gresham, *Houdini: The Man Who Walked Through Walls* (New York: Holt, 1959), 67.

CHAPTER 7

1. *Conjurers' Monthly*, II, no. 5 (January 1908): 105.

CHAPTER 8

1. *Saint John Sun*, June 5, 1896, 4.
2. *Saint John Sun*, June 27, 1895, 8. Note: This was a year before Houdini's visit.
3. "Some appliance needed," *Saint John Sun*, July 10, 1895, 8. Note: This was a year before Houdini's visit.
4. *Saint John Sun*, June 5, 1896, 4.
5. Ibid.
6. Ibid.
7. James Williams Elliott, introduction in *Elliott's Last Legacy: Secrets of the King of all Cards* (New York: Adams, 1923), 15.

CHAPTER 9

1. Geo. A. Hetherington, *Report of the Superintendent of the Provincial Lunatic Asylum at St. John, NB For the Year 1896*, 1897, 14.
2. Ibid.

3. Signor Blitz, *Fifty Years in the Magic Circle: An Account of the Author's Professional Life* (Hartford, CT: Belknap & Bliss, 1872), 268.

4. *Conjurers' Monthly Magazine*, II, no. 5 (January 15, 1908): 155.

5. Ibid.

6. Steeves, Jas. A.E. *Report of the Medical Superintendent of the Provincial Lunatic Asylum at Saint John, N.B. for the Year 1894* (Saint John, NB: "Progress" Electric Printing and Publishing Office, 1895), 17. PANB.

7. Ibid., 18.

8. *The Reporter* [Fredericton weekly], June 10, 1896, 1.

CHAPTER 10

1. "Addressing an Audience," *MUM* (Amer. Soc. of Magicians), XII, no. 7 (January 1923): 143-144.

2. *Saint John Daily Telegraph*, June 9, 1896, 2.

3. *Saint John Sun*, June 9, 1896, 8.

4. Ibid.

CHAPTER 11

1. *Saint John Globe*, June 3, 1896.

CHAPTER 12

1. *Saint John Globe*, June 10, 1896, 8.

CHAPTER 13

1. Samri Samuel Baldwin, *An Interesting Account of Prof. Samri S. Baldwin*. 1906. Twenty-plus-page booklet in the Houdini Collection at Library of Congress (BF1405. H6).

CHAPTER 14

1. *Saint John Globe*, June 10, 1896, 3.

2. *Saint John Sun*, June 6, 1895, 8.

3. Letter from Baldwin (77 Pike St. Port Jervis, NY) to James Harto, March 6, 1915.

CHAPTER 15

1. *Saint John Sun*, June 10, 1896, 8.

CHAPTER 16

1. Houdini diary entry, June 11, 1914. Quoted in Bernard C Meyer, *Houdini: A Mind in Chains* (New York: Dutton, 1976), 11.

2. Kellock and Houdini, *Houdini: His Life Story*, 52.

CHAPTER 17

1. *Saint John Daily Telegraph*, June 13, 1896, 3.

CHAPTER 18

1. Direct quote is from the *Saint John Globe*, June 13, 1896, 2. Variants in other papers including the *Saint John Gazette,* June 13, 1896, 5.
2. *Saint John Sun*, June 13, 1896, 8.
3. *Fredericton Daily Gleaner,* June 15, 1896, 4. Discovered by and sent via email transcription by Rob Gilmore at PANB.

CHAPTER 19

1. This *Mirror* story was republished in "A caustic view of the city of Halifax," *Acadia Recorder* (Halifax, NS), July 27, 1886, 4. The actor is not named in the newspaper. Instead they describe him as "One of the actors of the King-Handley Co., who was in this city a few weeks ago, writes to the New York Mirror of last Saturday his impressions..."
2. *Halifax Herald,* June 22, 1896, 1.
3. *Chatham World*, June 6, 1896, 3.

CHAPTER 20

1. Kellock and Houdini, *Houdini: His Life Story*, 79.
2. *Acadian Recorder*, June 25, 1896, 2.

CHAPTER 21

1. *Chicago Record Herald*, November 17, 1906. Note: This is a clipping from a scrapbook at NYPL, Robinson Locke Collection. Paper and date inscribed with pencil.
2. Undated list of sixty-one restraints. Patrick Culliton has identified it as the Defiance Handcuff Act list. Harry Ransom Center.
3. One-page undated letter (list of eleven restraints missing keys, etc.) at the Harry Ransom Center.
4. One-page undated letter (list of eleven restraints missing keys, etc.) at the Harry Ransom Center.
5. Multi-page letter dated March 25, 1908, Buffalo, NY, Harry Ransom Center.
6. Kellock and Houdini, *Houdini: His Life Story*, 78.

CHAPTER 22

1. *Halifax Herald*, June 25, 1896, 8.

CHAPTER 23

1. *Conjurers' Monthly Magazine*, II, no. 5 (January15, 1908): 155.

CHAPTER 24

1. William Lindsay Gresham, *Houdini: The Man Who Walked Through Walls* (New York: Holt, 1959), 40.
2. *Morning Herald*, January 30, 1883, 3
3. *Morning Herald*, January 31, 1883, 3.

CHAPTER 26
1. *Acadian Recorder*, June 30, 1896, 3.
2. Dooley obituary, *Conjurers' Monthly Magazine*, II, no. 9 (May 15, 1908): 261.
3. Ibid.

CHAPTER 27
1. *Echo*, July 13, 1896, 5.
2. *Halifax Mail*, November 4, 1936. 3.
3. Ibid.
4. *Conjurers' Monthly Magazine*, II, no. 5 (January 15, 1908): 155.

CHAPTER 28
1. Handwritten entry entitled "Prohibiting Obscene Placards," Truro Town Bylaws, November 7, 1895, 321. Sourced at Colchester County Archives.
2. *Truro Daily News*, July 11, 1896, 3.
3. *Truro Daily News*, June 23, 1894, 4.
4. Harry Houdini, *Magical Rope Ties and Escapes* (London: Will Goldston, 1915), 7.
5. Ibid.
6. Ibid., 8.
7. Ibid.
8. Houdini letter to Powell, December 30, 1916. Roger Dreyer collection.
9. *Acadian Recorder*, July 28, 1896, 2.

CHAPTER 29
1. Kellock and Houdini, *Houdini: His Life Story*, 108-109.
2. James C. Young, "Magic and Mediums Houdini, man of many tricks, tells of duplicating feats of spirit workers," undated clipping in Q. Kilby Houdini scrapbook, in Boston Public Library Rare Books and Manuscripts.
3. Kellock and Houdini, *Houdini: His Life Story*, 109.
4. *Springhill Advertiser*, July 30, 1896. 5.
5. Ibid.
6. Letter (three-page report) from W.J. McConnell to his superior at the Bureau of Mines; Morris N. Young collection. Note: I found a partial transcription in Silverman's notes at YIVO, Institute for Jewish Research.

CHAPTER 31
1. *Amherst Daily News*, July 27, 1896, 1.
2. *Amherst Daily News*, August 3, 1896, 1.
3. Walter Hubbell, *The Haunted House: A True Ghost Story; The Great Amherst Mystery* (Saint John, NB: Daily News Steam Publishing Office, 1879), 47.

CHAPTER 33
1. *Chignecto Post*, December 10, 1891.

CHAPTER 35

1. *Moncton Daily Times*, August 17, 1896, 4.
2. *Daily Transcript*, August 13, 1896, 4.
3. *New York Clipper*, September 19, 1896.

CHAPTER 36

1. Kellock and Houdini, *Houdini: His Life Story*, 89.
2. Ibid.
3. Shakespeare, Sonnet xviii, quoted in Otis Skinner, *Footlights and Flashes* (Indianapolis: Bobbs-Merrill Company, 1924).

EPILOGUE

1. *Bimbo of Bombay* programme, September 13, 14, and 15, 1897. New York Public Library Collection.
2. Letter from Dooley to Houdini, August 30, 1900, Harry Ransom Center.
3. Letter from Dooley to Houdini, September 5, 1903, Harry Ransom Center.
4. *Conjurers' Monthly Magazine*, II, no. 9 (May 15, 1908), 261.
5. *MUM magazine* (Amer. Soc. of Magicians) March 1924. Article transcribed by Patrick Culliton.
6. *The Magician Annual,* no. 3 (1909-1910), 3.
7. *Acadian Recorder*, December 28, 1903, 3.
8. *Acadian Recorder*, July 6, 1903, 2.
9. Don Bell, *The Man Who Killed Houdini* (Montreal: Véhicule Press, 2005), 59.
10. Ibid., 228.
11. Ibid., 60.
12. Ibid., 37.

Baldwin, Samri S. *The Secrets of Mahatma Land Explained: Teaching and Explaining the Most Celebrated Oriental Mystery Makers and Magicians.* Brooklyn, NY: T.J. Dyson & Son, 1895.

Bayer, Constance Pole. *The Great Wizard of the North: John Henry Anderson.* Watertown, MA: Ray Goulet's Magic Art Book Co., 1989.

Bell, Don. *The Man Who Killed Houdini.* Montreal: Véhicule Press. September 2005.

Blakeley, Phyllis R. *Glimpses of Halifax: 1867-1900.* Halifax, NS: The Public Archives of Nova Scotia, 1949.

Blitz, Signor. *Fifty Years in the Magic Circle: An Account Of The Author's Professional Life; His Wonderful Tricks And Feats; With Laughable Incidents, And Adventures As A Magician, Necromancer, And Ventriloquist.* Hartford, CT: Belknap & Bliss, 1872.

Bordman, Gerald. *American Musical Theatre A Chronicle.* 2nd ed. New York: Oxford University, 1992.

Brandon, Ruth. *The Life and Many Deaths of Harry Houdini.* New York: Random House, 1993.

Burlingame, H.J. *Leaves from Conjurers' Scrap Books.* Chicago: Donohue, Henneberry, 1891.

Byers, Conrad. *Our Parrsborough Shore Heritage Scrapbook.* N.p.: Printed by author, n.d.

Cartlidge, Ron. *Houdini's Texas Tours 1916 & 1923.* Austin: Ron Cartlidge Publications, 2002.

Centennial Book Committee. *Heritage Homes and History of Parrsboro.* Parrsboro, NS: Centennial Committee, 1988.

Christopher, Milbourne. *Houdini.* New York: Gramercy Books, 1976.

————. *Houdini: The Untold Story.* Markham, ON: Simon & Schuster, 1969.

Clowes, J. Arthur. "The First System 1896-1897," *The Street Railways of Moncton, NB.* N.p.: n.d.: 3-7.

Conjuring Arts Bulletin 1, no. 2 (2007).

Conjurors' Magazine: Hardeen Memorial Issue. New York: Conjurors' Press, 1945.

Constitution and By-Laws of St. Peter's Catholic Total Abstinence and Benevolent Society of Dartmouth, NS. Halifax, NS: Alex Moody Printer, circa 1892.

Cooke, Louis E. "Walter L. Main; America's Best Railroad Shows." *Circus Historical Society Bandwagon* 11, no. 4 (1967): 3-9.

Culliton, Patrick. *Houdini—The Key.* Marina del Rey, CA: Kieran Press, 2010.

"David Price Writes from Egyptian Hall Museum, Nashville Tennessee." *Genii, The Conjurors' Magazine: In Loving Memory of Harry and Bessie Houdini.* (Geraldine Larsen-Baker) 26, no. 2 (October 1961).

Dexter, Will. *The Riddle of Chung Ling Soo.* London: Arco, 1955.

Dooley, E.J. *The Maria Immaculata, a Collection of New Music for the Roman Catholic Church.* Boston: Oliver Ditson Company, MCMIV.

Doyle, Sir Arthur Conan, *AC Doyle: The New Revelation*. New York: George H. Doran Company, 1918. From Ken Silverman's notes, YIVO Institute for Jewish Research, New York City.

Dramatic Compositions Copyrighted in the United States: 1870-1916, Volumes 1 & 2. N.p.: Library of Congress Copyright Office, 1918.

Du Maurier, George. *Trilby*. New York: Harper & Brothers, 1895.

Duggan, Thomas, S. *The Catholic Church in Connecticut*. New York: The States History Company, n.d.

Elliott, James Williams. *Elliott's Last Legacy: Secrets of the King of all Card Kings*. New York: Adams, 1923.

Emmons, S.B. *Spiritualism Exposed*. New York: United States Book Company, circa 1890.

Frank, Gary R. *Chung Ling Soo: The Man of Mystery*. Granada Hills, CA: Fantastic Magic Co., 1988.

Furst, Arnold, and Patrick Culliton. "Houdini: A Review of His Show at the Maryland Theatre," *Genii, The Conjurors' Magazine: Houdini, A Re-creation of His Complete Show*. (Geraldine Larsen-Baker) 27, no. 2 (October 1962).

Gibson, Walter B. *Houdini's Escapes*. Toronto: Bantam, 1930.

Gibson, Walter B. *The Original Houdini Scrapbook*. New York: Corwin Sterling Publishing, 1976.

Gibson, Walter B. and Morris N. Young, eds. *Houdini on Magic*. New York: Dover, 1953.

Goldston, Will. *The Magic Annual, 1909-1910*. Accessed in Ken Silverman's notes at YIVO Institute for Jewish Research.

Goss, David. *150 Years of Caring*. Saint John, NB: Unipress, 1998.

Gresham, William Lindsay. *Houdini: The Man Who Walked Through Walls*. New York: Holt, 1959.

Halifax Chronicle. "Yarmouth and Western Nova Scotia." June 30, 1896.

Harkness, Leonard. *History of the Amherst Police*. N.p.: Printed by author, 1989.

Hatfield, Leonard F. *Simon Gibbons: First Eskimo Priest*. Hantsport, NS: Lancelot Press, 1987.

Heffernan, Jean. *Recollections of a Nova Scotia Town*. Springhill, NS: Springhill Heritage Group, circa 1995.

Henning, Doug. *Houdini: His Legend and His Magic*. New York: Times Books, 1977.

Herrmann, Prof. *Herrmann's Art of Magic*. New York: Wehman, 1897.

Hetherington, Geo. A. *Report of the Superintendent of the Provincial Lunatic Asylum at St. John, NB For the Year 1896*. Fredericton, NB: Printed for the Legislature, 1897.

Heritage Trust of Nova Scotia. *Lakes, Salt Marshes and the Narrow Green Strip*. Halifax, NS: Heritage Trust of Nova Scotia, 1979.

Hermann's Little Jokes and Some Amusing Tricks. New York: Excelsior Publishing House, 1897.

Higgins, William, Peter McGahan, and Gerald Wallace. *The Saint John Police Story; Vol. I-IV*. Saint John, NB. New Ireland Press, 1991.

Houdini, Harry. *The Adventurous Life of a Versatile Artist*. N.p.: 1922.

_____. ed. *Conjurers' Monthly Magazine*. (The Conjurers' Monthly Magazine Publishing Company), 1906-1908.

_____. *Handcuff Secrets.* N.p.: n.d.

_____. *Houdini: A Magician Among the Spirits.* New York: Arno, 1924.

_____. *Houdini Exposes the Tricks Used by the Boston Medium "Margery."* Boston: Adams, 1924.

_____. *Houdini's Paper Magic.* New York: Dutton, 1922.

_____. *Magical Rope Ties and Escapes.* London: Will Goldston, 1915.

_____. *Miracle Mongers and Their Methods.* New York: E.P. Dutton, 1920.

_____. *The Right Way to do Wrong: An Exposé of Successful Criminals.* N.p.: Printed by author, 1906.

_____. *The Unmasking of Robert Houdin.* New York: The Publishers Printing Company, 1908.

Hubbell, Walter. *The Haunted House: A True Ghost Story; The Great Amherst Mystery.* Saint John, NB: Daily News Steam Publishing Office, 1879.

Jay, Joshua. "Tragic Magic: A Survey of Fatal Conjuring 1584-2007." *Gibecière* 5, no. 2 (2010): 71-129.

Kalush, William, and Larry Sloman. *The Secret Life of Houdini Laid Bare.* Pasadena, CA: The Conjuring Arts Research Center & Mike Caveney's Magic Words, 2007.

_____. *The Secret Life of Houdini: The Making of America's First Superhero.* New York: Atria Books, 2006.

Kellar, Harry. *A Magician's Tour: Up and Down and Round About the Earth, Being the Life and Adventures of the American Nostradamus.* Chicago: Donahue, Henneberry, 1891.

Kellock, Harold and Beatrice Houdini. *Houdini: His Life Story.* New York: Blue Ribbon Books, 1928.

Larracey, E.W. and Alexander C. Pincombe. *Resurgo: History of Moncton, Vol. 2.* Moncton, NB: City of Moncton, 1991.

Lindley, Harry. *Merely Players.* Toronto: Printed by author, circa 1900.

Magic: Featuring the Manny Weltman Houdini Collection. New York: Swann Galleries, 2002.

Mahatma (1895-1898). Found in the Boston Public Library.

Martin, John Patrick. *The Story of Dartmouth.* Dartmouth, NS: Printed by author, 1957.

Matheson, Trueman. *A History of Londonderry.* Londonderry, NS: Printed by author, 1983.

McKnight, H.A. *The Great Colliery Explosion at Springhill, Nova Scotia, February 21, 1891.* Springhill, NS: H.A. McKnight, 1891.

Meyer, Bernard C. *Houdini: a Mind in Chains.* New York: Dutton, 1976.

Milner, W.C. *History of Sackville, New Brunswick.* Sackville, NB: The Tribune Press Ltd., 1934.

Morrow, R.A.H. *Story of the Great Disaster at Springhill Mines, Nova Scotia, Feb. 21, 1891.* Saint John, NB, 1891.

Moses, Arthur. *Houdini Speaks Out.* N.p.: Printed in United States of America, 2007.

New York Clipper Almanac/Annual (1890s editions). Found in the Boston Public Library.

New York Dramatic Mirror (1880-1890s editions). Found in the Boston Public Library Microtext Department.

Pallme, Hermann. *Entertaining by Magic.* New York: M. Witmark & Sons, 1906.

Quinpool, John. *First Things in Acadia*. Halifax, NS: First Things Publishers Limited, 1936.

Randall, Gerald A. *Handcuffs and Ploughshares*. Sackville, NB: Printed by author, circa 1992.

Randi, The Amazing & Bert Randolph Sugar. *Houdini: His Life and Art*. New York: Grosset & Dunlap, 1976.

Rapaport, Brooke Kamin. *Houdini: Art and Magic*. New Haven: Yale University Press, 2010.

Robinson, Wm. E. *A Few of Robinson's New Ideas*. New York: Wm. E. Robinson, circa 1890.

_____. *Spirit Slate Writing and Kindred Phenomena*. New York: Martinka, 1898.

Sawyer, Thomas A. *S.S. Baldwin and the Press*. Santa Ana, CA: Printed by author, 1993.

Scott, Bertha Isabel. *Springhill: A Hilltop in Cumberland*. Springhill, NS: Printed by author, 1926.

Shettel, James W. "They Bought a Circus," *The White Tops*, January/February, 1946.

Sila, James P., Auctioneer. *Catalogue of the Entire Household Furniture, Jewelry and Effects: "Herrmann the Great."* New York, 1899.

Silverman, Kenneth. *Houdini!!!: The Career of Ehrich Weiss*. New York, NY: Harper Collins, 1997.

Skinner, Otis. *Footlights and Spotlights*. Indianapolis: Bobbs-Merrill Company, 1924.

_____. *Mad Folk of the Theatre*. Indianapolis: Bobbs-Merrill Company, 1928.

Skinner, W.E. *Wehman's Wizards' Manual*. New York: Wehman, 1891.

Smith, Lloyd K. "Londonderry Letter," *Truro Weekly News*, August 28, 1952.

Smith, Mary Elizabeth. *Too Soon the Curtain Fell: A History of Theatre in Saint John 1789-1900*. Fredericton, NB: Brunswick Press, 1981.

Sobol, Louis with Hardeen. "The Voice of Broadway." *New York Evening Journal*, November 25, 1933.

Steeves, Jas. A.E. *Report of the Medical Superintendent of the Provincial Lunatic Asylum at Saint John, N.B. for the Year 1894*. Saint John, NB: "Progress" Electric Printing and Publishing Office, 1895.

Steinmeyer, Jim. *The Glorious Deception*. New York: Carrol & Graf, 2005.

_____. *Hiding the Elephant: How Magicians Invented the Impossible and Learned to Disappear*. New York: Barnes & Noble, 2003.

_____. *The Last Greatest Magician in the World*. New York: The Penguin Group, 2011.

Stewart, W. Brenton. *Medicine in New Brunswick*. New Brunswick Medical Society, 1974.

Vickery, Gary. *"The" Joggins: Its History and Its People*. N.p.: Printed by author, n.d.

Weltman, Manny. *Houdini: Escape Into Legend: The Early Years: 1862-1900*. Van Nuys, CA: Finders/Seekers Enterprises, 1993.

Wiley, Barry H. *The Indescribable Phenomenon*. Seattle: Hermetic Press, 2005.

Professor Wormwood's Monkey Theatre
46, 49, 52, 270, 295, 299, 305, 311,
312, 317, 335
Projea, the Wild Man of Mexico (Houdini
stage name) 37
Prouty, Jed 236
Providence RI 209, 299

Q

Queen Hotel (Halifax) 188, 208, 209
Queen of the Air illusion 78

R

Rahner, Wilhelmina (Bessie Houdini)
(wife) 6, 7, 10, 11, 28-33, 35-41, 44,
45, 47, 56, 67, 72, 73-78, 88, 98, 111,
114-115, 117, 130, 153, 156-157,
158, 159, 161, 164, 165, 167, 171,
178, 187, 189, 191, 193, 194, 195-
198, 201, 209, 212, 214, 221-223,
226, 230, 235-237, 241, 244, 247,
248, 250, 252, 253, 257-262, 270-
272, 274, 279, 280, 283, 287, 288,
292, 293-295, 297, 298, 299, 302,
303, 306, 311, 315-317, 319-322,
325, 329, 333-335, 338
Randi, James (magician) 123
Redemptionist Mission Church (Boston)
61
Reed, Norton 157
Rhodes, Curry & Company 287, 288
Richmond VA 301
Richmond, Officer Samuel 270
Right Way To Do Wrong, The 145
River Hebert 293
Robb's Hall (Dorchester) 304
Robert-Houdin, Jean (magician) 25-26
Robinson, William (magician) 264-266
Rochester NY 267
Rocket Boy 181
Ross, Officer Neil 190
Roterberg, August (advisor) 71, 200, 205,
206, 230, 334
Roterberg, Mrs. 71
Royal Hotel (Halifax) 162

Royal Hotel (Springhill) 272
Royal Nova Scotia Yacht Squadron 226

S

Sackville NB 84, 297-301, 304, 306
Saint Croix Courier 85
Saint John NB 8, 43, 46, 59, 78, 81-85,
86, 90, 95-99, 101-106, 108, 109,
111-113, 115, 117, 118, 121-125,
127, 129-131, 133, 135, 136, 143,
145-148, 151-154, 159, 161-165,
167, 171, 172, 174, 175, 177-181,
188, 189, 212, 220-223, 231, 258,
259, 270, 286, 312, 317, 319, 334
Saint John Gazette 98, 123, 164, 165, 178
Saint John Globe 81, 82, 122, 133, 146
Saint John Progress 122, 177
Saint John River 101
Saint John Sun 85, 97, 121, 130, 131,
136, 159, 178
San Antonio TX 257
San Francisco CA 35, 195
Scientific American 114, 115, 154, 266,
315, 340
Scott Act 285, 294, 304
Scott's Bazaar (Yarmouth) 65, 67, 73
second sight act 272-274, 277
*Secrets of Mahatma Land Explained:
Teaching and Explaining the Most
Celebrated Oriental Mystery Makers and
Magicians, The* 139, 229, 231
Semon, Zera (magician) 58, 83, 181, 298-
301, 317
Shamrock Grounds (Saint John) 171,
174, 175
Shanahan, Peter 291
Shaw, Robert G. 121
Shea's Theatre (Toronto) 335
Shediac NB 311
Sheridan, Jas 309
Sing Sing prison 32, 304, 307, 309
Skinner, Alfred Osbourne 84
Skinner, Willis (Markos) (magician).
See Markos (magician)
sleight-of-hand tricks 24